Sustainability in Sub-Saharan Africa

Sustainability in Sub-Saharan Africa

Problems, Perspectives, and Prospects

Edited by
Jennifer L. De Maio, Suzanne Scheld, and
Mintesnot Woldeamanuel

LEXINGTON BOOKS
Lanham • Boulder • New York • London

Published by Lexington Books
An imprint of The Rowman & Littlefield Publishing Group, Inc.
4501 Forbes Boulevard, Suite 200, Lanham, Maryland 20706
www.rowman.com

6 Tinworth Street, London SE11 5AL, United Kingdom

British Library Cataloguing in Publication Information Available

Library of Congress Cataloging-in-Publication Data

Names: De Maio, Jennifer L., editor, author. | Scheld, Suzanne, editor, author. | Woldeamanuel, Mintesnot, editor, author.
Title: Sustainability in Sub-Saharan Africa : problems, perspectives, and prospects / edited by Jennifer L. De Maio, Suzanne Scheld, and Mintesnot Woldeamanuel.
Description: Lanham : Lexington Books, 2019. | Includes bibliographical references and index.
Identifiers: LCCN 2018043250 | ISBN 9781498573955 (cloth : alk. paper) | ISBN 9781498573962 (electronic)
Subjects: LCSH: Sustainable development—Africa, Sub-Saharan. | Africa, Sub-Saharan—Economic conditions—21st century.
Classification: LCC HC800.Z9 E57988 2019 | DDC 338.9270967—dc23
LC record available at https://lccn.loc.gov/2018043250

♾™ The paper used in this publication meets the minimum requirements of American National Standard for Information Sciences—Permanence of Paper for Printed Library Materials, ANSI/NISO Z39.48-1992.

Printed in the United States of America

Contents

Introduction

Sustainable Development and Sub-Saharan Africa

Jennifer L. De Maio, Suzanne Scheld, and Mintesnot Woldeamanuel[1]

2015 was a watershed year for promoting sustainable development in the world, and Africans and African organizations played a prominent role in this milestone. In July, Ethiopia hosted the Third International Conference on Financing for Development (FFD3) which produced the *Addis Ababa Action Agenda* (AAAA). The AAAA lays the groundwork for retooling global financial practices and generating the financing for sustainable development. Then, in September, nearly 150 world leaders signed off on the 2030 Agenda for Sustainable Development plan, which includes the 17 integrated Sustainable Development Goals (SDGs) and 169 other targets. The process of defining the 2030 Development Agenda was guided by the high-level panel co-chaired by Ellen Johnson Sirleaf, the president of Liberia. And, negotiations among world leaders were mediated by the Intergovernmental Negotiations (IGN) committee, which was co-facilitated by Ambassador Macharia Kamau of Kenya. The G77+China contributed significantly to the negotiations, and this committed was spearheaded by H. E. Mr. Luwellyn Landers, deputy minister of International Relations and Cooperation of the Republic of South Africa. In addition to this, Sirleaf took the lead in producing the Common African Position (CAP) on the Post-2015 Development Agenda (UNECA, 2014). The CAP received input and support from the African Union (AU) and other influential Africa-based organizations (e.g., New Partnership for Africa's Development [NEPAD], the Africa Development Bank [AfDB], the Economic Commission for Africa [UNECA], and the UN Regional Bureau for Africa, among others). The year ended with the UN Convention on Climate Change (COP21) in Paris, where the international community sought to write a global agreement to keep global warming below 2°C, and made plans to return to Marrakech, Morocco for a follow up meeting in 2016. In sum, African leaders were key participants in the conferences and conversations that produced the new global sustainable development goals. What is sustainable development and why were African nations particularly invested in defining the new global agenda for sustainable development?

WHAT IS SUSTAINABLE DEVELOPMENT?

For the last three decades, the concept of sustainable development has been the focus of almost every environmental literature and development program involving in social and economic issues. It is developed not only as a concept but also as a goal, a practice and, in many cases, as a movement and it became a central theme to the mission of countless international organizations, national institutions, corporate enterprises, and cities (Kates, Parris, and Leiserowitz, 2005). The frequently cited definition of sustainable development is from the Brundtland Commission's report *Our Common Future* which is stated as "development that meets the needs of the present without compromising the ability of future generations to meet their own needs" (United Nations General Assembly, 1987). Soon after the publication of *Our Common Future*, scholars argued that the definition is vague, impractical, too general, and too narrow. The definition also criticized for focusing too much on balancing environmental protection and economic development. With this, some argued sustainability through environmental protection should not be achieved with the cost of economic development. For example, Michael Porter and Claas Van der Linde (1999) argued that pollution is a sign of inefficient resource use; therefore, win-win opportunities for the environmental protection and economic development can be captured through improvements which reduce pollution in production processes (Porter and Van der Linde, 1999). Moreover, this broad definition limited the scope of sustainability to environmental protection and economic development neglecting the social equity issue. Although the intergenerational equity is stated in the definition, the intra-generational social equity was not part of the broad definition of sustainable development.

The social equity component of sustainable development emerged later when the *triple-bottom-line* was the accepted understanding of sustainability. The triple goals of sustainable development include environmental protection, economic development, and social equity. The overall goal of sustainable development is the long-term stability of the economy and environment, and, according to Emas (2015), this is only achievable through the integration of the two with social concerns throughout the decision-making process. Harris (2003) offered a detailed explanation of the three sustainable development goals. An *economically sustainable* system must be able to produce goods and services on a continuing basis, to maintain manageable levels of government and external debt, and to avoid extreme sectoral imbalances which damage agricultural or industrial production. An *environmentally sustainable* system must maintain a stable resource base, avoiding over-exploitation of renewable resource systems or environmental sink functions, and depleting nonrenewable resources only to the extent that investment is made in adequate substitutes. This includes maintenance of biodiversity, atmospheric stability, and other ecosystem functions not ordinarily classified as economic resources. A *socially sustainable* system must achieve fairness in distribution and opportunity, adequate provision of social services including health and education, gender equity, and political accountability and participation. Harris (2003) acknowledged the complex and multidimensional nature of the simultaneous effect of the three components of sustainability.

These three elements of sustainability introduce many potential complications to the original, simple definition of economic development. The goals expressed or implied are multidimensional, raising the issue of how to balance objectives and how to judge success or failure. For example, what if the provision of adequate food and water supplies appears to require changes in land use that will decrease biodiversity? What if non-polluting energy sources are more expensive, thus increasing the burden on the poor, for whom they represent a larger proportion of daily expenditure? Which goal will take precedence? (Harris, 2003)

The complexity of sustainable development was also sufficiently discussed in a study by the Board on Sustainable Development of the US National Academy of Sciences. Its publication *Our Common Journey: A Transition toward Sustainability* reviewed broad literature and explained the complex relationship between the two sustainability and development, and among the three components of sustainability. Kates, Parris, and Leiserowitz (2005) discussed this complexity by analyzing the literature reviewed in *Our Common Journey*. According to their analysis, the Board identified three major categories of things to be *sustained*—nature, life support systems, and community—as well as intermediate categories for each, such as earth, environment, and cultures. Most of the literature in Kates, Parris, and Leiserowitz's analysis emphasize on life support systems, which defined nature or environment as a source of services for the utilitarian life support of humankind (although some of the sustainable development literature valued nature for its intrinsic value rather than its utility for human beings). There were also parallel demands to sustain cultural diversity, including livelihoods, groups, and places that constitute distinctive and threatened communities. Similarly, there were three quite distinct ideas about what should be *developed*: people, economy, and society. Much of the early literature focused on economic development, with productive sectors providing employment, desired consumption, and wealth. More recently, attention has shifted to human development, including an emphasis on increased life expectancy, education, equity, and opportunity. There are also calls to develop society that emphasized the values of security and well-being of national states, regions, and institutions as well as the social capital of relationships and community ties (Kates, Parris, and Leiserowitz, 2005).

Although the above discussed components of sustainability seem to be hard to measure, there are studies that developed models to quantify sustainability. ARCADIS, a global design and consultancy firm for natural and built assets is the latest to quantify the three dimensions of sustainability by analyzing several aspects of communities. The analysis led to the creation of a sustainability index to understand the viability of cities as places to live, their environmental impact, their financial stability and how these elements complement one another. The 2016 ARCADIS Sustainable Cities Index ranks global cities on three dimensions of sustainability: people (social), planet (the environment), and profit (economic). These represent social, environmental, and economic sustainability and offer an indicative picture of the health and wealth of cities for the present and the future. It is worth to note that four African cities (three of them from the sub-Saharan Africa) are among the list of the top 100 sustainable cities of the world. The study shows that cities around the world are not effectively balancing these three pillars of sustainability. Instead, many demonstrate split personalities. While taking the lead in some areas, cities often underperform in one element of sustainability which negatively impacts their overall performance (ARCADIS, 2016).

In sum, sustainability is a call for planning, programs, policies, and actions that brings lasting relationships among society, the environment, and the economy. This results in the creation of sustainable communities with enduring resources for long-term survival. So, where is the sub-Saharan Africa in the conceptual and practical discourse of sustainable development?

SUSTAINABLE DEVELOPMENT AND SUB-SAHARAN AFRICA

Since the relationship between economic development and environmental degradation was first placed on the international agenda (on the United Nations Conference on Human Environment in 1972), sustainable development remained a far-off goal for many African countries. Poverty has been a major problem while war, deforestation, and climate change continue to challenge sub-Saharan Africa. Colonization and the historical pattern of resource exploitation have contributed to sub-Saharan Africa's inability to promote sustained economic growth, environmental protection, and improved social capital. The absence of critical infrastructure, social services, utilities, and lack of access to modern energy services have all been further obstacles to sustainable development. For a long time, Africa was not part of the discussion about sustainable development, and if sub-Saharan Africa was mentioned in the sustainability discourse, poverty eradication was on the forefront of the discussion. The Millennium Development Goals (MDGs) yielded mixed results, and with that Africa's voice got louder in recent years and contributed to the development of the SDG and other African-led sustainable development initiatives.

While there are diverse African perspectives on sustainable development, we can point to several shared attitudes. For example, there is widespread agreement that a focus on sustainability needs to be a part of the development discourse. It is commonly accepted by diplomats, scholars, development workers, and lay people that development planning in sub-Saharan Africa must simultaneously address economic, environmental, and societal issues, and that problems and solutions in one of these domains have implications for the other domains. As we indicated at the beginning of this chapter, African nations played a significantly large role in this process of re-defining the global development agenda for 2030. Many key committees that negotiated the new SDGs were chaired by African leaders. Several important conferences and meetings were held in Africa. In addition to this, the CAP became a special feature of the SDGs. It outlines six pillars of sustainable development specific for Africa (i.e., structural economic transformation and inclusive growth, science and technology, people-centered development, environmental sustainability, peace and security, and financing), and it symbolizes the extent to which Africa had a unified and particularly influential voice in the process of defining the SDGs. Some argue that the African voice was leveraged in the negotiations of SDGs due to the lack of success of the MDGs in Africa and the fact that African leaders felt they lacked the capacity to participate in defining the previous global development agenda (Quint, 2014). It is also noted that African leaders demanded a bigger role in the SDG negotiations since six out of the top ten fastest growing economies between the years 2000–2010 and 2011–2015 were African countries (The Economist, 2011). Much of this growth is attributed to internal structural changes that sparked domestic economies. Therefore, African leaders wanted greater participation in the negotiations of the SDGs in order to better leverage possibilities for strengthening the private sector and private-investments. Motivations for elevating African participation in defining the SDGs appear to be diverse from an "on the ground" perspective. There is widespread agreement, however, that the inclusive dialogue among Africans indeed resulted in strengthening an African voice in the SDG discourse, and in fact resulted in creating development goals that specifically address urbanization and the need for creating peace and security. That said, while Africans celebrated the production of the

CAP and the multiple ways in which African voices contributed to defining the SDGs, other participants in the process have characterized the numerous consultations and conversations in Africa as "hyper-participatory" and as a "convoluted" process.

In May 2012, African heads of states, in collaboration with public and private sector partners, held a two-day summit where sustainability was at the center of the deliberations. The summit resulted in the Gaborone Declaration for Sustainability in Africa, where countries committed to implementing all conventions and declarations that promote sustainable development. The declaration demonstrated how African nations and their investment partners understand, manage, and value natural capital to support and improve human well-being. The aim was to take a practical, results-focused approach, with African nations leading and encouraging investment partners to provide support in a coordinated and coherent fashion. They agreed that the value of natural capital—the wealth of benefits provided to people by biodiversity and ecosystems, like watersheds, forests, coral reefs, and grasslands—must be fully accounted for and integrated into national and corporate planning, as well as reporting practices, policies, and programs (Seligmann and Andelman, 2012).

Moving forward, sub-Saharan Africa's participation in the planning of sustainable development need to be translated into action. With the implementations of SDG and other declarations, pledges, and initiatives lay ahead, sub-Saharan Africa keeps playing a key role in ensuring that there is a balanced economic growth and environmental protection that can render social equity and well-being of its people.

THE NEED FOR A POST-SDG BOOK

This book is intended to advance the understanding of the relationship between sustainability and the promotion of prosperity in sub-Saharan Africa. When the United Nations' adopted the 17 SDGs in 2016 it issued a universal call to mobilize efforts to end poverty, fight inequalities, and combat climate change in ways that meet the needs of the present without compromising the ability of future generations to meet their own needs. Nowhere is the question of sustainable development more pressing than in sub-Saharan Africa. As the result of its unique set of historical, socioeconomic, political, and environmental challenges, sub-Saharan Africa demands our attention and focus on how to build an inclusive, sustainable, and resilient future. In this book, we examine how strategies that build economic growth, social inclusion, and environmental protection are being implemented throughout the region. We consider how experiences of inequality, access to healthcare, economic growth, cities and human settlements, environmental terrorism, climate change, sustainable consumption and production, and peace and justice have impacted sustainability in sub-Saharan Africa and evaluate strategies that have developed to promote equitable social development and the sustainable management of natural resources and ecosystems.

Each chapter of this book is intended to advance the discourse on sustainable development in sub-Saharan Africa. A variety of disciplines are represented to allow for a discussion of sustainable development in Africa from different perspectives. Every region of sub-Saharan Africa is represented in order to provide a broader consideration of challenges to sustainability and efforts that are being made to implement the SDGs. We have divided the chapters to align with specific sustainable development goals as outlined by the UN. The plan of the book is as follows: Part I provides a historical overview and regional context for a discourse about sustainability in sub-Saharan Africa. Chapter 1 highlights the development of sustainable development practices in general and the history of African sustainability in particular. In chapter 2, the ethical challenges of designing and implementing sustainable development programs are considered against the backdrop of post-genocide Rwanda. Chapter 3 contributes to the understanding of the regional context for sustainability by focusing on the environmental crisis and mining terrorism in Congo. Congo hosts the largest segment of the legendary pristine forest of Central Africa. At the same time, it is the land of the global "gold rush" for access to strategic minerals useful for our digital technologies. This chapter explores the crisis of mining pollution in the Katanga province and the shrinking of the rain forest, while reflecting on the political and social implications economic development that fails to promote equity and inclusion. In chapter 4, the relationship between governance and economic development is explored, using recent events in Zimbabwe to assess the long-term prospects for the sustainable development goals.

Part II applies the sustainable development goal of climate action and institutional partnerships to the discussion of attitudes of Africans toward climate change in chapter 5 and grassroots partnerships for sustainable development in chapter 6. More specifically, chapter 3 examines how climate change is conceptualized by publics in sub-Saharan Africa where the impacts of a changing climate are increasingly discernible. To investigate Africans attitudes regarding climate change, the chapter's authors employ multivariate analysis of public opinion data to examine the attitudes of those residing in a region of the world that is heavily dependent on environmental stability for economic survival. The chapter aligns with the UN's recognition that fostering sustainable development requires confronting the realities of climate change. Indeed, sustainable development cannot be achieved without climate action. In chapter 6, the authors focus on domestic resource mobilization

(DRM) which remains a challenge for many reasons in the world's poorest countries. The chapter reviews some of the obstacles to increasing DRM across sub-Saharan Africa and suggests that international cooperation on tax is, in fact, the key to mobilizing the domestic public resources required to achieve the SDGs. The chapter also draws upon Africans critiques not only to highlight the shortcomings of the current reform process but also to advance an alternative set of proposals.

Part III of the book turns its attention to the issue of sustainable cities and communities. Here the authors of chapters 7, 8, and 9 examine bridging the gaps in healthcare disparities, assess the impact of changes to transportation on urban development, and discuss the issues surrounding the promotion of open green spaces in African cities. This set of chapters relies on case study evidence to advance our understanding of how cities, towns, and villages can be planned and managed as drivers of sustainable development. Chapter 7 looks at the case of Holy Innocents Children's Hospital Mbarara, Uganda (HICH) which provides holistic, integrated, and sustainable health care to children. HICH's community health outreach programs involve collaborations with a local women's NGO and American Study Abroad programs to supply health information for disease prevention, especially in geographically isolated locations and rural communities. In chapter 8, the author considers how cities in Africa have implemented sustainable practices in their transportation planning in order to avoid the negative socio-environmental consequences of a developing autocentric culture. Chapter 9 explores the current status of open green space in Dakar, Senegal. It explains how urbanization, privatization, and local communities' appropriation of neglected open green space has changed the use of and meanings associated with these socially and culturally significant urban spaces and the impact this has had on the social sustainability of urban communities.

With their multidisciplinary approach to understanding sustainable development in sub-Saharan Africa, the chapters realize synergies from the links between health, water, climate change, transportation, natural resources, urban design, land use, and economic growth. Sustainable development has remained elusive for many African countries, but there have been effective responses in several settings. This book addresses the challenges to sustainable development in sub-Saharan Africa while also discussing the important progress that has been made across the region. It is our hope that this will advance a framework for sustainability that will emphasize the role of community-based partnerships as well as regional and international collaborations to promote sustained economic growth and sustainable development.

NOTE

1. The editors are grateful for the support of colleagues at the California State University, in particular Harry Hellenbrand, Stella Theodoulou, Lii Yii, Matthew Cahn, Tom Spencer-Walters, Theresa White, Yan Searcy, and Liam Espinoza-Zemlicka, and members of the ISAMP. We also thank Emily Roderick and Alison Keefner at Lexington who guided this project through the publication process. Thank you to all of our friends, colleagues, and relatives in Africa; without their support, this book would not have been possible.

REFERENCES

ARCADIS. (2016). Sustainable Cities Index 2016: Putting People at the Heart of City Sustainability. https://www.arcadis.com/en/global/our-perspectives/sustainable-cities-index-2016/.

Board on Sustainable Development Policy Division of National Research Council. (1999). *Our Common Journey: A Transition toward Sustainability*. Washington, DC: National Academy Press.

Emas, R. (2015). *The Concept of Sustainable Development: Definition and Defining Principles*. Florida International University, Brief for GSDR.

Harris, J. M. (2003). *Sustainability and Sustainable Development, Encyclopedia of Ecological Economics: International Society for Ecological Economics*. http://isecoeco.org/pdf/susdev.pdf.

Porter, M. E., and Van der Linde, C. (1999). Green and Competitive: Ending the Stalemate. *Journal of Business Administration and Politics*, 73(5), Sept–Oct 1995, 120–134.

Quint, R. (2014). Levaeraging Africa's Voice: Determining the Post-2015 Development Goals. *SAIS Review of International Affairs* 34(2): 113–20.

Robert, W. K., Thomas, M. P., and Anthony, A. L. (2005). What is Sustainable Development? Goals, Indicators, Values, and Practice. *Environment: Science and Policy for Sustainable Development* 47(3): 8–21.

Seligmann, P. A., and Andelman, S. J. (2012). Sustainability in Africa. *ArcNews*, http://www.esri.com/news/arcnews/fall12articles/sustainability-in-africa.html.

The Economist. (2011). Africa's Impressive Growth, January 6, 2011, http://www.economist.com/blogs/dailychart/2011/01/daily_chart.

United Nations General Assembly. (1987). *Our Common Future, Report of the World Commission on Environment and Development*. United Nations General Assembly, Development and International Co-operation.

Part I

HISTORY AND REGIONAL CONTEXT FOR SUSTAINABILITY DISCOURSE IN SUB-SAHARAN AFRICA

Chapter 1

The History of Sustainable Development and the Emerging African Voice

Suzanne Scheld and Mintesnot Woldeamanuel

On May 25, 2018, 50 African heads of states and 41 former leaders gathered in Addis Ababa, Ethiopia, to celebrate the Golden Jubilee, or the 50th anniversary of the African Union (formerly called "the Organization of African Unity" [OAU]). The OAU was formed in 1963 and played a critical role in the decolonization of Africa and the emergence of African voices in international relations. In addition to celebrating this historic moment, the Golden Jubilee provided an opportunity to set a new agenda for transforming Africa in the coming 50 years. There is a growing critique among Africans that the continent has abandoned the principles laid out by the founders of the OAU. Many lament the structural inequalities within the global economy that produce poverty in the continent, promote negative stereotypes of Africa that mask these inequalities, and limit unity among African States. Many argue that donors providing loans and aid to African countries largely set the agenda for development in Africa. How can Africans get back to the foundational principles and goals of the OAU, and take charge of shaping the Africa that Africans want? How would the concept and goals of sustainable development be defined in the context of Africans determining the future of Africa?

In this chapter we discuss the concept of sustainable development—a contemporary and refined variation on the broader concept of development—and its emergence and application in Africa over time. There is a tendency to believe that poverty and a poor quality of life characterizes the circumstances for all Africans everywhere in the continent, and development has not been possible because circumstances within the continent prevent improvements from being made (e.g., life in Africa is perceived as too chaotic due to wars, too backward due to low levels of education, and too wracked by disease due to harsh natural environments and the lack of environmental awareness).

In the pages below, we show how the goal of effecting development in Africa has been a cover for legitimizing foreign interventions and the maintenance of unequal political and economic relationships between Africa and Others over time. We believe the goals of sustainable development have a possibility of creating positive change in Africa. However, this will not be due to the new focus on the sustainability of development. Rather, change will be possible if Africans have a greater say in defining the sustainable development agenda and its implementation.

DEFINING SUSTAINABLE DEVELOPMENT

Sustainable development is a recent variation on the concept "development," a term that has been in use since the mid-1800s. The roots of the concept of sustainable development lie in the history of the Enlightenment, a European intellectual movement of the seventeenth and eighteenth centuries that promoted the notion that the power of reason is a means to understand the universe and to attain knowledge, freedom, and happiness. The movement became a driving force behind European exploration, the emergence of nation states and the concept of democracy, as well as the development of the scientific method. Philosophers of the Enlightenment promoted the use of rational thought, science, and technology as markers of social progress, and embraced capitalism as a system with the potential to improve the human condition as long as there was free competition and limited government intervention. Adam Smith (1723–1790) best articulates these beliefs in the power of capitalism in *The Wealth of Nations* (1776), a text that is often viewed as laying the foundations for development debates.

As it is discussed in the introduction to this book, today's most widely acknowledged definition of sustainable development is articulated in the Brundtland Commission Report published by the United Nations in 1987. This report defined sustainable development as "development that meets the needs of the present without compromising the ability of future generations to meet their own needs" (WCED, 1987). This broad definition was derived from two basic ideas: the need for countries to be able to strive for economic development now and in the future, and the need for natural resources to be available in order for these goals to be met. Since the publication of the Brundtland Commission Report, numerous interpretations of sustainable development have emerged. In 1999, the landmark study of sustainable development commissioned by the National Research Council, *Our Common Journey: A Transition Toward Sustainability*, sought to give order to the unwieldy body of emerging concepts. They created a comprehensive typology of the variety of definitions for sustainable development. They highlight that sustainable development has largely been conceived as an economic and ecological phenomenon. Social capital and social phenomena eventually made their way into the discourse. Based on the report, definitions tend to vary in terms of the conceptualization of what is to be sustained, what is to be developed, and for how long phenomena need to be sustained and developed. In addressing what is to be sustained, definitions varied in emphasis on nature (e.g., earth, biodiversity, and ecosystems), life support (e.g., ecosystems, resources, environment), and community (e.g., cultures, groups, places). In addressing what is to be developed, definitions also varied in emphasis on people (e.g., child survival, life expectancy, education, equity, equal opportunity), economy (e.g., wealth, productive sectors, consumption), and society (e.g., institutions, social capital, states, regions). Definitions further varied in terms of the scope of time in which phenomena should be sustained and/or developed, and the extent to which phenomena should be sustained and/or developed (e.g., only, mostly, and, or, etc.) (Kates et al., 2005). They also varied in terms of their stated goals (Redclift, 1992). Kates et al. (2005) note that sustainable development goals can vary in terms of scopes of time in which one should expect to see change. For Kates et al. (2005), the United Nations Millennium Declaration of 2015 represents short-term goals (i.e., effect sustainable development by 2035). The Sustainability Transition of the Board of Sustainable Development, part of the US National Academy of Sciences, conceives of sustainable development taking at least two generations in order for goals to be reached. And, The Great Transition of the Global Scenario Group, formed by the Tellus Institute in Boston, Massachusetts, and the Stockholm Environment Institute of Sweden, perceived of change taking place over an undefined "long term."

In 2002, the World Summit on Sustainable Development resulted in the clarification of several shared themes in the definitions, which went on to be considered the three pillars of sustainable development: economic development, social development, and environmental protection. The definition that emerged from these meetings also emphasized the notion of a collective responsibility to address sustainable development at the local, national, regional, and global levels. This definition shifted the long-standing association of the sustainable development with merely ecological and economic concerns. At the same time, it expanded the scope of the concept by highlighting the need to address sustainable development on diverse scales. That said, a quick Web search reveals that there are also diverse concepts of the three pillars of sustainable development, especially the "social" pillar. Some definitions focus on social development, social progress, human development, human well-being, social justice, and equity. These terms are similar but not necessarily interchangeable as they have distinct histories and therefore propose distinct definitions of sustainable development.

African scholars and leaders' definitions of sustainable development to some extent echo the broader debates. Some are in favor of a definition based on the three-pillar notion. Some place an accent on one pillar over another. Others suggest the lack of a unified view contributes to the ineffectiveness of sustainable development initiatives. Godwell Nhamo, of the University of South Africa, argues that morality and ethics are missing elements of current sustainable development definitions. He writes, "Sustainable development goes beyond the three founding principles of sustainability that include the economic, environmental and social pillars. Human beings simply need to adhere to what is right, and do it simply because it is right" (Nhamo, 2017: 228). Nhamo is concerned that the emergence of an African voice in determining the sustainable development agenda signals to many a level playing field and encourages people to ignore the historical factors that generated poverty, environmental degradation, and the marginalization of African voices from the discourse in the first place. In short, from the African perspective, the definition of sustainability not only needs to attend to the environmental, economic, and social relationships, there is a moral obligation to appreciate the historical underpinnings of sustainable development. Without this, progress is unlikely to be achieved.

MEASURING AND CLASSIFYING SUSTAINABLE DEVELOPMENT

Sustainable development implies the notion of change; therefore, practitioners of sustainable development need tools to assess progress. Many of the available tools, however, do not always capture the realities in Africa or set up reasonable comparisons between African and other countries. For example, some of the tools that are commonly used to measure sustainable development include per capita gross national product (GNP), the gross national income, human poverty index, gender development index, infant mortality rate (IMR), the human development index, and the human freedom index, to name a few statistical approaches. These measurements reflect a drive to aggregate the measurement of a variety of indicators in order to present sustainable development in comprehensive and manageable terms. However, development is a complex phenomenon that in many ways defies statistical summary. Efforts to represent this ongoing, holistic phenomenon with statistics inevitably create distortions. But aside from this, bureaucracies in Africa are relatively ill-equipped for undertaking comprehensive surveys and censuses, and for adequately storing data. As a result, timely statistics from a broad range of institutions are often unavailable or inaccurate, which makes it difficult to create aggregated statistics for comparison as well as evidence-driven policies (Jerven and Johnston, 2015). The poor quality of statistical data from African countries is a problem that affects many domains of social life. To give one example of the consequences, in 2014 Nigeria surpassed South Africa overnight as the African country with the largest economy. A decision was made to rebase the calculation of the gross domestic product (GDP). Normally, rebasing is done every three to five years; however, it had not been done in decades in Nigeria. In effect, Nigerian policies had been based upon inaccurate statistics for many years, and our understanding of the order of economies and relationships among African countries was skewed for many years.

In addition to this, traditional metrics have perpetuated the view that African countries are always on the bottom rungs of any system of classification. In the past, the term "Third World" was often used to describe "developing" countries, while "First World" was used to describe "developed" countries. This system of classification was created during the Cold War when First World countries were those aligned with the North Atlantic Treaty Organization, and Second World countries were those aligned with the Communistic Bloc (e.g., Soviet Union, China, Cuba and friends), and Third World countries were others that didn't fit with the definition of the First and Second World categories. These countries tended to be poor, so the category Third World country soon became associated with poverty and hence African countries. Even when this classifying system fell out of favor due to the dissolution of the Soviet Union in 1991, the Third World label remained and became a convenient code to refer to African countries.

In the 1990s, the United Nations adopted "developed" and "developing" as terminology for classifying countries. Developing countries was further parsed into "less developed country" and "underdeveloped country." These categorizations are based on levels of industrialization, technology, GNP, and the visibility of a host of shared features that are intertwined with these economic factors such as levels of poverty, IMRs, and access to education. This system of classification has been criticized for its ethnocentric presumption that high levels of industrialization and technology are universal markers of development when these markers of progress are particular outcomes of specific historical trajectories that not all countries have followed; in addition, there are other markers of social progress that are not taken into consideration such as cultural creativity, and levels of ingenuity for solving problems with human "infrastructure" instead of technology or material forms of infrastructure (Robinson, 2002; Scheld, 2003; Simone, 2004).

Since the 1990s, social scientists have challenged this dichotomous categorization of nations by pointing out evidence of uneven development within regions and individual countries. To give one example, Ghana is currently among the fastest growing economies in Africa. In 1994, the economy's growth rate was 3.3 percent. It peaked in 2011 at 14 percent due to oil production. Since then, its growth has leveled off at 6.3 percent, which is a higher growth rate than the average African country (Africa Development Bank Group, 2018). As a result of this growth, the national poverty rate has dropped from 56.5 percent in 1992 to 24.2 percent in 2013 (Cooke, Hague, and McKay, 2016: 1). However, while the poverty rate in urban areas significantly improved within this period of time, the rural poverty rate significantly increased nearly fourfold (ibid). In some ways, Ghana is beginning to show the signs of a "developed" nation, while other signs suggest it is a "developing" nation. There are similar examples of uneven development in countries that are presumed to be fully developed, suggesting these labels are limited for characterizing and comparing social progress, and illuminating at least one reason why the World Bank does not have an official definition for these categories and announced in 2016 that it would no longer employ these terms because they are more convenient than analytical terms.

An alternative to using developing and developed terminology is "Global South" and "Global North." These terms emerged because many poor countries are located in the Southern Hemisphere, and many of these countries are marked by colonialism and neocolonialism and other social transformations that have resulted in large inequalities, poor living standards, and limited access to resources. That said, as we have suggested in the earlier paragraphs, there are many differences between African countries as well as within them, which suggests that these terms are homogenizing. The changing systems of classification reflect an increasingly nuanced understanding of differences among countries in the world and the need for more precise ways to measure development. At the same time, it draws attention to the political aspect of naming and ordering countries in relationship to development, a multidimensional and challenging phenomenon to characterize.

The earlier discussion of metrics and classification systems is crucial to understanding Africa's initial absence in the discussion of global development agenda. They show how African countries have been poorly understood as well as constructed as inferior and insignificant nations, and therefore relegated to being passive participants in determining sustainable development agendas. Meanwhile, African countries have provided an abundance of resources that have helped the advancement and improvement of statistics of other societies in the world. For this reason and from the African perspective, it is problematic to conceive of African countries as aid "recipients" instead of equal partners, as indebted to others instead of leading or contributing to others. As the African perspective has come to be recognized, a demand for strengthening the tools and mediums for representing Africa has also emerged.

SUSTAINABLE DEVELOPMENT IN HISTORICAL PERSPECTIVE OF AFRICA

As the concept and approaches for measuring and classifying sustainable development have changed over time, these shifts signal a moment of change in the history of sustainable development in Africa. How did sustainable development emerge in Africa? Why are Africans demanding to have a voice in sustainable development debates today? Why haven't their voices been heard since the founding of the OAU?

Pre-colonial versions of sustainable development and early African voices

The term "sustainable development" was not likely to have been used in the pre-colonial era; however, Africans were concerned with the sustainability of natural resources and the prosperity of their societies during this time. Understanding African in the pre-colonial period is challenging, though, due to limited sources and the wide range of interpretations of available information. For example, Astrid Meier (2007) illustrates how two highly regarded researchers, the historian George Brooks and the meteorologist Sharon Nicholson, use the same sources but arrive at vastly different conclusions about the time frames for the wet and dry seasons in the Western Sahel in the eleventh to seventeenth centuries (218; see McCann for similar observations, 1999: 264). Another reason it is difficult to conjure an accurate picture of Africans in the pre-colonial period is this history is highly mediated by Western perspectives. Europeans who wrote about the first encounters in Africa, feared Africans because they were unfamiliar. As a result, they often cast Africans in a negative light, describing them as primitive, backward, and uncivilized. Some went to the extreme in the opposite direction and cast Africans of pre-colonial times as nobles, and extraordinary for their ability to live in perfect harmony with pristine nature. These views, although intended to be positive, were over-romanticized and at times patronizing. Either way, due to a lack of familiarity with Africa, Europeans socially constructed exaggerated images of Africans, which led them to inaccurately convey their relationships with their natural and social environments prior to colonialism. Today's researchers are aware of these biased frameworks and must exercise caution when examining sources from the pre-colonial period.

Today, at least two bodies of literature are consulted for imagining the antecedents of sustainable development in Africa. First, the archaeological record documents many forms of environmentally conscious adaptations in Africa, reflecting Africans' concerns for resource conservation and interest in planning for the future. For example, the record includes evidence of innovative approaches to hunting and food foraging, swidden (slash-and-burn techniques), terracing, divisions of labor across and within communities, and vegetation and marine life management (see Allan, 1965; Clark and Brandt, 1984; Sutton, 1989). Africans employed these adaptations within diverse forms of political structures, such as the band, tribe, chiefdom, and early state structures. Each of these forms entails a different system for decision-making (e.g., consensus, informal leadership, hereditary leadership, and bureaucracy). Such diversity of political structures suggest some African societies were not only concerned about survival and environmental conservation but invested in expanding the size of their size and its economy. Scholars debate the interpretation of the archaeological record, however, and caution readers from assuming that all evidence of complex societies does not necessarily reflect that a society is driven to expand. For example, archaeologists argue evidence of terracing at Nyanga hills in eastern Zimbabwe and at Engaruka in the northern Tanzanian rift over time reflect efforts for societies to adapt to ecological pressures so as to remain insular rather than expand (Sutton, 1989: 6). Archaeologists also caution readers from interpreting the typology of diverse forms of adaptations as an indication that African societies developed along in a linear progression, and contemporary food foragers, for instance, reflect a lack of adaptation and evidence of traditional societies being stuck in the past. There is evidence that some societies, such as the Hadza of Tanzania, shifted from a simple to more complex form of social organization, and then reverted back to a simple form as a strategy for adapting to harsh environmental conditions (Marlowe, 2002). In other words, the "devolution" of a social formation can be a "development" strategy employed for the sustainability and prosperity of a society in the context of Africa.

While anthropological literature helps us to imagine the innovativeness of Africans in the pre-colonial period, it leaves us to wonder about the role the environment played in shaping societies during this time. In much anthropological research referred to above, the environment is cast as a static entity. Yet landscapes in Africa are constantly changing, and at times they have exerted more influence over humans than humans have exerted over the landscape. For example, the Inter-tropical Convergence Zone (ITCZ), a high pressure belt of approximately 30 degrees latitude from both sides of the equator, is an important natural phenomenon that shapes Africa's physical environments as well as the social interactions within them. The ITCZ impacts rainy and dry seasons in Africa, which researchers now prefer to refer to as "levels of aridity." In *Landlords and Strangers* (1993), George Brooks argues shifting levels of aridity played a significant role in human interactions in the Sahel in the pre-colonial period. As the location of rains shifted over time, cereal farming tended to move from the edge of the savannah to the north. This in turn extended the political boundaries of ruling elites associated with the farmers, and intensified relations along Saharan trade routes. At the same time, less arid temperatures fostered the growth of grasses and increases in tsetse fly populations. Swarms of tsetse flies dissuaded warrior horsemen in the north from raiding villages in the south, thereby permitting new social relations to develop in a context of limited conflict. In other words, aspects of the environment produced change within nature and society. This example illustrates how the environment in the pre-colonial period was as much an agent of promoting and creating a need for sustainable development as Africans (for additional examples see Beinart, 2003; Maddox, 2006; McCann, 1999; Sheridan, 2009).

One area of research that has received significant attention in discussions of conservation in the pre-colonial period is the history of sacred groves (Beinart et al., 2000; Beinart, 2003; Leach and Mearns, 1996; Maddox, 2006; Sheridan and Nymaweru, 2008; Sheridan, 2009). A sacred grove is a natural area that is protected by communities for spiritual and cultural reasons. Today, such areas may be large (e.g., the Royal Mile of Uganda, the Osun-Osogbo of southern, Nigeria, and Jaagbo and Anweam of Ghana) or smaller "islands" of forested areas such as those on the coast of Kenya. They may also be individual trees, such as specific baobab trees in various towns in Senegal (Ross, 2008). Many view sacred groves as the untouched relics of larger, formerly pristine forests that were undermined during the colonial and post-colonial periods. It is argued sacred groves illustrate the role religious belief systems, customs, and cultural taboos play in safeguarding against excessive killing of animals and over use of agricultural lands (Ntiamoa-Baidu, 2009). On the one hand, this view elevates the status of African indigenous knowledge as enduring wisdom and a sign of the strength of indigenous cultures since the pre-colonial period. On the other hand, it renders Africans as passive in relationship to the natural and social forces that have threatened African landscapes.

Sacred groves are proving to be more complex than this, however. In recent years, they have become an international symbol of African conservation. UNESCO and other international organizations contribute to this status as they deem certain sacred groves as sites for historic preservation and pour funds into the preservation of these areas. Stewards of sacred groves now vie for this classification and the resources that come with it, and as a result, the sacredness of some groves is being created in the twenty-first century and is not an aspect of pre-colonial history (Sheridan and Nyamweru, 2008). Although sacred groves are socially constructed and do not offer a precise prism through which to view the pre-colonial past, they underscore that African responses to sustainable development are mediated by the political arrangements and power structures and specific environmental circumstances. They also underscore that a global perspective is relevant to understanding the antecedents of sustainable development. Before contact with Europeans, Africans were certainly decision-makers who exercised voice with respect to the conservation and management of their own resources.

Early European Encounters: Silenced African Voices

Early encounters with Europeans took place during the time of the emergence of nation states in Western Europe and the rise of triangle trading between Europe, the Americas, and Africa (1600–1900s) which fueled their formation. During this time, the term "development" began to appear in common parlance and environmental conservation was a recognized practice; however, African voices were not among those invited to define either of these concepts. In fact, Africans began to lose control over resources on the continent and were actively silenced by Europeans in international conversations regarding development.

As nation states began to form in Western Europe, there was a great need for land and resources to strengthen these societies. Thus, Europeans established a network whereby they brought slaves from Africa to the Americas and the Caribbean for farming cotton and sugar. These goods were then exported to Europe and used to manufacture textiles and other goods which were then exported back to Africa and the Americas for consumption. This arrangement of trading networks was highly lucrative for Europeans as they were able to offset the cost of imports by the gains made with exports. The triangle of trade was extremely disadvantageous to Africa, however. Estimates suggest between 10 and 12 million Africans were taken into slavery during these years. Such a loss destroyed traditional farming systems and any equilibrium between human needs and the environment they had fostered. Although African elites made small gains from the transatlantic slave trade by participating in setting up slave ports and supplying traders with slaves in exchange for arms, wine, textiles, and other goods, overall, the slave trade undermined African societies (Curtin, 1969; Inikori, 1992; Klein, 2010; Rodney, 1981). What is more, it positioned Africa as a supplier of resources to the global economy and foreshadowed the need to socially construct African societies as in need of development, dependent on Europeans for development, and as having no historical experience or authority to take the lead in defining the terms of development.

By the mid-nineteenth century, Europeans questioned the morality of slavery and argued for it to end. These arguments, however, coincided with the reality that the slave trade was also no longer lucrative. Nevertheless, it was "abolished," but triangle trade relations remained intact. These relations were re-invigorated by the rise of industrialization in Europe and the United States, and the need for oils to grease industrial machinery. This shift, then, prompted the emergence of the concept of development and its modern association with economic growth. European traders set up colonies in Africa in order to efficiently facilitate the extraction of palm oil, peanuts, cacao, and other vegetable products for the development of industrialization in Europe. The development of the colonies also included setting up cash crop agricultural systems, mining operations, and systems of forced labor as well as taxes for Africans to pay if they did not allocate their lands and labor to this new European endeavor. Conservation efforts that folded into development goals also disfavored Africans. For example, it was often declared that African traditional farming practices were the cause of soil erosion. Scientific studies of plants and soils were employed to legitimize mandates to stop traditional African farming practices (Beinart and Bundy, 1987: 18). In South Africa, in order to protect endangered animals, policies were created to relegate African herders to designated land area, even though wide-ranging mobility is central to the pastoralist approach to subsistence. Such policies, again, undermined traditional African adaptations to the land, limited Africans access to their own lands, and increased colonial administrators control over Africans (Beinart and Bundy, 1987: 17).

Throughout the European colonies, these and other similar policies were backed and funded by governments in the metropoles. Indeed, the British Empire dedicated a large department within its government to oversee and develop its colonies throughout the world. The Colonial Development Act of 1929, which permitted the Crown to provide significant funding to develop the British colonies in Africa, was therefore not unusual. Rather, this policy foreshadowed a dynamic of contemporary development that was to become common in Africa, namely, the sponsorship of development by foreign governments. The creation of such policies and provision of funding also highlighted how Africans were not the intended beneficiaries of development nor given a say in defining the goals of development.

Early Post-Colonialism (1960s–1970s): Thwarted African Voices

In the 1960s–1970s, many African nations were liberated from colonial rule and the OAU was formed. It appeared that Africans would finally have a say over the terms of development in their emerging nation states. In the international arena, however, African voices were somewhat thwarted.

The hegemony of "modernization theory" contributed to curtailing African voices in the early post-colonial period. "Modernization theory" is a concept that asserts with the end of colonialism, less developed countries would improve their standards of living if they followed in the footsteps of developed countries and modernized their industrial sectors (Larrain, 1989).

Industrial development was expected to give African countries a boost by permitting the capitalist sector (i.e., urban sector) to draw off surplus labor from the non-capitalist, subsistence, or "inefficient" sector (i.e., rural sector). Profits created in the urban sector would eventually be reinvested in the rural sector, thereby a creating a well-integrated dual sector economic system. This theory of economic development was offered by an American economist, W. A. Lewis, in *The Theory of Economic Growth* (1955). In many African countries, however, this theory resulted in stark uneven development. Resources were poured into developing infrastructure and amenities in cities, while rural sectors were neglected. Even when the international development field recognized the lack of attention being paid to developing agricultural sectors, the solution was to gift technology (e.g., tractors, fertilizers, etc.) rather than capacitate African farmers with knowledge of how to repair and maintain such technology and access special supplies in the long run. As a result, injections of agricultural technology did little to improve rural economies. This situation became problematic over time as opportunities for a better life were perceived to be attainable in cities and incentivized rural-to-urban migration, leaving rural sectors with less skilled labor, capital, and capacity for developing.

Modernization theories fell short in Africa in another way. Since industrialization was thought to be the key to development, many African countries implemented import substitution policies and sought to nationalize their economies. Some of the light manufacturing was successful for a while. For example, success was initially seen with textiles, beverage, and soap production. But manufacturing was limited due to a lack of capital, updated technology, and skilled labor. Domestic markets were small, transportation across borders was not highly developed, and many goods were unable to compete in the global market. As a result, industrialization in the 1960s and 1970s did not provide the powerful boost that was necessary for the economic autonomy of African countries. This "incomplete" development, rather, reinforced the perception that African countries were better suppliers of natural resources to the global market than manufacturers.

The myth of modernization theories is further illuminated through a view of international relations leading up to the decolonization of Africa. After World War II, Western European countries needed significant assistance, and without external aid, they would have collapsed and negatively affected the world economy. Therefore in 1944, the United States organized the Bretton Woods conference in New Hampshire, where 700 delegates from 44 allied nations gathered to discuss strategies for stabilizing the global economy. At this conference, the International Monetary Fund (IMF) and World Bank (WB) were created as international organizations that would set the agenda for the global economy and provide loans and aid to rehabilitate countries in need of support in order to be able to contribute to the global economy and its potential for growth. In 1948, the United States strategically added to these efforts by implementing the Marshall Plan, a policy that permitted the government to provide over 12 billion to rebuilding Western Europe countries. Bretton Woods and the Marshall Plan signaled the beginning of a new era when states and supra-state organizations would pro-actively provide aid for the uplift and development of countries that were needed for the maintenance and growth of the global economy. In addition to boosting countries and maintaining the global economy, aid and loans created particular power relations within the international arena as these forms of assistance were often delivered with conditions, such as the requirement of using loans to purchase goods that are manufactured in donor countries. Many African countries were required to pay back loans that were generated by colonial administrations before Independence. In other words, while development in Africa was touted as a desirable form of modernization, and held the promise of putting African countries on a level political and economic playing field with Western European countries and the United States, it masked the reality that governments of the former colonies were redefining their relationships with emerging African countries, and diminishing their obligations to pay for development in Africa. African leaders accepted this responsibility, but they did so while import substitution economies were not yet viable, producing curtailed African voices in the international arena.

Second Stage Post-Colonialism (1980s–2000s): Defiant African Voices

If the political voices of African leaders were thwarted in the late 1970s, they would become defiant in the mid-1980s. In the late 1970s, a global oil crisis and rising prices of commodities propelled the world economy into a recession. Developing countries experienced increased unemployment and poverty. In Africa, the effects were much worse as they were compounded by water and food shortages in West Africa, the spread of HIV/AIDS in east and southern Africa, political conflict in Central Africa, and apartheid in South Africa. Many African heads of state did not respond well to the growing and varied problems in Africa. Since the Cold War they were sent down a path of allocating public funds for personal use and receiving special favors from entities from the United States, Western Europe, the Soviet Union, and the Eastern bloc vying for power and influence in Africa. By the early 1980s, many African countries were heavily in debt and were experiencing any economic growth. The World Bank and IMF sought to bail out African countries implementing Structural Adjustment Programs (SAPs). These programs intended to alleviate poverty. However, in exchange for loans and aid, African countries were required to devalue their currencies, diminish the size of the public sector by instituting government austerity and cost-sharing measures for education, health, and other public services. Open borders and tax breaks for foreign companies were also required.

SAPs were a controversial approach to development. Because most African countries did not experience any economic growth since their implementation, many were critical of these neoliberal policies. Some however, argue while SAPs did not alleviate poverty, they did not exacerbate it—without SAPs, the quality of life in Africa could have been much worse. Others argue that economies were more depressed than ever. Public services were in decline, private services were unaffordable to many, and environmental destruction was on the rise (see Babb, 2005; Williams, 1994). Ordinary citizens sided with the negative view of SAPs, and as a result, many protests were organized throughout Africa to protest SAPs and the WB and IMF in the mid-1980s and 1990s. There were students protests in Benin (1989), Niger (1990), Nigeria (1986, 1988, 1989, 1990, 1992), Sudan (1987), Uganda (1990), Zaire (1989), Zambia (1981), among other countries (Danaher and Yunus, 1994; Dwyer and Zeilig, 2012). These protests directly critiqued economic policies, but they were also joined by other dissenting voices that critiqued the accelerated exploitation of natural resources as a result of development policies of the 1980s. In Kenya in the mid-1980s, for example, Wangari Maathai organized the Green Belt Revolution. Rural women experienced food insecurity as their water supplies were drying up and soils were eroding due to climate change and the exploitation of natural resources. Maathai led women in a social movement that entailed planting trees in order to address the environmental issues while also promoting women's rights. At the time, women in the Green Belt movement were not taken seriously, and in fact were ridiculed by Daniel Toroitch arap Moi, the president of Kenya, for planting trees (Dater and Merton, 2009). The Survival of the Ogoni People in Nigeria in the 1990s is another example of African voices challenging the effects of development policies on the environment in the 1980s and 1990s. In this case, Ken Saro-Wiwa, a well-known Nigerian writer and television producer, mobilized the Ogoni in a protest against Dutch Shell Oil who was drilling for oil on Ogoni native lands. As a result of the oil, pollution, environmental degradation, and poverty increased. Violence in the region also increased as Saro-Wiwa and other activists were executed as a tactic for mitigating the protests. In short, these dissenting voices expressed an intense dissatisfaction with the ineffectiveness of SAPs and the reality that this development strategy was devised and imposed upon African countries by international organizations. SAPs appeared to perpetuate unequal political and economic relations within the global economy, as well as silence among African leaders in international development debates.

That said, at the level of the United Nations, conversations had begun in the mid-1980s to reflect on the concept of development and the means to promote economic growth while ensuring the long-term viability of natural resources as well as the stability of communities who produce natural resources for the global market. In 1983, the United Nations General Assembly appointed Gro Harlem Brundtland, the former prime minister of Norway, to bring together countries that would need to rethink development and devise an approach to development that took into consideration the future. The Brundtland Commission was formed, and through their work they coined the concept "sustainable development."

Post Post-Colonialism (2000s to the Present): Coalescing Voices

Since the Brundtland Commission's report introduced a new focus on the sustainability of development, there has been a growing recognition of the need to pay attention to the needs and expressions of local communities for community development and empowerment is central to the sustainable environmental practices that effect economic growth. At the international level, the emphasis on listening to the people "on the ground" was interpreted as incorporating the voices and perspectives of African leaders in international conversations regarding sustainable development. Thus, the first African, Kofi Annan, as elected to serve as the seventh secretary general of the United Nations in 1997. The president of Namibia, Sam Nujuma, with the president of Finland, Tarja Halonen, presided over the Millennium Summit of 2000 where 150 world leaders gathered to discuss world peace, equality, and the eradication of poverty. At this meeting, the Millennium Declaration was drafted, a document which lay the foundation for defining the Millennium Development Goals and promoting them in the years to come. African activists were also brought into the conversation. For example, Maathai was appointed to be a part of the Millennium Development Goals Advocacy Group in 2010.

Although African leaders had been in the margins of decision-making processes related to global sustainable development efforts for too long and playing a prominent role in defining the Millennium Development Goals (MDGs) gave voice to African perspective, the conceptualization of MDGs continued to convey African and other developing countries were customers or clients of services, rather than stakeholders affecting change. For example, several of the eight MDGs for 2015 are framed in highly specific terms. The goals of MDGs call for "halving extreme poverty rates" and "halting the spread of HIV/AIDS." Economists and authorities of the UN and governments around the world may view these goals as benchmarks to aim for. However, individuals in Africa with lives marked by poverty and HIV/AIDS among other problems, hear these goals as promises and services to be delivered.

In 2015, MDGs were replaced by the 2030 Agenda for Sustainable Development and its new goals (i.e., SDGs), reflecting the integration of sustainability with development, and a shift from conceiving the agency of African countries in international development. For example, the agenda recognized that poverty eradication must go hand-in-hand with addressing social needs and protecting the environment. The agenda also has intentions of knowledge sharing and capacity building, which Africa needed. What is more, the SDGs are conceived as guiding an inclusive world where countries share universal goals for development. The 17 goals of the SDG are universal in nature, and therefore applicable to all countries, suggesting African countries are on a level playing field (see http://www.un.org/en/africa/osaa/peace/sdgs.shtml). The shift in focus on "needs" to "rights" (e.g., environmental rights, human rights, the right to economic security) (Redclift, 2005) provides language that is applicable to all countries.

Of special significance to Africa is the strategy for implementing the 2030 SDGs. Here too, Africans are taking the lead in determining an approach. In 2015, world leaders met in Addis Ababa, Ethiopia, for the Third International Conference on Financing for Development. This meeting resulted in a 68-page documents, the Addis Ababa Action Agenda (AAAA) which advocated for a new focus on finance, technology, and capacitating development. This document provided the foundation for discussions and decisions regarding the means for implementing the 2030 SDGs. The first paragraph of the AAAA states,

> We, the Heads of State and Government and High Representatives, gathered in Addis Ababa from 13 to 16 July 2015, affirm our strong political commitment to address the challenge of financing and creating an enabling environment at all levels for sustainable development in the spirit of global partnership and solidarity. (http://www.un.org/esa/ffd/wp-content/uploads/2015/08/AAAA_Outcome.pdf)

The effort to align the 2030 Agenda (a global agenda) with the AAAA reflects the growing power of Africa's voice in international discussions of sustainable development. This does not mean that all voices of Africa are audible. For example, Africa's proposal for restructuring the global economic governance of international tax cooperation which is overseen by the OECD was rejected by the European Union and the United States. As it is discussed in chapter 6, the proposed new global tax body would have helped Africa mobilize domestic resource and combat illicit financial flows (Lawan, 2015). Nevertheless, it appears that there are more opportunities for the Africans to take the lead and shape the international conversation on sustainable development. For example, the Common African Position is an African Union

(AU) technical report that was published in 2014. The document articulates a unified African perspective on the problems in Africa, the need for structural transformation, and is a call for a more people-centered approach to sustainable development. This document was influential in the negotiations of the SDGs for 2030. It was followed by the technical report, "Agenda 2063: The Africa We Want," released at the 24th Ordinary Assembly held in Addis Ababa, Ethiopia, in January 2015. Agenda 2063 is a vision and action plan for Africa. Its 20 goals align with the 17 SDGs, is broader in scope, and encompasses social, environmental, economic, and sustainability issues. It outlines the implementation tools of SDGs. And in 2017, African leaders validated the 78 indicators that track performances of the Agenda 2063 and the SDGs.

Africa is a continent of 54 countries with different issues, so the voices, priorities, and nation-specific needs should be addressed. To this end, The Africa Regional Report on Sustainable Development Goals, which is the follow-up of Africa Rio+20 and the post-2015 development agenda consultative processes, listed sustainable development priorities for the five subregions of Africa—North, West, Central, Eastern, and Southern Africa. In addition to common issues the continent faces such as governance and institutions, peace and security, financing, capacity development and technology transfer, countries need to work on specific regional issues and key subregional sustainable development priorities identified by the report (refer to *Africa Regional Report on Sustainable Development Goals*, United Nations, 2015).

Looking Ahead: The Africa Africans Want

Africa is in a position to benefit from the implementation of SDGs providing the history of Africa's relationship to the concept of development and sustainable development is not forgotten, and African leaders continue to maintain a voice in the international arena. The Agenda 2063 is meant to put into action the goals that Africans have articulated. But the question remains: given the past track record of AU and individual African nations in following through promises, what is the guarantee that ensures the implementation of Agenda 2063? It is to be seen, but the bottom-up approach of the implementation of the Agenda 2063 and Agenda 2030, and the laying out of indicators as tracking performances leave one with hope that the future is different for Africa. What is more, reforming the political, economic, and social relationships that create, shape, and perpetuate problems in Africa will be necessary to solving these problems (Fofack, 2015; Himmelstrand, Kinyanjui, and Mburugu, 1994; Monga and Lin, 2015; Nyamo-Hanga, 2013). Moving forward, Africa should continue play a key and active role in shaping the global agenda on sustainable development in many fronts. From reducing poverty, child mortality and social inequality to controlling its population growth to a "genuine" green economic development, Africa needs to find itself in the global sustainability discourse as a stakeholder, and most importantly as a beneficiary.

As the population growth rate in Africa is larger than anywhere else in the world, the continent expects to have 2.4 billion people by 2050. Some fear this growth may reverse the gains of MDGs. But, Africa's economy is growing fast as African countries now comprise ten of the most rapidly growing economies. Some countries exhibit a double-digit GDP growth for the last few consecutive years. Yet, there is some evidence that this growth creates social and economic inequality.

Besides, the population growth increases the rural-to-urban migration that causes rapid urbanization. This brings several challenges to African cities and complicated some sustainable development efforts. Inefficient land use and uncontrolled urban growth is becoming a norm, which is proven to be unsustainable in the long run and cause traffic congestion, air and water pollution, unbalance distribution of resources and social inequality. Some argue that urbanization can be beneficial for economic development, but the unintended consequences need to be addressed sooner than later to create healthy and livable cities that residents of urban Africa deserves.

Urban or rural, sustainable development is not just an economic slogan for Africa, but an essential component of its survival. As Kumi Naidoo, the executive director of Greenpeace International, puts it, "Africa is at the frontline of climate change. One can already see the impacts: drought, conflicts in areas such as the Horn of Africa, increased migrations and compromised food security. We can no longer sit back and watch it happen."[1]

Worth mentioning, Africa also need to tap into a long-lived indigenous conservation practices through institutional and financial supports. Therefore, there is an immediate need for better resource management and institution building. But there is hope in the potential for change.

NOTE

1. Interview with Kumi Naidoo, executive director of Greenpeace International; By Africa Renewal Online "Only our collective voice will be heard."

BIBLIOGRAPHY

African Development Bank Group. (2018). Ghana Economic Outlook. https://www.afdb.org/en/countries/west-africa/ghana/ghana-economic-outlook/, accessed on July 26, 2018.

Allan, W. (1965). *The African Husbandman*. Oliver & Boyd.

Babb, S. (2005). Social Consequences of Structural Adjustment: Review of Evidence and Current Debates. *Annual Review of Sociology* 31: 199–222.

Beinart, W. (2003). *The Rise of Conservation in South Africa: Settlers, Livestock, and the Environment, 1770–1950*. New York: Oxford University Press.

Beinart, W., and Bundy, C. (1987). *Hidden Struggles in Rural South Africa: Politics and Popular Movements in the Transkei and Eastern Cape, 1890–1930*. London: James Currey; Johannesburg: Ravan Press; Berkeley: University of California Press.

Beinart, W., Beall, J., McGregor, J., Potts, D., and Simon, D. (2000). African Environments: Past and Present. Special issue of *Journal of Southern African Studies* 26(4): 595–855.

Brooks, G. (1993). *Landlord and Strangers: Ecology, Society and Trade in Western Africa, 1000–1650*. Boulder, CO: University of Colorado Press.

Clark, J. D., and Brandt, S. (1984). *From Hunters to Farmers: The Causes and Consequences of Food Production in Africa*. Berkeley, CA: University of California Press.

Cooke, E., Hague, S., and McKay, A. (2016). The Ghana Poverty and Inequality Report: Using the 6th Ghana Living Standards Survey. UNICEF. https://www.unicef.org/ghana/Ghana_Poverty_and_Inequality_Analysis_FINAL_Mach_2016.pdf, accessed on June 25, 2018.

Curtin, P. D. (1969). *The Atlantic Slave Trade*. Madison, WI: University of Wisconsin Press.

Danaher, K., and Yunus, M. (1994). *Fifty Years is Enough: The Case Against the World Bank and the International Monetary Fund*. New York, NY: The Global Exchange.

Dater, A., and Merton, L. (2009). *Taking Root: The Vision of Wangari Maathai*. Marlborough, VT: Mongrel Media.

Dwyer, P., and Zeilig, L. (2012). *African Struggles Today: Social Movements since Independence*. Chicago, IL: Haymarket Press.

Fofack, H. (2015). The Idea of Economic Development: Views from Africa. In *The Oxford Handbook of Africa and Economics: Volume 1: Context and Concepts*, edited by C. Monga, and J. Lin. Oxford University Press, pp. 271–302.

Himmelstrand, U., Kinyanjui, K., and Mburugu, E. (1994). *African Perspectives on Development: Controversies, Dilemmas and Openings*. London: Palgrave Macmillan.

Inikori, J. E., and Engerman, S. L., eds. (1992). *The Atlantic Slave Trade: Effects on Economies, Societies and Peoples in Africa, the Americas, and Europe*. Durham, NC: Duke University Press.

Jerven, M., and Johnston, D. (2015). Statistical Tragedy in Africa? Evaluating the Data Base for African Economic Development. *Journal of Development Studies* 51(2): 111–15.

Kates, R., Parris, Thomas M., and Leiserowitz, Anthony A. (2005). What is Sustainable Development? *Environment: Science and Policy for Sustainable Development* 47(3): 9–21.

Klein, H. S. (2010). *The Atlantic Slave Trade: New Approaches to the Americas*. Cambridge: Cambridge University Press.

Larrain, J. (1989). *Theories of Development.* Cambridge: Polity Press.

Lawan, S. (2015). *An African take on the Sustainable Development Goals.* Brookings Institute.

Leach, M., and Mearns, R. (1996). *The Lie of the Land: Challenging Received Wisdom on the African Environment.* Oxford: Currey, 1996.

Lewis, W. A. (1955). *The Theory of Economic Growth.* R. D. Irwin Press.

Maddox, G. (2006). *Sub-Saharan Africa: An Environmental History.* ABC-CLIO.

Marlowe, F. (2002). Why the Hadza are Still Hunter-Gatherers? In *Ethnicity, Hunter-Gatherers, and the "Other": Association or Assimilation in Africa*, ed. Sue Kent. Washington, DC: Smithsonian Institution Press, pp. 247–75.

McCann, J. C. (1999). Climate and Causation in African History. *The International Journal of African Historical Studies* 32(2): 261–79.

Meier, A. (2007). Natural Disaster? Droughts and Epidemics in Pre-Colonial Sudanic Africa. *The Medieval History Journal* 10 (1 & 2): 209–36.

Monga, C., and Lin J. (2015). *The Oxford Handbook of Africa and Economics: Volume 1, Contexts and Concepts*, Oxford University Press.

National Research Council. (1999). *Our Common Journey: A Transition Toward Sustainability.* Washington, DC: National Academy Press.

Nhamo, G. (2017). New Global Sustainable Development Agenda: A Focus on Africa. *Sustainable Development* 25(3): 227–41.

Ntiamoa-Baidu, Y. (2009). Indigenous Beliefs and Biodiversity Conservation: The Effectiveness of Sacred Groves, Taboos and Totems in Ghana for Habitat and Species Conservation. *Journal for the Study of Religion Nature and Culture* 2(3): 309–26.

Nyamo-Hanga, G. B. (2013). The Role of Rural Electrification in Poverty Reduction. Paper presented at National Poverty Policy Week, November 25–27, Dar es Salaam.

Redclift, M. (2005). Sustainable Development (1987–2005): An Oxymoron Comes of Age. *Sustainable Development* 13: 212–27.

Robinson, J. (2002). Global and World Cities: A View from Off the Map. *International Journal for Urban and Regional Research* 263: 531–54.

Rodney, W. (1981). *How Europe Underdeveloped Africa.* Washington, DC: Howard University Press.

Ross, E. (2008). Palaver Trees Reconsidered in the Senegalese Landscape: Arboreal Monuments and Memorials. In *African Sacred Groves: Ecological Dynamics and Social Change*, eds. Michael Sheridan and Celia Nyamweru. Columbus, OH: James Curry and Ohio University Press, pp. 133–48.

Scheld, S. (2003). The City in a Shoe: Redefining Urban Africa Through Sebago Footwear Consumption. *City & Society* 15(1): 109–30.

Sheridan, M. (2009). The Environmental and Social History of African Sacred Groves: A Tanzanian Case Study. *African Studies Review* 52(1): 73–98.

Sheridan, M., and Nymaweru, C. (2008). *African Sacred Groves: Ecological Dynamics and Social Change.* Athens: Ohio University Press.

Simone, A. (2004). *For the City Yet to Come.* Durham, NC: Duke University Press.

Sutton, J. E. G. (1989a). Editor's Introduction: Fields Farming and History in Africa. *Azania* 24(1): 6–11.

Sutton, J. E. G. (1989b). History of African Agricultural Technology and Field Systems. *Azania* 24: 89–112.

United Nations. (1947). *Economic Development in Selected Countries: Plans, Programmes and Agencies*. New York, NY: United Nations.

United Nations. (2015). *Africa Regional Report on the Sustainable Development Goals: Summary*. Addis Ababa, Ethiopia: United Nations Economic Commission for Africa.

Williams, G. (1994). Why Structural Adjustment is Necessary and Why it Doesn't Work. *Review of African Political Economy* 60: 214–22.

World Commission on Environment and Development (WCED). (1987). *Our Common Future*. Bethesda, MD: Oxford University Press.

Chapter 2

Ethical Dilemmas in International Relief and Development Work

Blaine D. Pope

This chapter highlights the occasional ethical dilemmas of international relief and development work. To be more precise, it is about the ethics of working in the field of integrated political, economic, and social development in Africa. The setting used here will be the operations of a US-based nongovernmental organization (NGO) operating in the East African nation of Rwanda. The period is the mid-1990s. Many things have changed for the better in Rwanda, in Africa, and in the world since that turbulent time. However, I am arguing here that the ethical dilemmas posed by my brief-but-disturbing period in Rwanda are ultimately "timeless." Scenarios like these have been encountered many times in the past, and they will likely be encountered many more times again in the future.

This chapter is therefore designed to help students of business, government, and the social sciences, or who otherwise may one day be involved in complex, large-scale service delivery, and/or emergency relief operations. It is intended as a practical guide designed to facilitate the long-term impact, or sustainability, of such operations. The concept of sustainability—sometimes also referred to as "sustainable development"—plays a key role here. The concept of "sustainability" is a double-edged sword. It has both positive and negative aspects, which need to be unpacked and examined.

The following background discussion on Rwanda and Africa is of secondary to the larger points I will make here. Those larger points highlight the role of ethics and morality in business management.[1] I will also argue that explicit inclusion of business ethics issues in program planning, design, and implementation is critically important in the overall process of management. The extreme circumstances posed by the Rwandan Civil War and Genocide of 1994 serve as backdrop to highlight these issues. By throwing them into stark contrast under the extreme conditions imposed by Rwanda at that time, one can more easily see their essential nature. These issues remain, however, a constant challenge in the world program management, especially in resource scarce environments.

DETAILS

Background and Context

For many years, CARE International (together with its flagship subsidiary, CARE USA) has been one of the industry leaders in the delivery of integrated social, economic, and emergency relief programming in the developing world. In the immediate months after World War II, however, CARE began implementing its very first programs in war-torn Europe. It is from this successful, large-scale, post-World War II activity in Europe that the term "CARE package" entered the American lexicon. At that time, the acronym "CARE" stood for "Cooperative for American Remittances to Europe."

Since the late 1940s, CARE has grown and evolved. In the latter twentieth century the acronym would come to stand for "Cooperative for Assistance and Relief Everywhere." From its website dated 2017 it stated, "CARE operates in 94 countries reaching more than 80 million people through nearly 1000 lifesaving projects." By most traditional measures, CARE has been a highly successful, private nonprofit organization. The current headquarters of CARE USA—the oldest and largest of the various national offices in the CARE International confederation—is in Atlanta, Georgia.[2]

I started working for CARE in the early 1990s. Although I had been hired to be deputy regional director for East Africa, I had become de facto acting regional director for a few brief months, due to unforeseen staff turnover. Additionally, I was also the first person of color to ever work in CARE's Regional Management Group (excluding the mostly female support staff, a majority of whom were women of color). The vast majority of management-level staff throughout the entire organization was White Americans. Many of the people in the regional management group (which saw itself as the core of CARE's operations) had attended prestigious Ivy League universities, as had I. This meant that, at a cultural level, I would also have to navigate a wide array of internal organizational norms (often in the form of unspoken rules), some of which would have been initially familiar to me, and some not.

I came to CARE academically well prepared, however. I had formal training in African studies from the School of International and Public Affairs, at Columbia University. I was also the first regional director to be fully trained in the main indigenous language of the East Africa region, Swahili. My knowledge of Swahili would come to play a critical role in my new world at CARE HQ and in the field, as I will attempt to demonstrate here.

At the time, CARE's East Africa Regional Management Group included the following countries: Egypt, Sudan, Somalia, Ethiopia, Kenya, Uganda, Rwanda, Comoros Islands, Madagascar, and Mozambique. As a direct result of the crisis in Rwanda CARE would establish a Rwandan refugee camp in Tanzania in 1994, eventually leading to full-service country operation there. Also, during this time, in 1993, the newly established nation of Eritrea would be carved out of Ethiopia's northern littoral along the Red Sea, leaving Ethiopia (one of the oldest countries in the world) now landlocked.

During this time, parts of eastern Africa had become extremely politically volatile. What I didn't realize then—and would only come to understand years later—was the powerful role environmental factors had played in driving both political and economic events in the region. A devastating drought affecting the Horn of Africa had contributed to the political-economic turmoil and eventual collapse of two East African governments—Somalia and Ethiopia respectively.[3]

Elsewhere in the region, Joseph Kony and his group known as *The Lord's Resistance Army* was still terrorizing civilian populations in northern Uganda.[4] In southern Sudan, the Sudanese People's Liberation Army was fighting a seemingly endless struggle against the government of Omar al-Bashir. Further to the south, the Mozambican rebel group going by the acronym "RENAMO" was still a force to be reckoned with. Together with its allies and sponsors in then-Apartheid South Africa, RENAMO had laced many of the country' rural roads with land mines, making them impassible. It was still attacking some remote, outlying towns. At that time, Mozambique was like an archipelago of towns and cities, surrounded by a sea of occasional insecurity in the countryside.

It is important to mention what was taking place in CARE's East Africa region, writ large. This will help contextualize organizational decision-making. This is mentioned with specific regard to contextualizing CARE's work in Rwanda, and our initial approach to it. In each of the situations outlined above, large numbers of people were dislocated and physically on the move. Among the general population in the United States, there has been a tendency to refer to all such people as refugees. According to international law, however, people dislocated to due to extreme events of any kind (whether human-caused or natural) but who stay within their national boundaries are designated "internally displaced persons" (or IDPs for short); while those who end up crossing international boundaries for the same reasons are designated as "refugees." These distinctions are important. Selected donor funding streams were attached to each of these legal designations.

In the early 1990s, eastern Africa was awash with large numbers of IDPs and refugees. From a headquarters perspective, as seen from CARE USA in Atlanta, many of these populations appeared highly fluid and dynamic.[5] They were fluid because IDPs could morph into refugees and vice versa. They were dynamic because it was often difficult to know exactly where these mobile populations would end up. The numerical equivalent of an entire town could be on the move all at once. It is into this context in which organizational decision-making—about where to intervene when and with how many resources—would be made. In other words, from an organizational headquarters perspective, there was a virtual "continuous background noise" of reports on IDPs and refugees ebbing and flowing in selected zones within the East Africa region.

In this context, CARE USA headquarters staff were often inundated with various types of reports on refugee populations—numerical projections, geographic directions, public health status, prevailing weather and environmental conditions, military-security factors, and so on. There seemed to be a never-ending stream of update reports that had to be sent out to large-scale donors like the various branches of the United Nations (UN) and the US Agency for International Development (USAID—a subsidiary unit of the US State Department), to name but a few.[6] It was in this context in which I received what was supposed to be a routine update phone call from our Rwanda country director, in the spring of 1994. Political violence seemed to be escalating in the capital city, Kigali, he had stated. Things were starting to look very bad in Rwanda, in short.

It would take one or two more long-distance phone calls from Kigali before I would comprehend that what was taking place in Rwanda was qualitatively different. Again, this had to do with our ability to perceive the nature of "bad things" in Rwanda, given that we sometimes operated in an overarching context of bad things in the region. There was an almost constant background noise of either disaster or imminent disaster. In this regard, it was not uncommon to sometimes hear a kind of gallows humor with the Regional Management Group. We each found various ways of coping with the semi-frequent human tragedies we encountered, during our weekly work activities.[7]

A 2017 page from the CARE USA website read as follows:

> CARE Rwanda is currently working in 27 out of 30 districts in all provinces of Rwanda. From 1984 to 1994, CARE Rwanda implemented a range of development projects, including maternal health care, forestry and water and sanitation activities. As a result of the civil war in Rwanda, we closed our Kigali office from April to July 1994 while conducting cross-border relief from Uganda to 150,000 displaced people in eastern Rwanda.[8]

I was a part of the four-person CARE team that initially went into northern Rwanda while the civil war and genocide was still raging in the south, during that fateful spring and summer of 1994. I had had a direct hand in that act of "conducting cross-border relief from Uganda to 150,000 displaced people in eastern Rwanda," noted in the quote above.[9] To borrow a literary trope from the writer, Joseph Conrad, it would also become my own brief personal journey in the heart of darkness.[10]

THE JOURNEY INTO RWANDA: WHAT WE ACTUALLY SAW, PART I—PREPARATION

As I packed my bags in preparation for departure from Hartsfield Airport, in Atlanta where I was living at the time, I had absolutely no clue of an impending side trip into Rwanda. I had no inkling that I would somehow end up behind rebel lines in a war zone, with a group known as the Rwandan Patriotic Front (RPF). Instead, I correctly saw myself as coordinating logistics of CARE's annual East Africa Conference in tandem with my colleagues at CARE Kenya. I enjoyed CARE's conferences, and this event gave me a chance to shine as I could use my diplomatic skills, my Swahili language skills, and my management and administrative skills, all in one very beautiful beach hotel setting on the Kenyan coast. That near idyllic beach location on the Indian Ocean would soon enough be replaced with something a bit starker, and eye opening.

It is one thing to see tumultuous events in the news, it is quite another to experience the impact of those events first hand. My first exposure to what was actually taking place in Rwanda came from CARE's Rwandan staff who had somehow managed to get out of Rwanda to attend our conference.[11] For the first time, I had a chance to meet with people whom I knew personally regarding what was taking place in their home country. The news was not good. In recent weeks, the violence had become extreme—and brutal. Some of our own staff in Rwanda had recently been reported as "missing" by this time.

As our Kenyan conference got underway, the hotel newsfeeds from CNN began reporting escalating levels of violence from the other side of Lake Victoria, in Rwanda. There were calls for the both UN and the United States to intervene militarily, as had been the case in Somalia roughly two years earlier.[12] The much-hoped-for western intervention would not be forthcoming, however. The intervention such as it was would be an entirely African affair; moreover, it would be coming from Rwanda's northern neighbor, Uganda.

Events began to accelerate significantly. Perhaps two or three days into our East Africa Regional Conference, CARE's vice president of programs gathered together a number relevant CARE staff, including myself, for a brief "emergency" meeting. In short, we were informed that he wanted a team to go into northern Rwanda, to assess the condition of our various project sites there. We would have couple of days to prepare, but he wanted us in Rwanda as soon as possible so that we could report back to him. I recall the exact moment I was told to go into Rwanda. The hotel conference room in which I'd been working seemed to quietly spin around my head for a few seconds. It seemed a profoundly unreal moment, and I had a strong hunch more such moments would soon be coming.

THE JOURNEY INTO RWANDA: WHAT WE ACTUALLY SAW, PART II—ON THE ROAD

From where we spent the night, in Kabale, in southern Uganda, it was to be a relatively short ride the next morning, by four-wheel drive vehicle, to the Rwandan border. It had been an adventure getting from Mombasa, Kenya, to neighboring Uganda. In the intervening time, we had secured some modest emergency relief supplies for our immediate staff, if we should happen across any while in Rwanda. Beyond this, we had also made prior arrangements for some medium-scale emergency relief shipments—enough to supply roughly 150,000 people—for Rwandan IDPs.[13]

We were up at dawn to begin our trip by road from Uganda into Rwanda. There was a low-lying mist in the air, blanketing the forested hills of southern Uganda. It was a stunningly beautiful sunrise over those hills, too. The beauty of that morning seemed to stand in stark contrast with the nature of the assignment facing us, on that particular day.

Southern Uganda and northern Rwanda are both regions characterized by lush green hills and mountains. Where urban Americans might describe their homes according to local neighborhoods or street blocks, rural Rwandans would typically describe their homes by according to which hills they lived on. It was a hill culture, so to speak. Moreover, like human beings in many places around the world, Rwandans routinely negotiated a complex set of social relations. Such relationships could be defined by family, by hill, by age, by gender, by religion, by ethnicity (a.k.a., "tribe"), and by socioeconomic class. These relationships would play out in interesting ways, in how people would choose to help one another during the unfolding crisis.

The section of northern Rwanda that our team was tasked with inspecting was not under the control of the Government of Rwanda. It was under the control of the RPF, a revolutionary movement which fought for the overthrow and replacement of that Government. The escalating violence in Rwanda had graduated to full-blown civil war by this time, and staff of CARE Rwanda had been caught in the middle of it. The RPF was very well organized, managerially, and had its own diplomatic outreach section based in Uganda which could assist us. A member of that diplomatic section had been assigned to accompany us, as we inspected CARE project sites in the zones it controlled in the north. That person would vouch for us at the numerous RPF highway checkpoints. Working in tandem with that RPF liaison officer, our team's mission was to determine the status of CARE staff and project sites in the region.

What we saw in northern Rwanda, for the most part, was the complete absence of human life—ghost towns, abandoned villages, empty roads. We did not see the grisly piles of bodies (or body parts) along the roadside—images that the western press had recently gotten hold of. That was a little further south. What we saw, instead, was evidence of massive and sudden human flight. In some cases, the last embers of stove fires were still smoky. A dog or a cat would dart in and out of an open front door of someone's house. Farm tools and cooking implements appeared to have been left or dropped in odd places. It was like a scene from a science fiction movie, wherein all the people had suddenly vanished. They had.

Northern Rwandan place names like "Butaro," "Ruhengeri," and "Byumba" still resonate with me; although I can no longer easily distinguish them in my mind due to the passage of time. The general image from northern Rwanda was this: most villages and small towns had been abandoned; however, in some instances a town of perhaps 5,000 people could have temporarily swollen to around 35,000 people. People decided to congregate in large numbers in just a few towns in the north, for relative safety. This would have also made it easier for RPF forces to watch over them in a few concentrated areas (rather than spread themselves thin, watching over a more dispersed population).

The first "internal crisis" of our Rwandan road trip came about late morning. A British-born CARE USA colleague assigned to work in Rwanda but who was now traveling with me (we will call him "Bill"—not his real name) became agitated. Our team discovered that the RPF had commandeered one of our rural family planning project offices, and attached storehouses, to use as a temporary soldiers' quarters and weapons depot.

Bill, upon seeing this, could not conceal his disappointment and anger. When Bill asked the officer in charge about how soon the RPF might return the project site back to CARE (a site at which Bill himself had worked, previously), the soldier told him he didn't know, and it shouldn't concern him anyway, as this was RPF official business. At that point, things began to get heated, as Bill continued to press this guerilla fighter for a more definitive reply. The soldier, starting to lose patience, insisted that he could tell him no more about the matter.

In this rapidly escalating verbal exchange (which initially took place in English), strong words between these two men soon turned to shouting. It was that kind shouting wherein human hands were also flying about, aggressively. I quickly noted that the RPF soldier shouting at Bill had his AK-47 automatic rifle on his shoulder, slung across his back (and not across his chest, where he might have quicker access to its trigger). I thought I saw him reach back over his shoulder, as if quickly checking the position of his gun. My pulse quickened. Not wanting to see anyone get shot that day, I decided to intervene and somehow redirect the discussion. I signaled to the soldier that I'd like to speak some meters away from where Bill was standing. Speaking rapidly in Swahili, something very much like the following conversation transpired:

Me (stepping forward): *Brother! Brother, please excuse my colleague here. He doesn't really know how to talk to people respectfully, sometimes. He got a little upset when he saw what happened to his old project, here. So, he's just trying to . . .*
Soldier (now also in Swahili): *Yeah, well you better talk to him about that! This White man has got a really big mouth!*
Me (hands clasped together, almost as if praying): *Brother, I am so sorry if he disrespected you in any way. Please accept this apology on behalf of our team, today. Okay? Please. I know your work here is not easy, and that you are only doing your job, and . . .*
Soldier (calming down, but still annoyed): *All I know is that you had better watch him [points over at Bill, who had since walked away and started mumbling complaints to someone else in French]. That's not how you talk to people around here. Who does he think he is, anyway? This is a new day in Rwanda.*
Me (lower tone of voice, very deferential): *Yes, brother, yes. You are absolutely right. You know how that is, though. There are some cultural differences going on here, too. Europeans, you know, tend to view things a little, well . . . differently. You know what I'm saying, right?*

By and by, things did calm down at the health-post-turned-arms-depot. There were some awkwardly formal "good-byes" as we prepared to depart. People shook hands. Bill, the other members of the CARE team and I got back in our Land Cruiser, and off we went to our next project location. It was to be one of those long, quiet rides. We were all seemingly lost in thought about what had just occurred.

We did not find any of our Rwandan staff until later in the day, as late afternoon was approaching. It was a strange experience; made even stranger because we never knew quite what to expect. In the south, things were much more black and white. The security issues in the south were clear, and clearly horrific. In the north things were opaque, things were vague. In northern

Rwanda, one could feel disturbed less by what one could actually see, and more by what one couldn't see—the hints, the absences, the rumors.

It seemed to take a long time before we spotted any of our Rwandan staff. Then, in the corner of one large building situated in one of a handful of towns taken over by displaced people, we suddenly found our staffers. The small handful of people we found there looked tired but very glad to see us. One of them was someone whom I had just met on my first visit to Rwanda, one year earlier. He and his colleagues were now recipients of emergency assistance, rather than providers of emergency assistance. For a few tough seconds, I successfully fought against tears that had wanted to come.

We had been given instructions back in Mombasa that if we found any CARE Rwanda staff, we were to give them a standard package of emergency relief supplies (plastic bucket, blanket, hand soap, flip-flops, etc.), a termination letter thanking them for their service, and a severance check. As a manager, that was probably the most difficult set of termination notifications I ever had to deliver. These were employees who, through no fault of their own, had to be let go.

LESSONS LEARNED

Moral and Ethical Issues

What I learned from my days of working in Africa taught me a lot about life, about the human condition, and has made me better person. In general, my experience has taught me that the more difficult the lesson, the more profound. What follows here are some of the key lessons that I learned.

1. *The Law of Opposites*—Sometimes, in order to accomplish a long-term goal you feel is right, you may have to perform a few short-term tasks that you feel are wrong (or about which you may at least feel ambivalent). Whatever else one might say, we were still working directly with a rebel group with the stated purpose of overthrowing a standing government.
2. *The Law of Opposites, Part II*—Sometimes, what at first appears wrong on the surface can end up later appearing very right (and vice versa). The rebel group with whom we had been temporarily coordinating our activities was attempting to intervene militarily in order to halt what had escalated into genocidal violence, perpetrated by the government of Rwanda against one particular ethnic group—the Tutsi.
3. *Borders Have a Dual Quality: They Can Be Both Fictitious and Real*—Borders and boundaries of many kinds are creations of the human mind. They don't actually exist "out there" in the real world as much as they do inside

the heads and hearts of human beings. Human beings then agree among themselves to abide by them. But just because something exists in someone's mind doesn't mean it doesn't exist at all. Those so-called artificial borders can still be real things, with very concrete implications. People have been able to save their own lives (or lose them) based their ability to traverse borders.

Example: There were Tutsis and Hutus in both Rwanda and Uganda. The Ugandan Tutsi and Hutu were just as horrified as the rest of eastern and central Africa at the events taking place inside Rwanda. Said another way, there was nothing inherent in their ethnic history that would automatically lead these two groups of people to violence.

1. *Governments, Laws, and Policies Matter*—The distinction between the horrible violence between Tutsi and Hutu in Rwanda, and its complete absence in Uganda comes down to the difference between governments. Elements from within the Government of Rwanda had been using their positions of relative power and privilege to actively encourage acts of violence against Tutsi (along with any of their Hutu friends, political moderates, or "collaborators"). The Government of Uganda had had no such bellicose exhortations, and no corresponding social tensions between those two ethnic groups. Governments have the general ability to set the tone and pace by which we live our lives.
2. *Any one of us is a Potential Savior, Avoider, or Perpetrator*—Saviors are those who try to rescue others from difficult circumstances. Avoiders are those who routinely prefer to not get involved in the difficult circumstances of others. Perpetrators are those who in various ways endanger others, placing them in difficult circumstances, up to and including threatening someone's life. To my shock and dismay, I discovered that CARE had staff in each of these categories, in Rwanda.

Example: A colleague who had been responsible for all my logistical arrangements (flight, taxi, and hotel) in and around Kigali one year earlier turned out to be one of the alleged genocidal ring-leaders and was accused of coordinating many mass murders. This man was not a raving lunatic. He was very "normal" in his personal comportment, and that is exactly the point.

1. *The Dual Nature of the Human Psyche: Law of Opposites, Part III*—We all have the capacity to destroy and to (re)build, to engage in life depleting and life supporting activities, to play the roles both devils and angels.
2. *News and Information Matter*—Upon my return to the United States I was to encounter a different form of collective madness—the national obsession over the infamous O. J. Simpson trial. I was recently back

from eastern Africa, still trying to process the brutal deaths of 800,000 to 1,000,000 people. In the United States, I returned to find my compatriots from all walks of life consumed by the deaths of exactly two people. It felt as if those roughly 1,000,000 African people didn't matter very much; not in America, anyway.

ALTERNATE PERSPECTIVES ON DEVELOPMENT AND SUSTAINABILITY

After I had returned home to the United States, I found out that the principle donor to our family planning program in Rwanda, USAID, would be terminating its programs there. As a result of the genocide and civil war in Rwanda, the country had lost approximately 10 percent of its total population. This would be equivalent to the United States, with a population of approximately 320 million people losing 32 million people (in a span of roughly 3 months). In short, Rwanda wouldn't need any population control programs anytime soon, as a direct result of its sudden loss of population—or so the thinking apparently went.

This was unfortunate for the women and children served by those programs, however. Much like *Planned Parenthood* in the United States, those family planning clinics provided a wide range of important health services, far beyond simple birth control. With their sudden closure and defunding, women would have had to find alternate sources of service to meet their reproductive health needs.

In New York, at the UN, UN officials tried mightily to convince the Clinton Administration to officially label the terrible event in Rwanda as "genocide." The Administration never did. Before there could be any external military intervention via the UN, there would have to be a vote from the UN Security Council (UNSC) approving the action. Much like the distinction between refugees and IDPs, official declaration of genocide by all the relevant member of the UNSC could have triggered certain legal mechanisms and attendant funding streams. The UNSC needed the approval from its most important member, the United States, in order to do so however. That approval never came.

In the end, it was an all African intervention force—and *not* the United Nations—that entered Rwanda to finally halt the violence there. Paul Kagame, defense minister under President Museveni of Uganda, would lead the RPF forces from Uganda into northern Rwanda, taking over the capital, and then the rest of the country. Kagame had been part of a large cohort of Rwandan-Ugandans (Ugandans either of Rwandan birth or Rwandan ancestry) in the Ugandan Army. They had effectively been "released" by Uganda to prosecute the war in Rwanda. It was a costly but strategically shrewd move by President Museveni of Uganda, as he could assure himself of a loyal political and military ally along his southern border, in Rwanda.

What I gradually learned from subsequent political events in Rwanda and in Africa was that *it was important that Africans develop mechanisms to address African issues*—to liberate themselves, as it were. I am pretty sure that the African approach to addressing the Rwandan crisis took longer than the UN approach might have, if the UN had intervened in a timely fashion; but it didn't do so. This forced African people with some modest means to utilize their own resources. In the process of doing so, it also helped break some of the reliance of western assistance, or general foreign assistance, to which so many African governments had become accustomed.

I had been initially outraged that the United States would not act on Rwanda, as it had done in Somalia. As I look back, I can now also see that that United States and UN inaction forced African governments to respond to Rwanda differently. Indeed, as the angry soldier had conveyed during that tense moment at the commandeered family planning clinic, it was a new day. It was the law of opposites in action, once again. The terrible events in Rwanda in 1994 have forced people to rethink how they are going to live, how they are going to function in relation to one another.

EPILOGUE

Rwanda 25 Years Later: The Power of Restorative Justice and Forgiveness

There is not a single week that goes by that I do not still think of Rwanda, even if just for a fleeting moment. The horrors that I came to learn about—including our own CARE staff as both victims and perpetrators of genocide—shook me to my core. Since that time, and as a direct result of that experience, I have been in constant internal dialog with myself about what it actually means to be a human being.

Long after I had returned to the United States for good and had gotten out of relief and development work, I saw something on TV about Rwanda that shook me once again. On a documentary TV program, I saw how Rwandan's were continuing to be socially innovative. As a way of bringing about healing to Rwandan society as a whole, the government of Rwanda together with selected nongovernmental organizations (NGOs) had established a national program of restorative justice.

In short, the program was designed to pair up families of victims of genocide with families of perpetrators. In many instances, this has involved not just families, but the actual individuals involved in the killing, after being released from prison. Some involved NGOs running a series of workshops, with the explicit intent of bringing perpetrators and victims face to face with one another. The key was to get people to start talking with one another, again. After years of pent-up emotions (hurt, anger, rage, fear, guilt, etc.) had initially been given time for expression, people could then begin to move forward, emotionally. It was a large-scale group therapeutic process, conducted on a national scale. Many of those workshops eventually morphed into community service clubs, still involving the same sets of people, working together on an array of voluntary community service projects.

Observing these people sit down to together over lunch, talking about their lives, occasionally laughing, was a very moving experience indeed. I, more than most other Americans, had a profound appreciation for what it must have taken them to sit down and share a meal together. Sitting by myself in Los Angeles, watching this TV program, I found myself suddenly moved to tears by Rwandan people once again. They had learned how to forgive, and how to be forgiven, in a way that I can only describe as deeply sublime. In a very concrete way, and as a result of profound suffering, the people of Rwanda had taught me what it meant to be a complete human being.

NOTES

1. I am using the term "business management" in its most broad sense—the business of management. This by no means restricts its use to the academic field of business administration, only.

2. In 1993, CARE USA moved its headquarters from New York City to Atlanta. This was done to help lower its operating costs, by moving to a cheaper labor market in Georgia.

3. Like much of Africa at the time, both Somalia and Ethiopia were predominantly rural-based economies which remained heavily dependent upon rain-fed agriculture. When the rains stopped those economies collapsed, triggering the subsequent political collapse of the regimes of Siad Barre in Somalia 1990, and Haile Miriam Mengistu in Ethiopia in 1991.

4. The Lord's Resistance Army, or LRA, was a Christian fundamentalist terrorist group which employed many similar gruesome tactics that would later come to be associated with the Islamic State in Iraq and the Levant (ISIL), in the Middle East and North Africa in the early twenty-first century.

5. CARE USA eventually moved its East Africa Unit out of the United States, into East Africa. It is currently based in Nairobi, Kenya. This was a good move for at least two simple reasons: (1) it would lower operating costs even further (after initially moving the whole organization from New York City to Atlanta, Georgia); (2) it would allow regional managers (later re-named "regional directors") to be physically

and mentally closer to rapidly unfolding events in the region. In addition to lowering operating costs, this would presumably also improve the overall timeliness and quality of many management decisions.

6. Although seldom mentioned in professional settings, it had long been an open secret that many of the reports we wrote to US Government donors might eventually find their way into various branches of the US intelligence community. Regardless of one's own political views on such things, this was simply the context in which we had to work. People of left-leaning political sympathies—of which there were many in this business—would have to find a way to somehow reconcile this fact with the social welfare and social justice work that they were doing.

7. On at least two separate occasions, I had the difficult task of communicating with colleagues or next-of-kin on the death of a CARE staff member, in the field. One involved an automobile accident in Sudan; the other involved a truck driver driving over a landmine in Ethiopia.

8. Source: http://www.care.org/country/rwanda.

9. I seem to vaguely recall writing some of the original text, above, for this particular emergency relief operation, in my role as CARE's East Africa Deputy Regional Director. These words would have been rehashed and adjusted many times over the years, of course. However, it's also possible I might be quoting some of my own sentences or phrases here.

10. *Heart of Darkness* was originally published in 1899, by British author Joseph Conrad. It is a kind of tragic picaresque novel about the absurdities and contradictions of the human experience. One of its sub-themes is the brutal late nineteenth century colonial setting of the Belgian Congo. The immediate setting was the hero's existential riverboat journey up the Congo River. *Heart of Darkness* is considered by many to be a classic of English literature. It was later adapted by the US film-maker Francis Ford Coppola, as his monumental 1979 film about the Vietnam War, entitled *Apocalypse Now*.

11. Wars can be strange things. A country at war can see absolute Hell in one area, and not too many kilometers away, people continue on with "normal life," as best they can. Kids still can be in school. Farmers can still farm. Adults can still commute to work in the cities. People can still go out for drinks after work. Then, suddenly it all halts, and for three or four or five terror-filled hours people are huddled in their closets at home as bullets fly all around them from nearby streets. Then, just as quickly as the violence came it can also leave. In the liminal periods in between such episodic outbreaks of violence, people often try to do "normal" things—like travel. It was in this context that a few of our colleagues from CARE Rwanda managed to reach us, at CARE's conference in neighboring Kenya.

12. The Ridley Scott film, *Black Hawk Down* (2000), depicted the military escort operation designed to secure emergency food convoys in war-torn Mogadishu, Somalia. Those were UN operations, involving CARE working together with many other NGOs designed to help avert mass starvation in that African city.

13. Those supplies had been found and procured in Kenya, shipped by rail from Kenya to Uganda, to then shipped by truck from Uganda into Rwanda. Emergency relief work typically involved a lot of cross-border logistical planning.

Chapter 3

War, Environmental Crisis, and "Mining Terrorism" in the Congo

Prolegomenon for an African Philosophy of Sustainability

Mutombo Nkulu-N'Sengha

The aim of this study is to expound in broad strokes an African philosophy of sustainable development, using Central Africa and its great lakes region as a case study. Given the limited scope of this book, our goal is not to articulate a comprehensive and exhaustive philosophy, but rather to merely propound a prolegomenon. We shall limit ourselves to delineating the contours of such a philosophy by articulating its raison d'être and some of its basic tenets, as well as the sources needed for such an endeavor and the fundamental questions that ought to be raised.

By "African philosophy of sustainable development," we mean a way of theorizing sustainability from an African perspective according to African *modus vivendi* and *modus operandi*, and most importantly according to the epistemological norms of "African rationality" and ethics, by interrogating the existing cultural, economic and political modes of social organization and their patterns of consumption and resource use in light of people's pursuit of happiness. It emerges out of analytical and critical involvement which points out the aporia of existing development theories, raises questions regarding the conceptual underpinnings of indigenous beliefs, values, and languages pertaining to the human condition and human quest for well-being, as well as the questioning of modern development paradigms heretofore used in Africa and their outcome. This leads us to scrutinize the African historical trajectory and African ancestral traditions in order to uncover some wisdom and practices that may be useful for the articulation of an authentic African "philosophy of sustainability" which we will draw from the tantalizing wealth and astonishing clarity of twelve essential African concepts: Umoja (unity), ujamaa (family spirit, brotherly love), sha-bantu-ne-bintu (God as father of beings and things), Bumuntu (genuine personhood), mucima muyampe (good heart), Mfwintshi (witch, evil person), fadenya-badenya (the person as an individual and a person-with-others), mitshi (trees), ntanda-yonso (the whole world, the entire universe), bumi (life), lufu (death), bijila (taboos). This philosophy synthesizes the African Weltanschauung stemming mainly from cosmology, cosmogony, ontology, metaphysics, ethics, and the "sage king" political philosophy, as well as the long tradition of African resistance movements to oppression and exploitation, notably the struggle against genocide, ecocide, and cultural genocide generated by dictatorship, slave trade, and the social, physical, economic, and epistemic violence generated by colonialism, neocolonialism, and neoliberal globalism. As a subcategory of African philosophy in general, African philosophy of sustainable development draws from various trends, notably traditional philosophy (as expressed in Bantu Philosophy, Bumuntu Philosophy, Sage Philosophy, ancestral proverbs, and traditional religious Weltanschauung), and contemporary philosophical discourse expressed in pan-Africanism, Negritude, Ujamaa, post-colonial studies and various other trends.

We shall proceed in four steps; after the status quaestionis, we shall clarify the context of our discourse. This will be followed by some salient points of the African crisis, and finally a response to such a crisis in the form of African philosophy of sustainable development.

STATUS QUAESTIONIS

In 1939, Albert Einstein sent a letter to F. D. Roosevelt, the US president, urging him to give "particular attention to the problem of securing a supply of uranium ore for the United States" for the production of the atomic bomb. In this letter Einstein explicitly pointed out the Congo as that indispensable uranium country, "The United States has only very poor ores of uranium in moderate quantities. There is some good ore in Canada and former Czechoslovakia, while the most important source of uranium is in the Belgian Congo."[1] In fact, while the uranium from the Eldorado mine in the Northwest Territory of Canada, and from the Colorado Plateau contained only 0.02 percent of uranium oxide, and the uranium ores from the South African gold mines 0.03 percent, the uranium from the Shinkolobwe mine in the Congo had a staggering 65 to 75 percent of uranium oxide content. According to Susan Williams (a senior research fellow at the Institute of Commonwealth Studies, University of London), Shinkolobwe uranium mines remained the greatest single source of uranium for the United States in the late 1940s and early 1950s, despite all the strenuous efforts to find alternative sources of rich ore (Williams, 2016). Toward the end of 1940, 1,200 tons of the stockpiled uranium ore of

Shinkolobwe (with an oxide content of 70 percent) were shipped to New York. According to the US Atomic Energy Commission, in 1947 the United States obtained 1,440 tomes of uranium concentrates from the Belgian Congo, none from its own territory and only 137 tons from Canada. In 1951, the United States got 639 tons from the United States, 255 from Canada, and 2792 from the Congo (Williams, 2016: 253 and 269). Moreover, after the occupation of Belgium by Nazi Germany several tons of Congolese uranium were shipped to Berlin where Werner Karl Heisenberg, one of the fathers of quantum physics, was actively working on Hitler's atomic bomb. This uranium case illustrates well how the scramble for Congolese minerals placed the country at the heart of global market conflicts in the struggle of world powers for access to strategic natural resources. Moreover, this country which provided material for the atomic bombs of Hiroshima and Nagasaki finds itself in the crossfire of the global sustainability debate in an era where the entire world is now living in the fear of nuclear holocaust and where radioactive waste have a tremendously negative impact on the environment and people's health. But the Congo is relevant to the sustainability debate for many other minerals and for other reasons such as its rainforest, and its incredible wildlife and biodiversity.

In 2017, Thomas Wilson concurred and wrote unequivocally in Bloomberg News that "we'll all be relying on Congo to Power Our Electric Cars; Congo supplies much of the cobalt needed for electric vehicles" (Wilson, 2017). In an article published in 2016 in the Washington Post, Todd C. Frankel stated emphatically that "the world depends on Congo for Cobalt," a strategic mineral widely used for space vehicles, rocket engines, power plants, jet aircraft engines, and turbine blades for gas turbines. Todd C. Frankel's article offers the following specifics: "About 90 percent of China's cobalt originates in Congo, where Chinese firms dominate the mining industry. The Cupertino, Calif.-based tech giant acknowledges that an estimated 20 percent of the cobalt it uses comes from Huayou Cobalt, which is the parent company of Congo DongFang" (Frankel, 2016). It is estimated that about 60 percent of the world's cobalt lies in the Democratic Republic of Congo, and at the present time, the Congo supplies 63 percent of the world's cobalt. Congo also accounts for almost 70 percent of world reserve of col-tan, a mineral so strategic for our digital technologies. This connection between Congolese minerals and a global economy shaped by Cold War geopolitics is a good illustration of the problematic nature of the vast world's scramble for Congolese minerals which began during the colonial era, mainly cobalt, col-tan, copper, diamond, gold, and other natural resources such as rubber and ivory, as Frankel rightly observed: "60 percent of the world's cobalt originates in Congo—a chaotic country rife with corruption and a long history of foreign exploitation of its natural resources. A century ago, companies plundered Congo's rubber sap and elephant tusks while the country was a Belgian colony. Today, more than five decades after Congo gained its independence, it is minerals that attract foreign companies." Likewise, Helen Epstein concurs,

> Beneath Congo's soil lies an estimated $24 trillion in natural resources, including rich supplies of oil, gold, diamonds, the col-tan used in computer chips, the cobalt and nickel used in jet engines and car batteries, the copper for bathroom pipes, the uranium for bombs and power plants, the iron for nearly everything. This wealth is the source of untold suffering. Today, more Congolese are displaced from their homes than Iraqis, Yemenis, or Rohingyas. Yet their miseries are all but invisible, in part because the identities and aims of Congo's myriad combatants are mystified by layers of rumor and misinformation, which serve the interests of those profiting from the mayhem. (Epstein, 2018)

From the perspective of sustainability, the crucial point is that the exploitation of minerals has political and environmental implications. It is worth noting that the exploitation of both uranium and cobalt has a notoriously negative impact on the environment and human health as they are linked to radioactive pollution. In fact, Cobalt-60 is a commercially important radioisotope, used as a radioactive tracer and for the production of high energy gamma rays. But while cobalt contributes to the green revolution with electric cars, in the Congo its exploitation is linked to all sorts of obnoxious pollution. The situation is even graver with regards to uranium. Extremely rich in oxide content, the Congolese uranium of Shinkolobwe was very powerful and terribly toxic. According to Zoellner, while the uranium from the south-western United States gives a radioactive signature of about 40 picocuries per gram (about ten times the amount of picocuries per liter of air that is considered safe for humans to breathe), the Shinkolobwe remains emit a whooping 520,000 picocuries per gram (265). Studies done in Canada and in the United States have shown that radioactive waste from uranium have led to birth defects and various health problems, including prostate and breast cancer. At the Shinkolobwe mines Congolese worked without genuine protection leading to several deaths. Nowadays, there are widespread birth defects in the entire Katanga province due to radioactivity from uranium and cobalt mining.

If the African environment is threatened by mineral exploitation and deforestation, it is also worth noting that Africa has produced outstanding defenders and promoters of the environment such as Wangari Maathai. In fact, in 2004, the Nobel committee declared that it has awarded to Wangari Maathai the Nobel Peace Prize "for her contribution to sustainable development, democracy and peace." A Native of Kenya, Maathai, the founder of the Green Belt Movement (GBM) was the first person to receive the Peace Nobel Prize for her work on the environment, her GBM having planted over 51 million trees. In various parts of the continent, efforts are underway to protect lakes, rivers, and forests, while human rights activists and civil societies continue their struggle against human rights violations which include "environmental crimes."

CONTEXT

The context of the present study is the Central African region that goes from Angola at the Atlantic coast to Tanzania at the Indian Ocean. In other words, we intend to study the Congo basin and its great lakes region, with a particular focus on the Democratic Republic of the Congo which is the largest, the richest, and the most diverse country at the center of this strategic region.

Covering about one-fifth of the total land surface of earth, Africa is a vast landmass, the second largest continent after Asia. With its 54 countries, Africa is a land of great biodiversity. It has a vibrant population of about one billion people and vast natural resources, mainly oil, coffee, and abundant mineral deposits which are critical to our digital revolution, military might, and transportation, to name but a few sectors. And yet the African people are among the poorest of the poor in the world. Moreover, people suffer not only from economic exploitation and political oppression but also from the environmental degradation which stifles the prospects of sustainable development and aggravates the spiral of impoverishment of the people.

Regarding the environment, it is worth noting that although the African ecozone is endowed with four mighty rivers (Nile, Niger, Congo, and Zambezi), Africa has an ecosystem which is increasingly under severe stress. In the North the Sahara Desert alone covers about 9.40 million km^2, occupying almost one-third of the entire surface area of Africa (30 million km^2), while the southern part of the continent is squeezed by the Kalahari Desert which occupies 930,000 km^2. Given the progressive advances of both the Sahara and the Kalahari deserts, the Congo basin remains one of the most ecologically viable regions of the continent. Lying astride the equator, and covering a vast area of more than 3.4 million km^2, the basin of the Congo River is the largest river basin in Africa and the world's second largest river basin, after the Amazon basin. It is blanketed by the pristine equatorial rain forest, one of the major ecological fortresses of our planet, along with the Amazon and the Malaysian forest. The largest portion of both the Congo basin and the equatorial rainforest is found in the Democratic Republic of the Congo, which accounts for 53.6 percent of Africa's lowland rainforest area. The study of the environmental situation in this part of the great lakes regions is important not only for the sustainable development of Africa but also of the world.

Let us now briefly examine how the major challenges to sustainability in modern era, since the introduction of Africa in the "global market."

ENVIRONMENTAL CRISIS, GENOCIDE, AND "UNDERDEVELOPMENT"

A dominant narrative among development theorists has been that slave trade and colonization helped Africa enter into modernity and escape obscurantist traditions and poverty. A good succinct summary of this school of thought can be found in the writing of the famed German philosopher Hegel, who, in his Philosophy of World History, put it peremptorily as follows:

> Negroes are enslaved by Europeans and sold to America. Bad as this may be, their lot in their own land is even worse, since there a slavery quite as absolute exists . . . slavery is in and for itself injustice, for the essence of humanity is freedom; but for this man must be matured. The gradual abolition of slavery is therefore wiser and more equitable than its sudden removal. (Hegel, 1994)

More explicitly Hegel claims that the European slave trade is not to be abolished suddenly because it is the only thing that humanizes Africans and brings them to maturity: "We may conclude slavery to have been the occasion of the increase of human feeling among the Negroes."

The Hegelian Paradigm did not disappear with the abolition of slave trade. We find it again in the "civilizing mission" ideology of colonial empires articulated in the documents of the "International African Association" of King Leopold II and in the Acts of the Berlin Conference itself. From the standpoint of the African philosophy of sustainable development a careful analysis of the outcome of this introduction of Africa in the global market reveals a picture which is antithetical to sustainability. We can grasp this by examining some salient factors regarding the impact on the people and on the environment. For the sake of brevity we shall limit our analysis to two points: the environment and genocide.

The Environment

The slave trade affected more the people than the environment. Nonetheless, the introduction of 20 million guns of unprecedented power of destruction made warfare more lethal and was to play a crucial role in the process of destabilization of the social fabric. It is mainly with mining industries during the colonial and post-colonial era that the environment will be damaged. Industrialization has taken a heavy toll, accelerating deforestation, and a heavy pollution of air and rivers from oil companies and mining industries, mainly the exploitation of toxic minerals such as cobalt and uranium.

Regarding the environmental crisis, deforestation is a major factor. About 22 percent of Africa is forest and woodland, and only a small percentage of this acreage is protected. Incredibly important from a human standpoint because of their timber and water resources, these tree-dominated ecological landscapes are also reservoirs of outstanding biological diversity. Tropical Africa is about 18 percent of the world total covering 20 million km^2 of land in West and Central Africa. By 1985, 72 percent of West Africa's rainforests had been transformed into fallow lands and an additional 9 percent had been opened up by timber exploitation. Tropical timber became a viable alternative to European wood following World War II, as trade with East European countries stopped and timber noticeably became sparse in western and southern Europe. As a result, the region suffered deforestation and defaunation due to the activities of local farmers and international timber industry. The rain forests are shrinking everywhere in Africa. The actual rate of deforestation varies from one country to another and accurate data does not exist yet. Recent estimates show that the annual pace of deforestation in the region can vary from 150 km^2 in Gabon to 2900 km^2 in Cote d'Ivoire. Extrapolating from present rates of loss, botanist Peter Raven pictures that the majority of the world's moderate and smaller rain forests (such as in Africa) could be ruined in forty years. In Africa, the environment is heavily negatively impacted by desertification, industrial timber exploitation, traditional practices of burning the bush for hunting and agricultural purposes, toxic pollution emanating from mineral exploitations, and the dumping of toxic waste in Africa by foreign companies.

Genocide

By genocide, we simply mean the "great dying out" stemming from the colonial system of economic exploitation and political domination. In some cases, we have direct massacres by colonial soldiers or police forces. In other cases, we have dying by exposure to toxic minerals and dangerous chemicals from industries. And finally the system makes it difficult for people to have access to decent living conditions and means of subsistence through insufficient salaries or confiscation of arable land and excessive taxes. The slave trade and colonialism created a state of terror which played a crucial role in the process of "emptying" the continent. The impact on the population was dramatic.

Four salient points can help illustrate this state of terror: the slave trade and the kidnapping of millions of people, various phases of mass killings epitomized by two major genocides committed between 1890 and 1910, namely the genocidal regime of the Belgian King Leopold II in the Congo, and the Herero genocide committed by the Germans in Namibia where more than two-thirds of the population were decimated when Lieutenant General Adrian Dietrich Lothar von Trota issued his famous Vernichtungsbefehl extermination order. In the Congo, the population was reduced by half, between 1890 and 1910, by the "philanthropic" regime of King Leopold II (1865–1909). Leopold's colonial officials established a hard slave labor in order to maximize profit from ivory, rubber, and minerals. The Congolese population, estimated at about 40 million before the colonial regime, was reduced to more or less 20 million (Friedman, 1991: 81). Despite discrepancies on the exact number of the Congolese people at that time, many agree that between 1890 and 1910 the population of the Congo was reduced almost by half. Morel's book titled *Red Rubber* captures the tragedy of a "developmental project" which cost too much Congolese blood without generating any industrial revolution in the Congo itself, let alone a transfer of technology.

In 1992, Eric Fottorino, Christophe Guillemin and Erik Orsenna remarked that the African population which constituted 20 percent of world population at the beginning of the seventeenth century fell to 8 percent of world population in the twentieth century according to the studies done on the period between 1920 and 1930 (Fottorino et al., 1992: 17). They conclude that even the projected one billion and a half in the twenty-first century does not mean that Africa is overpopulated because the African population is only catching up with its lost demographic place among other nations, the demographic weight it had in the seventeenth century (Fottorino et al., 1992: 17). Thus, the Congolese "Holocaust" reflects a general trend of colonization in Africa which is clarified when we compare the evolution of population in Europe and Africa before and after the encounter between the two worlds. According to statistics by the United Nations (Carr-Saunders, 1956), in 1650 Europe and Africa had an equal population of 100 million people or 18.3 percent of the world population. But once established, the slave trade and the colonial "regime de terreur" the population of Africa declined dramatically. In 1950, Europe increased to 593 million people or 24 percent of world people while African population dwindled to 7.9 percent of world population (Stavrianos, 1981: 199). Likewise, the French scholar L. M. Diop-Maes has shown that the population of Africa which was evaluated at 600 to 800 million peoples in the sixteenth century dropped to 200 million between 1850 and 1870, and to 130 million people in 1930 (Diop-Maes, 1993). According to some other studies, in 1650, Africa had one hundred million people, while Europe had 105 million and Asia 257 million. However in 1900, the population of Africa represented 120 million while Europe counted 423 million and Asia 857 million (Rodney, 1992: 97). From the fifteenth to the twentieth centuries, the history of colonization appears essentially as an overt and covert practice of extermination, the very antithesis of sustainable development.

AFRICAN PHILOSOPHY OF SUSTAINABLE DEVELOPMENT

Philosophy is a hallmark of sophisticated wisdom in all cultures, in so far as the Homo Sapiens is an "animal rationabile." Philosophy is a particular way of thinking in which reason, rational thought, critical thinking, relentless pursuit of knowledge, truth, deep and broad understanding of the root causes of reality, and wisdom play a crucial role. As "love of wisdom," philosophy is a mode of thinking grounded in rational inquiry and a relentless pursuit of truth, wisdom, and genuine well-being. The ability to ask fundamental questions about the nature of sustainability and development is the hallmark of a philosophy of sustainability. For our approach to the issue of sustainability, we shall focus on the two pillars of philosophy, that is, rational critical thinking, and "wisdom" which implies the ability to pursue truth, goodness, and happiness.

The human being is an animal (having a material body shaped by the environment), endowed with reason and wisdom, with technological capacity to transform his environment, and living in a community that survives through careful political organization and rules of ethical conduct. An African philosophy of sustainable development draws upon various branches of philosophy, especially epistemology, cosmology, philosophical anthropology, moral philosophy, and political philosophy. For the sake of brevity we shall limit ourselves here to lessons from African cosmology and ethics we refer to as Bumuntu.

To better reflect on sustainability it is important to grasp the African understanding of the nature of reality and its global context or its cosmic setting. African societies have produced more than one thousand creation myths, the most widely known in the world being those by the Dogon of Mali and the Yoruba of Nigeria. What is relevant to the philosophy of sustainability is the fact that, in Africa as elsewhere in the world, at the core of most of these creations myths stand the notion of the common origin of all things and subsequently the notion of the fundamental unity and interconnectedness of all things in the universe. Dogon's astronomy starts with the theory that the earth is in the Milky Way, that the Milky Way has a spiral structure, that there are an infinite number of stars and spiraling worlds. Moreover, they likened the motions of heavenly bodies to the circulation of the blood and maintained that stars and planets have a major influence on life on earth. Among stars and planets, they described carefully Sirius ("Sigi tolo"), Sirius B ("po tolo"), Jupiter, Saturn, Venus, Sun, Moon, and Earth. However, it is Sirius B which occupies the central place in Dogon astronomy. For the Dogon, in the universe, the most important body is not our solar system, but the Sirius star system, and more specifically Sirius B, which they claimed to be one of the densest and tiniest of stars in our galaxy.[2] The Dogon maintained that "po tolo" (Sirius B) is the egg of the world, the beginning and ending of all things seen and unseen. Having found in Sirius B the key to the phenomenon of life on earth, the Dogons articulated the most sacred of their 700-year-old traditions primarily around this tiny star. They articulated their social life around a focal ceremony called "Sigui," that is "the ceremony of the renovation of the world" (or feast of world's rebirth) held every sixty years, time during which the orbital periods of the planets Jupiter and Saturn come into synchronization.

It is remarkable that the Dogon cosmology was articulated not around the earth, or the sun, but around Sirius B, an "exo-star" situated 8.5 light years away from us and invisible to naked eye. By moving beyond geocentrism and heliocentrism, the Dogon elevated African thought to the height of modern cosmology, now embraced by African astrophysicists such as Jean-Paul Mbelek and Thebe Medupe, and summarized in the documentary "Cosmic Africa" released in 2002, and in "African Cosmos: African cultural astronomy from Antiquity to the Present" edited in 2012 by the Smithsonian National Museum of African Art. It appears that African philosophy is not antithetical to modern cosmology and that it can take into account the new scientific discoveries in the ongoing tale of the origins of the universe.

Between 1980 and 2010, new technologies have enabled astronomers, astrophysicists, and geneticists to perform astonishing discoveries of the mysteries of the universe and the human body. Subsequently modern cosmology and genetics have given birth to a coherent creation story that throws helpful light on traditional notions of interconnectedness of all things and beings in the universe, namely the interplay between matter and energy, and the fact that matter is made up of the same basic elements defined by the standard model and the periodic table of Mendeleev, with hydrogen, oxygen, nitrogen, carbon, calcium, and iron playing a crucial role in the unity between humans and the entire universe.

We now know that it literally takes the whole cosmos to make a human, for every individual is made up of elements that were manufactured in the Big Bang, in the stars, and in supernovas. About 98 percent of the human body is made up of six major elements (65 percent oxygen, 18 percent carbon, 10 percent hydrogen, 3 percent nitrogen, 1.5 percent calcium, 1.2 percent phosphorus), followed by trace elements that include among others iron, potassium, magnesium, sodium, sulfur, and chlorine. It turns out that the most abundant elements in the human body are the same as those we find in large amount in the universe. Hydrogen, oxygen, nitrogen, carbon, iron, silicon, calcium, potassium, magnesium, sodium, sulfur, phosphorus emerge among the most abundant elements not only in the human body but also in the earth, the galaxies, and the entire universe. Indeed all the elements in the human body were manufactured in the universe, namely in the Big Bang, in the stars and in supernovas. As Carl Sagan and Neil de Grasse Tyson put it poetically,

> We are not figuratively, but literally star dust, we live in the universe and the universe is living within us, for the Oxygen we breathe, the nitrogen in our DNA, the calcium in our bones and our teeth, the iron in our blood cells, the Carbon in our muscles, the atoms of our bodies are traceable to stars that manufactured them in their cores and exploded these enriched ingredients across our galaxy, billions of years ago.

And our hydrogen comes from the big bang itself, 13.7 billion years ago. For this reason, we are biologically connected to every other living thing in the world, we are chemically connected to all molecules on Earth, and we are atomically connected to all atoms in the universe. "We are all connected to each other biologically, to the earth chemically, and to the rest of the universe atomically, we have a genetic kinship with all life on earth, an atomic kinship to all matter in the cosmos. The Cosmos is within us, we are a way for the cosmos to know itself." Moreover, in light of quantum physics many of the tales of African cosmological beliefs, including "animism" and telepathy that seemed hocus-pocus begin to make sense. According to Bantu Philosophy, there is no such thing as dead matter: every being, everything—be it only a grain of sand—radiates a life force, a sort of wave-particle; and sages, priests, kings, doctors, and artists all use it to help bring the universe to its fulfillment. In Africa, the realm of beings comprises God, the spirits, humans, animals, plants, minerals, land, air and water, the living and the departed, the visible and the invisible, past generations, present generations, and the generations to come. There is no radical dichotomy, and no radical separation between the self and the non-self or phenomenal world. Reality is a continuum, an uninterrupted chain of beings. All beings are intertwined and exist in unity and interact in order to achieve harmony. Reality is seen as life force, as a composite, unity and harmony of natural forces. Reality is a holistic community of mutually reinforcing natural life forces consisting of human communities (families, villages, nations, and humanity), spirits, gods, deities, and nature. Reality involves some intimate ontological relationships and interactions among beings. Reality is a totality comprising the celestial and terrestrial realms, it is the unified whole of all beings, and the interaction between them.

Traditional Africans see mountains, trees, rivers, and different animals as representations or embodiment of deities or spirits, and as such, they are divine, sacred, and are given due reverence. The natural and the supernatural are also seen as two aspects of a unified and harmonious ontological field. Supernatural entities or forces are part of the all-embracing nature. The fact that the human body is eminently part of the natural world reinforces the vision of oneness between humanity and the environment. In African worldview, *Shakapanga* (the father of creation) created not only humans but "*ntanda-yonso*," that is, all other nations and the entire universe. For that reason, he is referred to as "*Sha-Bantu-ne-Bintu*" (the father of things and human beings). Life (Bumi) comes from the creator through the ancestors and the parents, but it is sustained only through the natural world which provides nourishment and all the material necessary for medicine, shelter and clothing. The importance of the natural world (flora, fauna, rivers, and the rest of the natural world) was captured in the profound traditional reverence for nature which has been deemed "animism." The notion that trees, rivers, rocks, animals, birds, insects, the entire natural world are living beings with "a soul," and can be from time to time be the reincarnation of the spirit of the ancestors, the notion that the spirit is present in humans as well as in the natural world was well captured by Birago Diop in a poem which has gained worldwide fame. It is the best expression of that deep held African belief in cosmotheandricity:

"Those who are dead are never gone, they are there in the thickening shadow, under the earth, in the tree that rustles, in the wood that groans, in the water that runs, in the water that sleeps, in the hut, in the crowd, the dead are not dead" (Diop, 1960)· This poem underlines the cosmotheandricity of African Weltanschauung, the belief in the interconnectedness between the visible and the invisible world, the empirical and the metaempirical realm of reality, the material and spiritual realms, the feminine and the masculine dimensions of reality, and that deep-seated African belief that the natural world is "sacred" and that "I am in a tree and the tree is within me, I am in the river, lake, mountain, as they are within me." A series of "totems" and "taboes" were instituted to hamper random and indiscriminate destruction of nature, flora or fauna. It is worth noting that the notion of taboo (bijila) is not merely limited to prohibition that invites curse upon the violator. In the traditional worldview, the violation of a taboo is tantamount to being impolite, rude, and indeed, a "bad person." Destroying the environment, flora and fauna is one of the actions that make one lose his humanness. This brings us to the second pillar of the African Philosophy of sustainability, that is, Bumuntu or the notion of authentic personhood. African ethics embodies two critical point: (1) that the life of every human being is sacred and (2) that to be a genuine human being is predicated upon one's behavior vis-à-vis other human beings and the entire natural world.

According to an Akan proverb, "All human beings are children of Heaven, no one is a child of the earth" (*Nnipa nyinaa ye Onyame mma, obi nnye asase ba*). For the Baluba of the Congo-DRC, all human beings, men and women, are "*Bantu ba Leza*" (God's people), "*Bana ba Bidye Mukulu*" (children of the Great Spirit). This brings us to another dimension of the human being: the moral character. Already in ancient valley civilization we find the famous ethical principles of Maat (Lichtheim, 1976: 124–128) which state explicitly:

Hail to you, Great God, Lord of the Two Truths!
I have come to you, my Lord, bringing Maat to you, having repelled evil for you
I am pure, I am pure, I am pure

As for specific things deemed immoral the text states,

> I have not done crimes against people, I have not robbed the poor, I have not done any harm, I have not caused pain, I have not caused tears, I have not killed, I have not ordered to kill, I have not made anyone suffer, I have not raised my voice, I have not caused fear, I have given bread to the hungry, Water to the thirsty, Clothes to the naked, A ferryboat to the boatless. . . . I have not mistreated cattle, I have not deprived cattle of their pasture, I have not snared birds in the reeds of the gods, I have not caught fish in their ponds, I have not held back water in its season, I have not dammed a flowing stream.

It is remarkable that this "Egyptian Decalogue" explicitly mentions cattle and birds, fish and flowing streams. The environment is clearly included in this African ethical canon. Likewise cheating people in economic transactions is strictly prohibited. The notion of Maat was not limited to ancient Egypt. Elsewhere in Africa we find the same fundamental idea: to be human and humane is to be ethical. Such is the notion of Bumuntu. Good character stands as the hallmark of authentic mode of being. According to Yoruba wisdom, "A man may be very, very handsome; handsome as a fish within the water; But if he has no character, he is no more than a wooden doll. . . . Iwa Lesin! Good character is the essence of religion."

African personhood can be defined in a variety of ways. Important insights can be gleaned by examining man's attitude vis-à-vis (1) the ethical principles of good and evil, (2) the individual and the community, (3) women, (4) children, (5) persons with disabilities, (6) foreigners, (7) government, (8) economy, (9) the environment, and (10) the cosmos as a whole. All this is embodied in African proverbs. There are three fundamental concepts—Muntu, Kintu, and Bumuntu—involved in the definition of a human being in the African context. In Kiluba language, a human being (man or woman) is referred to as a "Muntu" (plural: Bantu). "Muntu" is not an ethnic concept but a generic term for every human being. It is found in closely related variants in other Bantu languages. The word "Kintu" refers to things, and to human beings who have lost their dignity. All over Africa, we find a clear distinction between genuine humans and bad ones. Thus, to the fundamental existential question, "What is a human being?" Africans respond, Bumuntu. This notion conveys the fundamental African understanding of genuine personhood (i.e., authentic humanity). It is indeed Bumuntu that defines sainthood, holiness, or gentlemanness. "Bumuntu" means the quintessence of personhood, that fundamental authentic mode of being humane. "Bumuntu" stands for the content of a Muntu, the moral character, the essence of genuine humanity, the essence of a deeply humane being. This word is widespread among Bantu languages. "Ubuntu" is another variant of Bumuntu found in the southern part of Africa.

The distinctive characteristic of Bumuntu is the feeling of humanity toward fellow human beings. As John Mbiti pointed out so eloquently, a genuine human being does not define his humanity merely in Cartesian cogito ergo sum terms. He rather focuses on those thoughts of goodness and compassion toward others. Thus, the Bumuntu is defined in terms of hospitality and solidarity: "I am because we are, and because we are therefore I am." The Bumuntu, as Bishop Desmond Tutu puts it, is the feeling that "my humanity is caught up, is inextricably bound up, in what is yours," that "a person is a person through other persons" as a proverb has it. Thus, Bumuntu is that good character that believes in a universal bond of sharing that connects all humanity. It is the ontological authenticity that governs the African quest for well being and the African celebration of the humanity of other fellow humans. Such solidarity is not a superficial condescension. It stems from the understanding of the common origin of humanity as defined in African cosmologies. Creation myths indicate that Bumuntu derives from the transcendent origin of human beings. As an Akan proverb has it, "All human beings are children of God, no one is a child of the earth (*Nnipa nyinaa ye Onyame mma, obi nnye asase ba*). For the Baluba people, as for the Akan, all human beings, men and women, are "*Bantu ba Leza*" (God's people) and "*Bana ba Vidye Mukulu*" (children of the Great Spirit).

It is because of this transcendent origin that the true nature of human beings consists of good character, which is the intrinsic attribute of Bumuntu. Luba Weltanschauung makes a distinction between the categories of Muntu (a genuine human being) and Kintu (a thing). According to Luba cosmology, every human being exists as a pendulum that swings between these two categories of being. A human being can lose his humanness and shift to the category of things (i.e., the animal state). Bumuntu is determined by a person's capacity to move from Ki-ntu to Mu-ntu states of being. This distinction is not limited to the Bantu-Luba worldview. It is found in many other regions as well.

From West Africa to South Africa, there is the widespread belief that people of bad character are not truly human. In Nigeria, the Yoruba say, "*Ki I se eniyan*" (He/she is not a person). In South Africa, we find the expression "*Ga se Motho*," and the Baluba people of Central Africa say, "*Yao Ke Muntu*" (He is not human) or "*I mufu unanga*" (He is a dead body walking). It is not possible here to explore the worldviews of each ethnic group. Among the Yoruba, the concept of personhood is expressed through the term "*Eniyan*." The Yoruba make a distinction between *Eniyan* as "ordinary meaning" of human being and *Eniyan* as "normative quality" of a genuine human being, exactly as the Baluba distinguish Muntu from Kintu.

For the Baluba, as for many other Africans, to be is to be ethical. This implies not only the capacity to distinguish good from evil, but the ability to choose to do good. An unethical person is "*muntu wa bumvu*" (a man of shame), a "*Muntu bituhu*" (a zero-person). In Kiluba language, ethics is expressed by "*Mwikadilo muyampe*" (A good way of being in the world) or *Mwendelo muyampe* (A good way of walking on the road of life). The notion of good heart (*Mucima muyampe*) includes virtues such as *buntu* (generosity), *butundaile* (hospitality), *bukwashi* (helpfulness), *butalale* (being peaceful, calm), *bwanahabo* (freedom, autodetermination), *buleme* (respect, dignity, integrity), *lusa* (compassion), *buswe* (love), *kanye* (sensitive heart), *boloke* (righteousness, rectitude), *Ngenyi* (intelligence, wisdom). As for vices, the notion of *Mucima mubi* (evil heart) includes things such as *bwivi* (theft, robbery), *mwino* (selfishness), *buzazangi* (hypocrisy), *mushikwa* (hatred), *bubela* (lie), *ntondo* (discrimination), *lwiso* (lust), *malaka* (envy), *bulobo*, *bukalabale*, or *nsungu* (violence, anger), *kwihaya* (killing), *butshi* (witchcraft), *kibengo* (insolence), *buhika* (enslavement), *busekese* (sexual misconduct), *makoji* (adultery), *bulembakane* (stupidity).

It should be noted, however, that the African religious ethic is holistic. It extends to the animals and the whole cosmos, precisely because the first principle of African cosmology is not the concept of Muntu, but rather that of *Ntanda* (the world). God first created the world, the universe, and then humans. God did not create only one village, but *ntanda yonso* (the whole world) and all its content. All human beings have but one single source of existence, and not only human beings, but all other creatures. Indeed, as the Mashi expression clarifies, God is "*Ishe Wabantu n'ebintu*" (father of human beings and things). The natural world is an extension of the human body, as the Yoruba orisha tradition makes it clear. This interconnectedness with nature marks the specificity of the African conception of both God and the human. Indeed for the Baluba, as for other Africans, religion is cosmotheandric. God's nature, as well as human nature, includes animals, trees—the whole cosmos is the home of the divinity. It is also the home of human beings. This is the foundation of the general solidarity that the Bantu feel with nature. Thus, a genuine human being, a person of Bumuntu, is one who has a good heart (*Mucima Muyampe*), one who extends his goodness to all human beings, animals, and the natural world. Bumuntu is manifested in four basic ways: good thought and good heart (*mucima muya*), good speech (*ludimi luya*), good actions (*bilongwa biya*), and a good way of looking at people and the world. Such is the art of becoming human and humane in African philosophy, according to the will of the ancestors and the will of *Shakapanga Vidye Mukulu* (the Great Spirit and Supreme Creator).

Another important component of African philosophical anthropology is the delicate balance between the individual and the community. A genuine human being is the one who succeeds in maintaining that delicate balance between individuality and the sense of community, for a genuine Muntu is, in the expression of the Mande, a Fadenya-Badenya—an individual and collective being.

Fadenya ("father-childness") is the centrifugal force of individuality. It orients human actions toward individual reputation and renown. The Fadenya force produces the heroes needed by the community: fearless people who can easily act against conventions and status quo. However, because the search for personal fame can easily lead to selfishness, self-aggrandizing passions, and anti-social behavior, Fadenya is feared as a force of social disequilibrium, envy, jealousy, abuse of power, competition, and self-promotion. The individual can find equilibrium only with the intervention of a counterpower, the centripetal force known as Badenya ("mother-childness"). This is a "conservative force," a force of stability, and cooperation; it brings the child to the mother's womb. Like the Chinese "Yin-Yang," and the Greek "Prometheus-Saturn" bond, Fadenya-Badenya cannot be reduced to masculine and feminine attributes, nor to a father and son hierarchy. It is a principle of being within every being. Fadenya corresponds to the Promethean impulse within the being: heroic, rebellious and revolutionary, individualistic and innovative, eternally seeking freedom, and autonomy. Badenya, on the other hand represents the Saturnian impulse: conservative, stabilizing, controlling, a force that seeks to contain, sustain, and maintain order. From Badenya arises social solidarity, benevolence, and altruism. Fadenya and Badenya stand as two sides of the coin that is the Bumuntu. What the Fadenya-Badenya paradigm indicates is that sustainable development is achieved when the welfare of the community and of each individual is taken into account. And community is not limited to human societies but extended to the environment, to flora and fauna, and to the entire cosmos as African cosmologies make it clear.

CONCLUSION

The Congo basin region remains part and parcel of the industrial and post-industrial revolutions in our world. Understanding this region of the world is critical to a genuine articulation of the African philosophy of sustainable development. The region is replete with vast mineral deposits and is the home of one of the most important rainforests of our planet. Rainforests are the great green heart of Africa, and present a unique combination of ecological, climatic, and human interactions. Africa is now suffering from deforestation and defaunation, while lakes and rivers are increasingly depleted of their fish. Moreover Africa has become the dustbin of the West. The dumping of electronic, chemical, and nuclear toxic waste in Africa by Western companies has reached alarming levels to such a degree that the United Nations has been forced to publicly denounce this dangerous dimension of global trade.

Sustainability like human rights is shaped by various cultural worldviews and is addressed in a variety of ways. For sustainability to be beneficial to Africans, it has to take into account the African context and the welfare of the African people.

The question of what ought to be sustained, why, how and by whom is eminently political. Sustainability cannot be achieved merely with the protection of the environment. It requires justice and the alleviation of poverty. In a world of unequal power relations and competing national interests, the discourse of development, universal human rights, and now environment and sustainability, is fraught with dangerous complexity. This is why African philosophy calls for a vision that supplements the economic and ecological models of sustainable development with cultural and political considerations. Africans who have a historical memory of the relationship between African and Foreign powers over the last four centuries, call for a vision of "sustainability of the people, by the people and for the people." It has been said by Africans that Westerners love human rights more than humans, and there is fear in some quarters that sustainability and environmentalism risk to become a dangerous ideology for the livelihood of Africans in some regions when environmentalist activists may use laws to protect trees, animals, and fish at the expense of human beings. Some would argue that it is for instance not helpful to forbid women from cutting trees for the purpose of cooking food without providing to village people alternative sources of energy or to forbid hunting in a region where people are starving or to forbid people's access to rainforest where medicinal plants are needed by healers in regions devoid of modern hospitals. Some fear that some environmental activists may move beyond vegetarianism and prohibit the consumption of not only meat but also vegetable. In this context, African philosophy calls for a balanced approach to environmentalism and sustainability. Likewise, there is need for a balanced approach to the usage of African rainforests and minerals for the benefit of humankind as a whole, without sacrificing the welfare of the African people. While national parks are necessary for the protection of the environment, the expropriation of people of the farmland cannot be done without providing alternative sources of livelihood to rural population.

From red rubber to blood diamond and blood iPhones, wars pertaining to access and control of minerals, land, water, oil, and other critical but dwindling natural resources, the pernicious effects of climate change, the tragic effects of chemical, nuclear, and other types of industrial pollution have made sustainability a "life and death" matter and put it at the center not only of development models and projects but also of the future of humanity itself. Having been for centuries the victim of all sorts of dangerous development programs and practices, Africa cannot afford the luxury of ignoring the grand debate of our time over sustainable development. It was the aim of this study to articulate, albeit in modest fashion, the African involvement in this debate, and to articulate the resources available for a genuine formulation of a systematic African philosophy of sustainable development. The best way to avoid that the love for the environment turns into a misanthropic ideology is for Africa to get involved in the global conversation and decision-making processes pertaining to sustainable development. An African philosophy of sustainable development is a paradigm shift that calls for a profound and holistic shift of thinking and consciousness, a new way of understanding the "mitsein" nature of humanity and the cosmos.

NOTES

1. The full transcript of the letter is available at http://www.atomicarchive.com/Docs/Begin/Einstein.shtml.
2. According to Cheikh Anta Diop, this one-year rotation on its own axis is not yet known to modern astronomers. They have not yet ascertained it, although they have confirmed the 50-year orbit the Dogon have given for another star circling Sirius.

REFERENCES

African Charter on Human and Peoples' Rights. www.achpr.org/files/instruments/achpr/banjul_charter.pdf.

Bujo, Benezet. (2001). *Foundations of an African Ethic: Beyond the Universal Claims of Western Morality*. Nairobi: Paulines Publications Africa.

Chimakonam, Jonathan O. ed. (2018). *African Philosophy and Environmental Conservation*. Abingdon-on-Thames, UK: Routledge.

Diop, Cheikh Anta. (1991). *Civilization or Barbarism. An Authentic Anthropology*. New York: Lawrence Hill Books.

Diop, Birago. (1960). *Leurres et lueurs*. Paris: éditions Présence Africaine.

Einstein, Albert. (1939). *Letter to President Roosevelt*. Available at http://www.atomicarchive.com/Docs/Begin/Einstein.shtml.

Fottorino, Eric, et al. (1992). *Besoin d'Afrique*. Paris: Fayard.

Frankel, Todd C. (2016). "The Cobalt Pipeline: Tracing the Path from Deadly Hand-Dug Mines in Congo to Consumers' Phones and Laptops." *The Washington Post*, September 30.

Hegel, G. W. F. (1994). The Philosophy of History. In *Great Books of the Western World Volume 43: Hegel, Kierkegaard, Nietzsche*, edited by Adler, Mortimer. Chicago: Encyclopedia Britannica, Inc.

Hochschild, Adam. (1998). *King Leopold's Ghost: A Story of Greed, Terror, and Heroism in Colonial Africa*. New York: Houghton Mifflin Company.

Kreamer, Christine Mullen, ed. (2010). *African Cosmos: African Cultural Astronomy from Antiquity to the Present*. New York: The Monacelli Press and Smithsonian National Museum of African Arts.

Lichtheim, Miriam. (1976). *Ancient Egyptian Literature. Vol. II: The New Kingdom*. London: Berkeley, Los Angeles: University of California Press.

Mbiti, John. (1990). *African Religions and Philosophy*. Portsmouth: Heinemann.

Mulago, Vincent. (1973). *La Religion traditionnelle des Bantu et leur vision du monde*. Faculté Catholique de Kinshasa, Presses Universitaires du Zaïre.

Olupona, Jacob K., ed. (1991). *African Traditional Religions in Contemporary Society*. New York: A New Era Book/Paragon House.

Pakenham, Thomas. (1991). *The Scramble for Africa*. New York: Avon Books.

Tempels, Placide. (1959). *Bantu Philosophy*. Paris: Présence Africaine.

Wangari, Maathai. (2014). "Nobel Lecture." http://www.nobelprize.org/nobel_prizes/peace/laureates/2004/maathai-lecture-text.html.

Williams, Susan. (2016). Spies in the Congo: America's Atomic Mission in World War II (Public Affairs Books, 2016).

Wilson, Thomas. (2017). We'll All Be Relying on Congo to Power Our Electric Cars. *Bloomerg News*, October 26, at https://www.bloomberg.com.

Zahan, Dominique. (1979). *The Religion, Spirituality, and Thought of Traditional Africa*. Chicago: The University of Chicago Press.

Chapter 4

Good Governance and Sustainable Development Challenges and Opportunities in Zimbabwe

Chipo Dendere

POST-INDEPENDENCE EFFORTS TOWARD SUSTAINABLE DEVELOPMENT GOALS

Beginning in the early 1960s when the first wave of African countries gained independence, there has been a lot of global concern on the state of development on the continent. The official terminology used has changed but the goals of finding long lasting solutions for sustainable development have remained the same. Top among these is the goal to end poverty. In the early 1990s when the last group of settler colonies gained independence, the continent was making strides toward development but serious economic challenges remained.

The poverty story of African countries has necessitated the development of global agendas aimed at alleviating poverty among the most vulnerable in our global community. These agendas began with the eight Millennium Development Goals (MDGs) developed in 2000 at the turn of the century. The eight goals were universally ambitious: to eradicate poverty, to achieve universal primary education, gender equality, reduce child mortality, to improve on maternal health to combat diseases, to ensure environmental sustainability, and ensure global development. By 2013, there was uneven success across the globe but it remained clear that poverty, disease, and environmental issues remained a real concern especially among African countries. In 2016, the United Nations developed the newest set of goals known as the Sustainable Development Goals (SDGs) generally referred to as the Global Goals. The new seventeen goals are an expansion of the MDGs with the same primary agenda to eradicate poverty, sustainable consumption and good governance among other priorities.

While good governance is included as one of the major goals for sustainable development, this agenda has received very little attention. And yet the majority of Africa's developmental problems stem from and are exacerbated by bad politics. This chapter focuses on Zimbabwe to explore the ways in which the deteriorating political situation have stunted economic growth thereby increasing poverty. Whereas sixty-four countries mostly in Europe, Asia, and the Americas have made some progress on the development goals, the majority, many of them in Africa, are still lagging behind. Countries that are still far behind are also some of the poorest countries hardest hit by conflict and political instability (Hodal and Holder, 2016). It is those countries, like Zimbabwe, for whom the new SDGs are targeted.

ZIMBABWE BACKGROUND AND OVERVIEW OF PATH TOWARD MEETING SDGS

Zimbabwe is now a low-income country following decades of poor economic management, political instability, and inconsistent land reform program and political sanctions leveraged by western countries. Zimbabwe gained independence in 1980 after almost a century of British rule and two decades of white minority rule. At independence, Zimbabwe was ahead of most of her peers in the developing world on measures of economic growth. While the majority of Zimbabwe's population resides in rural areas, there was universal access to health care, education, and clean water in most parts of the country. However, the government was failing to meet its goals to provide additional welfare to citizens especially those in rural areas who had suffered during the civil war for independence. In the early 1990s, Zimbabwe restructured its economy under the guidance of the World Bank's Structural Adjustment Programs. Over the next two decades, Zimbabwe would fail to pay its debts to the World Bank resulting in severe economic isolation. International isolation combined with the deteriorating political conditions made Zimbabwe into a pariah state.

Since 2000, Zimbabwe has failed to bring itself out of poverty. With agriculture production severely diminished, closures in the manufacturing industries soon followed resulting in over 90 percent unemployment rate. Weak institutions, increasing poverty, and a growing population have put pressure on the aging infrastructure and as a result overall quality of life has decreased.

Thus, Zimbabwe is unlikely to meet many of the 2015 United Nations SDGs. The resignation of longtime leader Robert Mugabe in 2017 brought Zimbabwe out of isolation, and there are promises from the international community to provide more aid more to Zimbabwe, however, three months after the transition less than $10 million has been donated. It is unlikely that small amounts of aid will accelerate the recovery process in Zimbabwe which is also headed into an expensive election season in the latter part of 2018. More Zimbabweans are in poverty now than twenty years ago. Food and commodity prices continue to rise ahead of wages and the country's currency remains unstable. In 2017, as the cash crisis intensified the government increased production of a new currency known as "bond-notes" adding it to the basket of currencies including the United States dollar which has been the formal currency since 2009 (Wilfred Kajese, 2017).

The majority of Zimbabweans who reside in the rural areas have been hardest hit by the twin political and economic crises and many of them depend solely on food aid for survival. There is some hope that the good rains in late 2017 and 2018 will result in better yields but most in the southern regions will likely remain on food aid programs.

Zimbabwe's hospitals are in a dire state. Most hospitals do not have basic medications. In 2017, the hospitals rationed pain medication accessible to patients. Zimbabwe's education has a strong foundation but even the education sectors are suffering. The majority of well-trained teachers along with nurses and other professionals continue to emigrate because of low and irregular remuneration. Rural schools are increasingly understaffed and under resourced. There is notable growth in private education but this is limited to the wealthy. Zimbabweans have less access to clean water now than at any other time in the country's history. The water crisis has contributed to major health issues; over the last four years typhoid and cholera outbreaks have become frequent.

Zimbabwe has made some strides toward addressing gender inequalities, climate change and energy but the twin forces of rising poverty and political instability have made it challenging to see any real improvements in the other areas of development. Governance is a very critical factor for Zimbabwe's path to sustainable development. In 2009, soon after the formation of the Government of National Unity (GNU) which brought in the Movement for Democratic Change to share responsibilities with the ruling ZANU PF, there was an immediate positive change in the economy. At the height of the Zimbabwe crisis in 2008, inflation hit 79,600,000,000 percent and drastically dropped to single digit numbers during the GNU. During the tenure of the GNU, the GDP per capita growth reached a 15 percent high before plunging back down after the 2013 election when ZANU PF won resoundingly ending the GNU. A few months prior to the signing of the GNU, Zimbabwe had experienced the worst cholera outbreak since independence but a month after the GNU was officiated the city of Harare was restored to health.

The rest of this chapter will discuss in greater detail the ways in which political stalemate has slowed down progress on the five key goals for sustainable development: no poverty, zero hunger, good health, quality education, and access to clean water. Although the focus will be on these five goals, I will show the connections between all seventeen SDGs and that the success of each one depends on overall success of the agenda.

TOWARD GOOD GOVERNANCE

Good governance is critical for reaching the sustainable development goals that the UN has set for the world. When asked about the general direction that their country is going in, 60 percent of Zimbabweans interviewed for the Afrobarometer surveys said the country was headed in the wrong direction. Zimbabweans identify the government's poor management of the economy (31 percent), high unemployment (53 percent), food shortages (20 percent), and poverty (13.6 percent) as the major challenges facing Zimbabwe (figure 4.1).

While the Zimbabwean government has blamed much of the country's woes on the sanctions targeting ZANU PF elites imposed by the United States, the majority of citizens blame corruption and the same elites for general mismanagement of funds. When asked to rank how well the government is doing on handling corruption, the majority, 69 percent, responded that they felt that the government was doing badly in managing the economy. Only 3.5

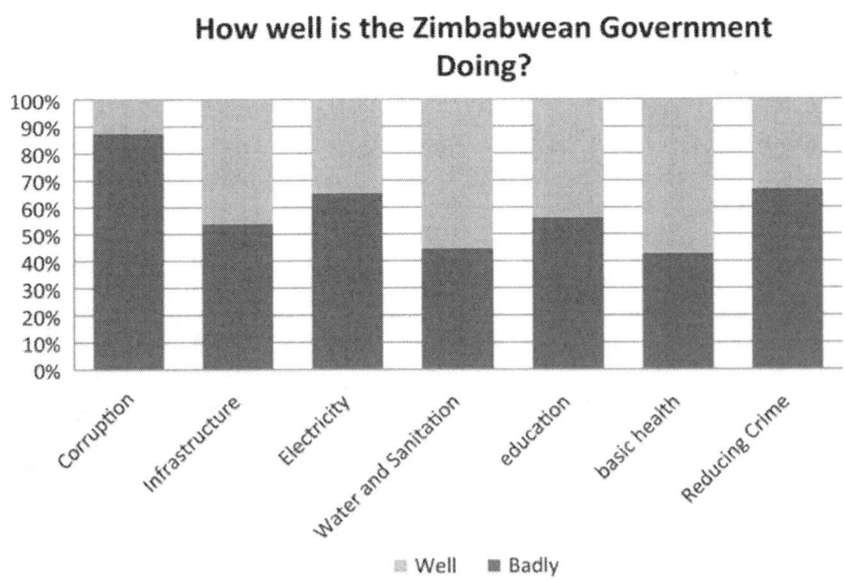

Figure 4.1 Public Opinion on the Performance of Zimbabwean Government. *Source*: Zimbabwe Round 6: Afrobarometer.

percent of Zimbabweans thought the government was doing a good job in managing corruption.

Corruption is an epidemic. In 2017, the Zimbabwe Revenue Authority reported that the country was losing billions from corruption. In the first half of the year, the agency had recovered $120 million in looted funds and only solved 21 out of 394 cases of corruption. Transparency International gives Zimbabwe a poor 2/10 on corruption evaluation and ranks the country in the top thirty most corrupt countries (*Reuters*, 2016). The new president, Mr. Emmerson Mnangagwa, has made tackling corruption his top most agenda since coming into office in November 2017. After three months of a targeted campaign to recover looted funds, his office has only received $250 million from the estimated $1.6 billion (Nyemudzai Kakore, 2018).

TOWARD UNIVERSAL ACCESS TO WATER: ACCESS TO WATER AS A GOVERNANCE ISSUE

Fewer Zimbabweans have regular access to water today than they did twenty years ago. In 1990, ten years after independence, 97 percent of the urban population had access to piped water; this decreased to 60 percent in 2008 and by 2016 less than 50 percent of urbanites had regular access to water (Manzungu et al., 2016). Greater access to water in urban areas was a product of colonial structures that limited urban residency to the white population and a very small black minority. Following independence, the black-majority government improved infrastructure in rural areas thereby also improving access to water for the rural population. In the years since independence, rural urban migration also increased facilitating the need for urban expansion. From public opinion data, the proportion of Zimbabweans who reported confidence in the government's handling of water issues has also declined. Whereas in 1999 only 20 percent of Zimbabweans reported to the Afrobarometer that the government was handling water issues badly, in 2016 the proportion of Zimbabweans dissatisfied had increased to 35 percent. If the new post-Mugabe government does not invest in water infrastructure development the numbers are more likely to increase.

Zimbabwe's new constitution passed with overwhelming support from citizens in 2013. The constitution guarantees every citizen access to safe and clean water as Section 77 reads: "Every person has the right to (a) safe, clean and portable water; and the State must take reasonable legislative measures, within the limits of the resources available to it, to achieve the progressive realization of this right." Five years on, the government's ability to provide this basic right has been diminished significantly. At the launch of the current

SDGs in 2016, Zimbabwe's ability to provide universal water access had a very low likelihood.

Most of Zimbabwe's burgeoning youth born after 1999 to poor parents in rural and urban areas alike are unlikely to associate water taps with running water. For most children in poor high-density areas, tap fixtures have no real function. In most countries, taking a daily shower is not a time-consuming activity; it is often a normal routine that most people do not think much about. In Zimbabwe most young citizens have never taken a shower. As access to running water has declined, the average Zimbabwean takes bucket baths. A family of five will often share a 20-liter bucket of water for their bathing, toilet and food preparation needs. In the majority of urban homes, it is now normal for families to have large plastic containers of water decorating the home. In high-income neighborhoods, citizens have resorted to digging boreholes on their premises as a way to ensure regular access to running water. The increase in demand for private boreholes has also created new environmental problems because boreholes are distorting the water tables (figure 4.2).

In 2018, the majority of citizens, many of whom are poor urban women, are spending most of their time in search for water. In low-income areas, there are not enough public or private boreholes to meet then needs of the growing population so the average woman travels about three kilometers to the nearest water sources and then typically spends at least six hours in line for water (Pahwaringira, Chaminuka, and Muranda-Kaseke, 2017). Women have the primary responsibility of ensuring that a family has enough water and many also carry the primary financial responsibility for their families.

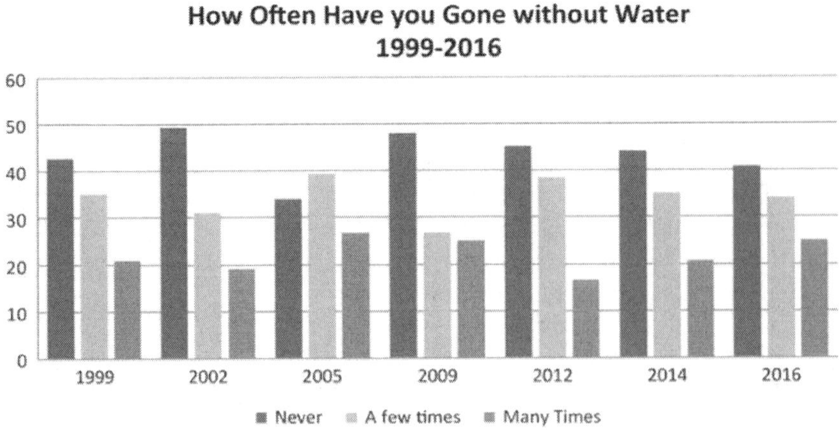

Figure 4.2 Public Opinion on Citizen Access to Water in Zimbabwe. *Source*: Zimbabwe Round 6: Afrobarometer.

An assessment project conducted by the World Bank in collaboration with the Government of Zimbabwe revealed that low water yield in Zimbabwe is primarily due environmental degradation and rotting water pipes (Government of Zimbabwe and the World Bank, 2014). In the city of Harare where nearly 16 percent of the population resides, water yield is less than 70 percent even with extensive water rationing efforts by the government. In Harare and surrounding areas of Chitungwiza and Ruwa, the majority of water infrastructure is in poor to terrible condition. While the major water reservoirs are in good condition, Zimbabwe loses the majority of its water to leakages of old steel pipes. Most of the water and sewer supply infrastructure is outdated as the government has not replaced most of the pre-independence structures. Most of the valves that would normally control water pressure are loose resulting in frequent pipe bursts. It is not uncommon to see multiple burst pipes around Harare's CBD which can go unfixed for months.

To restore Zimbabwe's water system toward the SDG goals would require billions of dollars. In 2014, the World Bank reported that in the metropolitan areas around Harare alone would need to replace over 100 km of transmission pipelines and almost 200 km of distribution pipelines to improve water access. Zimbabwe would also need to construct at least three new reservoirs to meet the water needs for the growing population. To fix the immediate water challenges, Zimbabwe would only need about $400 million which is not a highly prohibitive amount for this kind of project. As I will discuss later, however, a combination of bad governance and political will among the civil society has stalled Zimbabwe's water plans.

POOR GOVERNANCE AND PERSISTING DETERIORATING WATER CONDITIONS

Collier (2008) writes that the poorest in the world are victims of multiple traps including the *natural resource* trap and the *bad governance in small country* trap. Zimbabwe is failing to meet the goals to provide access to clean water because of the twin traps of bad governance and access to natural resources. In the last two decades, Zimbabwe has experienced some of the worst economic crises in recent history. As the political situation began to decline in 2000, the economy also went into free fall making it difficult for the government to address infrastructure issues that have worsened what would have normally been a manageable problem. At the same time, in 2009 Zimbabwe also discovered diamond deposits in the Eastern Highlands. The diamond revenue somewhat stabilized the economy but not for long due to endemic corruption and plundering of natural resources by those in power.

In Zimbabwe, addressing the water crisis has not been a priority until recently. Across Africa, citizens have easier access to cellphones than they do to clean water and toilets (Busani Bafana, 2017; Devarajan, 2010; Giridharadas, 2010). While there is a lot of civil society activity on political issues, human rights, gender equality, and even violence issues, there is very little civil society interest in water issues. As a result, the government has not been motivated to invest in clean water. The private sector has also seen very little utility or business sense in investing in water and sanitation projects. Between 2009 and 2014, the Government of Zimbabwe managed to raise $400 million toward water and sanitation upgrade but that was just a small fraction of the estimated $30 billion the government needs to upgrade the country's outdated infrastructure. The bill for a total water upgrade is about $4 billion (Mthandazo Nyoni, 2017). While Zimbabwe is a poor country, its poverty stands in stark contrast to the billions that are lost every year to corruption. The former president Robert Mugabe claimed in 2016 that at least $15 Billion from diamond revenue had been lost due to corruption (Peter, 2016). These numbers have not been verified but it is clear that the Zimbabwean reserve bank like the nation's water pipes is leaking millions of dollars.

The government continues to abuse funds earmarked for infrastructure development. In 2014, secured funding to revamp the water and sewage infrastructure from the Multi-Donor Trust managed by the African Development Bank an estimated $140 million (African Development Bank report, 2015). Of this amount, an estimated $16 million was for water-related development. The Government of Zimbabwe also received a loan from the Chinese Bank Exim of $144 million toward rehabilitation of Morton Jaffrey Harare's major water treatment center. Between 2012 and 2018, Harare's water problems have worsened. The Morton Jaffrey Center has fourteen pipes, but over the last decade less than half are in working condition at any given time. As a result, water production and access greatly diminished. The City of Harare Council received a loan of $144 million in 2012, but it was brought to light in early 2018 following citizen protests that the majority of funds had been stolen by officials. An audit of the Harare City Council conducted in 2013 revealed that funds earmarked for water rehabilitation were diverted, but it was difficult to ascertain how the funds had been used because the council had not created an account for the project. The audit also found that the council had overpaid for most of the materials used in the project and the committee could not account for most expenditures. The approved loan was $144 million but the council could only account for expenditures worth about $5 million even after including fancy cars bought for fifteen committee members and another six ghost members. The Chinese who have strict anti-corruption laws are unlikely to give more money to the project.

FINANCIAL CHALLENGES AND ACCESS TO WATER

Since 1999, Zimbabwe's ability to meet the majority of the SDGs has been compromised by a crippling economy and the massive exodus of health professionals. The economic challenges have resulted in shortages of important chemicals needed to treat water. Beginning in 2016, tap water in Harare has increasingly become highly contaminated and unsafe for drinking. Harare tap water has a brownish-greenish color and often carries moving particles. When the water is boiled, it turns a murky green (figure 4.3).

In December 2017, most Harare residents including this author took to social media to protest the poor quality of water. Popular activist Evan Mawarire pushed for a dialogue with the city mayor who until then had largely ignored citizen concerns over the quality of water. In earlier conversations with citizens, the Harare mayor had argued that there was nothing wrong with Harare water. He had said in a statement to the media that citizens should drink the water because the water is clean (Zimbabwe Citizen Post, 2017). However, after the citizens protested, he back tracked on this message saying instead that the city had been able to purchase the needed water treatment chemicals due to sever financial hardships. The city of Harare alone requires over $5 million to manage water treatment for the over one million Harare residents and surrounding areas. However, due to the foreign currency shortages in Zimbabwe the city councils tasked with providing clean water are unable to access the chemicals they need to treat the water. While the city is unable to meet the water treatment bill, the council is also heavily burdened by an unmanageable wage bill. The local council which employs just under

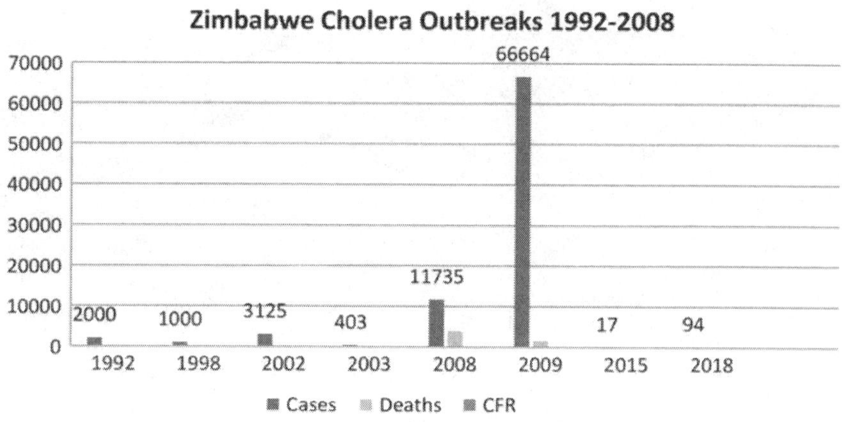

Figure 4.3 Cholera Cases and Deaths in Zimbabwe 1992–2018. *Source*: Data from (Mukandavire et al., 2011; MOHC, 2018).

10,000 employees had a wage bill of nearly $12 million. An audit of the council's wage bill revealed that the city council employees are paid nearly twice as much as same level employees in other government institutions. The highest grossing employees were taking home at least $15,000 per month including lavish perks such as fuel, a company vehicle, and tuition remission at expensive private schools (Newsday, 2010).

In late 2017, the council promised to slash the salaries of the top executives to align the wage bill with the needs of million tax payers, but until March 2018 they were yet to deliver on this promise. Zimbabwe, like most African countries, suffers under the burden of a huge wage bill that overshadows other development needs. At least 90 percent of the Zimbabwean budget goes to paying salaries (Gift Phiri, 2017). In the early 1990s, the World Bank and IMF forced African countries to readjust their economies by cutting the civil servant expenses. The error that the international aid agencies made back then was to focus on retrenching the middle level workers who earned very little. The majority of workers earn peanuts compared to the millions pocketed by political elites and top management. In 2014, the Zimbabwean government made attempts to cap the salaries of the highly paid officials to $6,000. Prior to this failed attempt, top officials had earned almost $30,000 a month, salaries higher than those earned by government officials in most developed countries. Zimbabwe has been able to borrow money from international lending agencies because of existing arrears. Additional aid would have allowed Zimbabwe to borrow money for development projects including water management. The IMF suggested to the Zimbabwean government that they reduce the wage bill and redirect those funds to paying their debt.

WATER, SANITATION, AND HEALTH CRISIS

Declining water conditions in Zimbabwe have serious consequences not only for Zimbabwe's ability to provide universal access to clean and fresh water but other priorities such as providing universal health care and ensuring that everyone has access to sanitary conditions. In 2008, eight years after the introduction of the MDGs, Zimbabwe suffered from a cholera outbreak. Cholera is a dangerous waterborne disease that causes an estimated 100,000 deaths a year globally (Taylor et al., 2015). Cholera outbreaks are often associated with poor hygiene and water shortages. The poorest countries with poor infrastructure also tend to be the ones most affected by these outbreaks. In 2008, Zimbabwe recorded over 11,735 cases of cholera resulting in over 4,000 deaths. The outbreak coincided with the worst economic crisis since World War II, and the most intense season of political violence and instability following the disputed 2008 March elections and the highly violent March re-run. Cholera was most prominent in densely populated poor urban areas. In Zimbabwe, the World Health Organization investigation revealed that the majority of deaths were as a result of citizens drinking contaminated water and food. The majority of Zimbabwe's urban poor can go for weeks without access to fresh running water. People are forced to hoard water in plastic bins and, in most cases, the water will rot before the next cycle of running water.

Since independence, Zimbabwe has experienced multiple outbreaks but disease outbreaks have increased in frequency. It is often the case that the outbreaks happen in densely populated urban areas were multiple families share access to the limited water sources (figure 4.4).

Since 2016, the most immediate water-related health threat is typhoid. Typhoid, "Salmonella *enterica* serovar Typhi (Typhi) is a Gram-negative bacterium that causes typhoid fever—a systemic illness of varying severity characterized by fever, headache, cough, abdominal pain, and other gastrointestinal symptoms"(Imanishi et al., 2014). Like cholera, typhoid is a waterborne illness that most frequently affects populations with poor access to safe drinking water. In 2016, at least 944 cases of typhoid were recorded around Zimbabwe (UN Report 2016, n.d.). Since then, incidences of cholera and typhoid have been reported all over the country with highest incidences being recorded in the same low-income high-density areas that suffered heavily from cholera in 2008. Since the end of the Unity Government in 2013, the Zimbabwean economy has gone back into depression. The poor have further emigrated into urban areas and the increased costs in rental housing have forced people to live in even smaller, squalid shared spaces.

The erratic water access is worsened by poor refuse collection. As a result of economic decline and corruption within the city councils, waste management is no longer a priority (Tsiko and Togarepi, 2012). Citizens in the

Figure 4.4 Residents Display Harare Water 1. *Source*: Evan Mawarire.

richer parts of the city can pay private refuse collection vendors to offset poor service delivery by the government. The poor are not as fortunate. As a result, in high-density low-income areas like Mbare, citizens are surrounded by mounds of rubbish. Decomposing rubbish contaminates the open sources of water.

Zimbabwe's waste management challenges have a long history dating back to colonial times. While the colonial government had stringent laws on refuse collection in white areas, black-majority areas were a low priority. After independence, waste management improved, but the lack of political consensus on political responsibility for environmental issues exposed weakness in the system. These weaknesses would become an even bigger concern when the country lost donor funding as the political crisis worsened (Tsiko and Togarepi, 2012). After 2009, a new and democratically elected council found itself facing a major cholera crisis. A combination of internal and external political crises has further weakened the council's ability to manage new challenges. The majority of Harare's official dumping sites have reached full capacity. As a result, most poor neighborhoods have overflowing trash all around people's homes. In 2017, members of the Combined Harare Residents Association reported that the city council had enough trucks to successfully collect refuge across the city. Chairperson Simbarashe Moyo said the real issue was poor management within the city council (Kadirire, 2017). Poor governance is at the center of every environmental and health challenges that Zimbabwe is facing.

The Gendered Impact of Poverty and HIV

Notwithstanding the political and economic crisis, Zimbabwe has made some significant strides on addressing major health challenges over the last two decades. However, despite recent declines and concerted efforts by the government, Zimbabwe remains burdened by the HIV crisis. In the post-2015 era, HIV related death have reduced by over 60 percent and HIV prevalence halved from a height of 30 percent to 15 percent in 2017, but Zimbabwe remains in the top five of most affected countries in the world even with these improvements (Gazimbi and Magadi, 2017; Kandawasvika et al., 2015; Pascoe et al., 2015).

Recent studies by Gazimbi and Magadi 2017, Lowenthal et al. 2014, Pascoe et al. 2015, and Simms et al. 2017 show that poor young women are more vulnerable to getting HIV. On the one hand, HIV testing uptake has increased; in a study of sex workers in Zimbabwe at 64 percent of women were aware of their HIV status and 67 percent of those were on ARVs resulting in reduced HIV related deaths. In the general population, however, most women—especially widows—have limited access to medication. Cultural norms, gender expectations, class and age influence one's ability to get medication (Gazimbi and Magadi, 2017). There is need for increased public education and awareness programs that challenge stigma associated with getting tested for HIV.

The HIV epidemic in the mid-1990s resulted in a huge number of orphaned children. The responsibility of caring for the family often fell on the shoulders of the oldest child in the family. Children who have been affected by HIV either because they are infected or because their family members were infected or both tend to suffer significant cognitive impairment (Kandawasvika et al., 2015). Children from poor HIV infected families are also at a greater risk of contracting HIV and other sexually transmitted diseases because poverty has forced them into prostitution. These issues are more prevalent in border-tourist towns and small rural areas. Rural citizens already face difficulties in accessing medication; minors who also serve as their head of home often feel pressured to have unprotected sex in exchange for very small payments.

The impact of HIV is gendered. In 2016, I conducted fieldwork in the small resort town of Victoria Falls where it was not uncommon to witness young school age girls selling their bodies to tourists in exchange for $5. One of these young women, a high school fourteen-year-old, explained that denying her customers unprotected sex was not an option. Demanding protected sex would result in a lower payment rate. A lower payment rate meant a lower income which would add strain on their already overburdened budget. The majority of these young women and their siblings are part of the large population of HIV orphans.

PROSPECTS FOR THE FUTURE

Zimbabwe has made some progress in opening up political space for women, but women's political participation remains low: women occupy only 35 percent of the parliamentary seats (HIVOS, 2017). None of the existing and viable political parties have met the 50 percent threshold of female leadership at any party level. The recent ouster and demise of former First Lady Grace Mugabe will likely further restrict women's participation in politics. That said, women have been actively creating space for themselves in politics, civil society, and business. A significant number of young women, the majority under thirty-five years of age, have committed to contesting the 2018 elections as independent candidates for local and national positions (Marima, 2017). These women are also changing the political landscape by actively engaging citizens on social media and crowd sourcing for campaign resources.

The government must continue working to align the country's laws with the constitution in an effort to increase female representation across all sectors of life. The combined efforts of the United Nations, World Bank, and donor governments and agencies have led to an increase in women owned business (ZNCC, 2018). Women are disproportionately impacted by violence and corruption. In 2016, when the government banned South African imports the majority of vendors negatively impacted were women. Beyond the economy, women are also the majority primary care givers and therefore the health and water crisis have a huge impact on their quality of life (Mangwiro and Tanga, 2016).

WILL ZIMBABWE REACH SDG GOALS?

The ouster of long serving leader Robert Mugabe in November 2017 has dramatically changed the political landscape in Zimbabwe. The citizens have become emboldened to speak out against mismanagement and the new administration seems anxious to stay in power thus engaging citizen concerns. The international community has also shown their confidence in the transition by offering financial support. Therefore, a combination of good governance practices that respect human rights and reduce corruption will have a positive and lasting impact on Zimbabwe's sustainable development goals.

REFERENCES

African Development Bank Report. (2015). "Zimbabwe Multi-Donor Trust Fund." African Development Bank. November 2015.

Afrobarometer Data, Zimbabwe, Round 6, 2016, available at http://www.afrobarometer.org.

Busani, Bafana. (2017). "Support IPS Inter Press Service on Razoo." *Inter Press Service* (blog), March 21, 2017.

Collier, Paul. (2008). *The Bottom Billion: Why the Poorest Countries Are Failing and What Can Be Done about It*. Bethesda, MD: Oxford University Press.

Devarajan, Shanta. (2010). "More Cell Phones than Toilets." Text. *AfricaCan End Poverty*, April 12, 2010.

Gazimbi, M. M., and M. A. Magadi. (2017). "A Multilevel Analysis of the Determinants of HIV Testing in Zimbabwe: Evidence from the Demographic and Health Surveys." *HIV/AIDS Res Treat Open J* 4(1): 14–31.

Gift, Phiri. (2017). "Reduce Wage Bill: IMF Tells Govt." *DailyNews Live*, July 8, 2017.

Giridharadas, Anand. (2010). "Where a Cellphone Is Still Cutting Edge." *The New York Times*, April 10, 2010, sec. Week in Review.

Government of Zimbabwe and the World Bank. (2014). "Greater Harare Water and Sanitation Investment Plan." Harare, Zimbabwe.

Hodal, Kate, and Josh Holder. (2016). "Poorest Countries Hit Hardest as World Lags behind on Global Education Goals." *The Guardian*, September 6, 2016.

Imanishi, Maho, Patience F. Kweza, Rachel B. Slayton, Tanaka Urayai, Odrie Ziro, Wellington Mushayi, Monica Francis-Chizororo, Lazarus R. Kuonza, Tracy Ayers, and Molly M. Freeman. (2014). "Household Water Treatment Uptake during a Public Health Response to a Large Typhoid Fever Outbreak in Harare, Zimbabwe." *The American Journal of Tropical Medicine and Hygiene* 90(5): 945–54.

Kadirire, Helen T. (2017). "Harare Grapples with Garbage Crisis." *DailyNews Live*, June 11, 2017.

Kandawasvika, G. Q., P. Kuona, P. Chandiwana, M. Masanganise, F. Z. Gumbo, M. P. Mapingure, K. Nathoo, and B. Stray-Pedersen. (2015). "The Burden and Predictors of Cognitive Impairment among 6- to 8-Year-Old Children Infected and Uninfected with HIV from Harare, Zimbabwe: A Cross-Sectional Study." *Child Neuropsychology* 21(1): 106–20.

Lowenthal, Elizabeth D., Sabrina Bakeera-Kitaka, Tafireyi Marukutira, Jennifer Chapman, Kathryn Goldrath, and Rashida A. Ferrand. (2014). "Perinatally Acquired HIV Infection in Adolescents from Sub-Saharan Africa: A Review of Emerging Challenges." *The Lancet Infectious Diseases* 14(7): 627–39.

Manzungu, Emmanuel, Margret Mudenda-Damba, Simon Madyiwa, and Vupenyu Dzingirayi. (2016). "Bulk Water Suppliers in the City of Harare-An Endogenous Form of Privatisation of Urban Domestic Water Supply in Zimbabwe?" *Water Alternatives* 9(1), 57–58.

Mthandazo, Nyoni. (2017). "Zim Requires $30bn for Infrastructure Revamp." *NewsDay Zimbabwe*, October 24, 2017.

Mukandavire, Z., et al. (2011). "Estimating the Reproductive Numbers for the 2008–2009 Cholera Outbreaks in Zimbabwe." *Proc Natl Acad Sci* May 24, 108(21): 8767–72.

Newsday. (2010). "Massive Salary Scandal Exposed." *NewsDay Zimbabwe* (blog), August 18, 2010.

Pahwaringira, Liliosa, Lillian Chaminuka, and Kwaedza Muranda-Kaseke. (2017). "The Impacts of Water Shortages on Women's Time-Space Activities in the High-Density Suburb of Mabvuku in Harare." *wH2O: The Journal of Gender and Water* 4(1). https://repository.upenn.edu/wh2ojournal/vol4/iss1/8.

Pascoe, Sophie J. S., Lisa F. Langhaug, Webster Mavhu, James Hargreaves, Shabbar Jaffar, Richard Hayes, and Frances M. Cowan. (2015). "Poverty, Food Insufficiency and HIV Infection and Sexual Behaviour among Young Rural Zimbabwean Women." *PLOS ONE* 10(1), 21.

Peter, Elisa. (2016). "Digging for the Missing $15 Billion of Diamond Revenue in Zimbabwe." *Huffington Post* (blog), June 2, 2016.

Simms, V., et al. (2017). "Community Burden of Undiagnosed HIV Infection among Adolescents in Zimbabwe Following Primary Healthcare-Based Provider-Initiated HIV Testing and Counselling: A Cross-Sectional Survey." *PLoS Medicine* 14(7): e1002360.

Taylor, Dawn L., Tanya M. Kahawita, Sandy Cairncross, and Jeroen H. J. Ensink. (2015). "The Impact of Water, Sanitation and Hygiene Interventions to Control Cholera: A Systematic Review." *PLoS ONE* 10(8). https://doi.org/10.1371/journal.pone.0135676.

Tsiko, Rodney, and Sydney Togarepi. (2012). "A Situational Analysis of Waste Management in Harare, Zimbabwe." *American Journal of Science* April, 8(4): 692–706.

UN Report 2016. (n.d.). "Zimbabwe Humanitarian Situation Report No 3, 31 March 2016." ReliefWeb. Accessed March 2, 2018.

ZimCitizen Post. (2017). "Ben Manyenyeni Water – Facebook Search." *Facebook*, November 2017.

Part II

CLIMATE ACTION AND INSTITUTIONAL PARTNERSHIP

Chapter 5

In the Hot Seat

The Impact of Vulnerability to Climate Change on Environmental Attitudes among Africans

Jennifer L. De Maio and Kristy Michaud

On June 4, 2011, about 1,000 people gathered in the Town Hall in Eldoret, a city in western Kenya, to watch the town's annual beauty contest. The year's theme: collective efforts in response to climate change. For the past several years, the Mr. and Miss. Environmental Beauty Contest has been arranged by youth organizations to create environmental awareness among young people on issues of pollution, waste disposal, and climate change. The event features local and national leaders from environmental institutions and organizations, including the Minister of Environment and the National Environment Authority. In addition, contestants and audience members can visit informational exhibits sponsored by environmental groups. The event attracts an average of 30 participants (20 women, 10 men) who compete in five categories: introduction, office wear, creative wear, traditional wear, and eveningwear. The winners who are chosen by a panel of four judges receive trophies, certificates, and cash awards. For the organizers, however, the greatest reward of the event is that the audience becomes sensitized to the need to protect the environment and learns about proper waste disposal and the consequences of pollution.

Events like this have been taking place throughout Kenya and the entire continent of Africa in recent years. They reflect the increasing concern among Africans about the impacts of climate change on their region. According to the International Panel on Climate Change's Fifth Assessment Report (2014), Africa is particularly vulnerable to the effects of climate change. This vulnerability stems not only from the many threats the changing climate poses to major economic sectors and to human health but also from the continent's weak capacity to adapt to these threats.

The Intergovernmental Panel on Climate Change (IPCC) reports that of the nine climate-related key regional risks identified for the continent, eight pose at least medium risk—even in systems without adaptation deficits. In the seven years that passed between the release of the fourth and fifth IPCC Assessment Reports, evidence of an increased warming trend across Africa increased, and the effects of climate change are already being observed across the continent. Africa faces or is already experiencing shifts in biome distribution, loss of coral reefs, reduced crop productivity, adverse effects on livestock, vector- and water-borne diseases, undernutrition, and migration. The impact of climate change on African agro-based economies is a major concern not only to African farmers but also to national governments, regional decision makers, and international organizations who acknowledge the threat to national security posed by environmental issues. Studies have suggested that global warming may increase the likelihood of civil wars in Africa, partly because of the potentially devastating effects on crop yields and scarce water resources (Burke et al., 2009).

The low adaptive capacity of many African states is largely a byproduct of problems in their economies, healthcare and education infrastructure, and governance (Low, 2005; Collier et al., 2008). Widespread poverty, ineffective governance and lack of institutional capacity, limited access to capital, infrastructure, technology, ecosystem degradation, and conflicts and disasters contribute to Africa's weak capacity to adapt to the threats posed by climate change. Resilience has thus been eroded by existing political and economic challenges, making the effects of climate change more severe.

In the face of these threats, Africans demonstrate considerable concern about climate change, as figure 5.1 shows. According to the fifth wave of the World Values Survey, the average level of unease about climate change among respondents in nine African countries is 83 percent, ranging from a global low of 65 percent among Zambians to a high of 96 percent among Burkinabe[1]. While high levels of concern are not unique in the global context (81 percent of Americans, 97 percent of Italians, 94 percent of Brazilians, and 82 percent of Chinese consider climate change to be a serious or very serious problem), they do present an opportunity to study the impact of vulnerability to climate change on individually held views about global warming and other environmental problems.

This chapter explores the link between vulnerability and environmental attitudes among Africans. Specifically, we are interested in examining the impact of a country's climate change risk factor and adaptive capacity on attitudes toward climate change and related environmental problems. We posit that people living in countries that are more vulnerable to the effects of climate change and have lower adaptive capacities are more likely to be concerned about environmental problems. By examining the attitudes of those

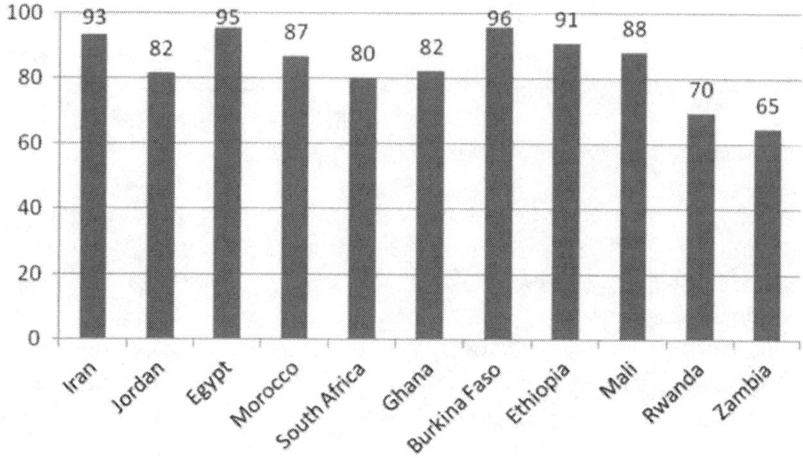

Figure 5.1 The View among Populations that Global Warming is a Serious Problem for the World (percentage). *Source*: World Values Survey 2005 Official Data File, v.20090901, 2009. World Values Survey Association.

residing in a region of the world that is heavily dependent on environmental stability for economic survival, this study contributes to the literature on risk, vulnerability, adaptive capacity, and environmental attitude formation.

THEORETICAL BACKGROUND

In its Sustainable Development Goals (SDGs), the United Nations identifies climate action (SDG13) as critical to mitigating the economic and social impacts of climate change. Addressing the threat of climate change is essential to achieving the SDGs and eradicating poverty and inequality (UNDP Sustainable Development Goals). The UN's collective call to action is focused primarily on the most vulnerable regions such as landlocked countries and island states. The United Nations Framework Convention on Climate Change (UNFCCC) requires developed countries to assist those developing countries that are particularly vulnerable to climate change with the costs associated with assessing, planning, and implementing adaptation measures in response to the effects of climate change (UNFCCC, Article 4). While the framework does not define what it means to be "particularly vulnerable," the IPCC characterizes vulnerability as a function of both the biophysical impact of climate change on a system and its capacity to adapt to the adverse effects of those climatic stimuli (Fussel, 2009: 6). As such, vulnerability in this context can be equated with concepts such as resilience, marginality, susceptibility, adaptability, fragility, risk, exposure, sensitivity, coping capacity, criticality, and robustness (Fussel, 2009: 3). In part to assist in the prioritization of financial assistance to at-risk countries, a number of national-level indices used to measure biophysical risks and social vulnerability to climate change have been created.

According to Fussel (2009), reviews of existing indices reveal that there are significant shortcomings in the construction of vulnerability indices, resulting in very little agreement regarding which countries are the most vulnerable. In one study of three indices, only one country (Cambodia) ranked among the twenty most vulnerable in all three indices, while only four others (Bangladesh, China, Iran, and Malawi) ranked among the twenty most vulnerable in at least two of the indices. Among the issues associated with aggregated risk indices is that they cannot adequately account for special circumstances—such as an economy that is strongly dependent on climate-sensitive activities—that make some countries more vulnerable to climate change than others (Fussel, 2009: 17).

Fussel's review of the literature assessing aggregated vulnerability indices leads him to conclude that vulnerability can be characterized by four factors—magnitude of regional climate change, biophysical sensitivity, socioeconomic exposure, and lack of adaptive/coping capacity due to poor governance (Fussel, 2009: 21). Based on these factors, it is likely that a number of African nations can be considered highly vulnerable to climate change.

Africa's vulnerability to climate change and its inability to adapt to its impacts may be most devastating to the agriculture sector, the main source of livelihood in the economies of most non-oil exporting African countries. African countries are particularly vulnerable as climate change presents a challenge for the continent's economic prospects. Despite the fact that African economies are slowly diversifying, they still rely extensively on agriculture: the majority of the population still works in farming and African farmers typically do not have irrigation—they rely on rain-fed agriculture. Between 2010 and 2020, the number of people employed in agriculture is expected to grow even as the share employed outside the sector continues to rise. Agriculture in low latitude developing countries is expected to be especially vulnerable because climates of many of these countries are already too hot. Further warming is expected to reduce crop productivity. The climate in Africa is predominantly tropical and is broadly classified into three climatic zones: humid equatorial, dry, and humid temperate. There are distinctive regional climates within these zones as determined by altitude and other localized variables. The climate also varies cyclically over decades, as well as from year to year. Most of the agricultural activities in African countries depend on the amount of rainfall. The IPCC's Fifth Assessment Report projects a reduction in rainfall over Northern African and parts of South Africa by the end of the twenty-first century which could threaten agriculture in those regions and compromise the livelihood of those dependent on it (IPCC). Moreover, the area of the continent suitable for agriculture is likely to decrease, particularly along the edges of semi-arid and arid regions. Climate change is expected to decrease food supply, thereby exacerbating the widespread poverty on the continent. Yields from rain-fed agriculture in some areas could decrease by as much as 50 percent by 2020, thereby compounding malnutrition and food security problems for an estimated 75 to 250 million people in Africa. Food supplies may also be affected by decreasing fish stocks as the result of rising water temperatures in lakes (Parry, 2007).

The impact of climate change will vary across the region. For example, global warming will make much of the western Sahel and southern and central Africa unsuitable for malaria transmission by 2050 (Ermert et al., 2013). Weather changes and forced migration, however, may bring the disease to densely populated areas of Zimbabwe as well as the highlands of Ethiopia, Kenya, Rwanda, and Burundi, which are currently malaria-free areas in these countries. While coastal areas will be vulnerable to rising sea levels, to more frequent and intense cyclones, and to the introduction of salt water into inland freshwater resources, other regions will be threatened by more variable precipitation patterns, which can result in more frequent and prolonged droughts and floods. Climate change in the arid regions of the continent is expected to increase desertification and result in a gradual decrease in forest cover. Rainfall is predicted to drop in the Sahara and Sahel regions, bringing soil degradation and an increasing number of dust storms. Across the continent, wetlands and wildlife are also threatened by drought (Parry, 2007).

What makes climatic variation particularly threatening for African countries is that vulnerability to climate change is only partially a function of environmental or geographic characteristics (Basher and Briceño, 2005). Flooding, drought, or other extreme weather events may be even more devastating for areas that are also marginalized from services, infrastructure, and levers of power that might otherwise help them in times of need. These areas may lack adequate roads, piped water, sanitation, and electricity. They may also have insufficient access to healthcare, education, and other basic services. The equation risk = vulnerability × hazard (Burg, 2008) considers vulnerability to be a component of risk which is defined as a function of both exposure to physical hazards and vulnerability. African countries are more vulnerable because they are more susceptible to the "potential for disruption or harm" (Wisner, 2004) and have "the reduced capacity to 'adapt to,' or adjust to, a determined set of environmental circumstances" (Cardona, 2004). This reduced capacity to adapt stems in large part, as Raleigh and Jordan note, from problems of poor governance and human agency (Raleigh and Jordan, 2008). A lack of political representation, weak governance, or a history of violence in the country can severely restrict its ability to recover from the adverse consequences of physical events. Climate shocks and natural disasters constitute more severe threats to domestic security in weaker or poorer states by compromising the government's ability to maintain peace and order. Looting and rioting to obtain necessities may result if relief supplies cannot be distributed quickly and efficiently and the destruction to infrastructure and interruption of services has been severe. An insufficient security presence may also provide opportunities for some to loot for personal gain. Moreover, citizens may use disasters as focal points around which to rally with grievances against the regime (Flores and Smith, 2010).

Recent research has found a strong causal link between climatic events and the likelihood of conflict across all major regions of the world (von Uexkull et al., 2014; Hsiang et al., 2013; Burke, 2009). With each 1 standard deviation change in climate toward warmer temperatures or more extreme rainfall, intergroup conflict increases by 14 percent. If global temperatures are expected to rise by 2 to 4 standard deviations by 2050, the impact of climate change on conflict is significant. While climate change and environmental crises may lead to a drop income, they alone do not explain why conflict is more likely to erupt. It is when these phenomena interact with perceptions that the government is responsible for the crisis (Gurr, 1970) and, even more critically, with preexisting social structures where ethnicity is a dominant cleavage around which political preferences are formed (Fearon, 2006; Posner, 2005; Horowitz, 1985) that economic hardship as the result of climate change will incite group mobilization toward conflict. Given that ethnicity has appeared to play a strong role in African politic as a source of conflict and division, ethnicity could play a powerful role in determining future vulnerability to the effects of climate change as well. In some cases, ethnic groups may be actively targeted by the government such that, in the event of an extreme weather event, ethnic groups at odds with the government may be deprived of essential relief services. In other cases, powerless and politically irrelevant groups may be ignored by the central government, should they find themselves subject to extreme weather events or other effects associated with climate change.

ASSESSING ATTITUDES TOWARD ENVIRONMENTAL ISSUES

In this project, we assess how attitudes toward environmental issues are impacted by a country's vulnerability and by its socioeconomic and political infrastructure which would allow it to adapt to climate change. We expect that more people will be concerned about the environment in countries that are vulnerable to climate change and have low adaptive capacity. Also significant is how dependent a country is on its agriculture. The United States, for example, has a large agricultural sector but only 0.7 percent of the labor force is engaged in farming and fishing. The majority of Americans work in the industrial and service sectors which could mean that most people perceive their livelihoods to be insulated from the effects of global climate change. The United States also has the political infrastructure and the economic and technological means to adapt to challenges and develop new modes of production. This adaptive capacity generates confidence and security among the population who as a result are less concerned with the impact of climate change. This is not the case in Burkina Faso, for example, where 90 percent of the population works in agriculture and where problems of poor governance and weak infrastructure inhibit the nation's adaptive capacity. Burkinabe express greater concern about climate change than Americans because they are more vulnerable and live in a country with low adaptive capacity.

METHODOLOGICAL APPROACH, THEORETICAL EXPECTATIONS, AND CASE SELECTION

We employ quantitative and qualitative methods in our examination of African attitudes regarding climate change. Specifically, we analyze cross-sectional public opinion data from the fifth wave of the World Values Survey to uncover the attitudes of sub-Saharan Africans in Burkina Faso, Ethiopia, Mali, and Zambia toward climate change. In addition, we conduct fieldwork in partnership with researchers at universities in the four African countries in question. By conducting focus groups and individual interviews, we uncover the mechanism that connects national-level characteristics and environmental conditions with people's views about the environment.

Based on the literature on risk and adaptive capacity, we expect that concern about climate change and related environmental problems will be highest among Africans in countries with high risk and low adaptive capacity. We posit that environmental concern will be greater the higher the magnitude of regional climate change, the greater the biophysical sensitivity and the socioeconomic exposure, and the lower the adaptive/coping capacity due to poor governance. We measure these factors using disaggregated indicators that are available in UN and World Bank data. These factors are then used to predict the environmental views of Africans in four countries—Burkina Faso, Ethiopia, Mali, and Zambia.

Our goal in selecting cases was to consider a set of countries that shared a number of basic socioeconomic, structural, and climate change risk characteristics yet had different outcomes in terms of the levels of concern about the impact of climate change. Burkina Faso, Ethiopia, Mali, and Zambia are among the poorest countries in the world. Each is landlocked, and all are heavily dependent on subsistence agriculture, with about 80 to 90 percent of the labor force engaged in farming and fishing. Furthermore, each of these countries are geographically located in the areas of the continent that are at the highest risk of variability in temperature and precipitation, drought, flooding, and disease epidemics associated with climate change.

In Burkina Faso, the main cash crop is corn. The country has few natural resources and an underdeveloped industrial sector. Burkinabe rely heavily on cotton and gold exports for revenue. 21.8 percent of the country is literate and the government spends 4.6 percent of GDP on education. Burkina Faso has begun privatizing state-owned businesses and has revised its investment code to attract foreign investment. This new code and other legislation favoring the mining sector have increased gold exploration and production in the country and by 2010, gold had become the primary source of export revenue.

In Ethiopia, where the main crop is coffee, the agricultural sector suffers from frequent drought and poor cultivation practices. All land in Ethiopia is owned by the state. Entrepreneurial growth in the industrial sector has been hindered because tenants must lease land from the government and are thus unable to use land as collateral for loans. Debt relief has been critical for the country's economy, but per capita income remains among the lowest in the world. Literacy rates are 42.7 percent and the government spends about 5.5 percent of the nation's GDP on education.

Like Ethiopia and Burkina Faso, Mali is heavily dependent on agricultural exports for revenue. Gold is another important commodity, but gold export levels have recently begun to fall (Peixe, 2017). The majority of industrial activity has traditionally centered on the processing of farm commodities. A regional drought in 2010 devastated the country's livestock and Mali is now developing its cotton and iron ore extraction industries in an order to diversify its revenue sources. The government has also been investing in tourism, but security concerns over the continued unrest in neighboring Cote d'Ivoire have limited the sector's growth potential. Mali's literacy rates are 46.4 percent and the government spends 4.4 percent of GDP on education.

While 85 percent of the country's labor force is engaged in farming, only 21.5 percent of Zambia's GDP comes from agriculture. Much of the nation's revenue derives from copper mining. Government-owned copper mines were privatized in the 1990s and this has resulted in increased mining output and profitability to spur economic growth. This combined with higher copper prices and greater foreign investment has led real GDP in Zambia to grow at about 6 percent per year. Literacy rates are 80.6 percent, though the government spends just 1.3 percent of GDP on education. Despite its economic growth, a high birth rate and a heavy HIV/AIDS burden have meant that poverty continues to be a serious issue in Zambia.

While the four cases share a number of important characteristics, as we will discuss below, they differ considerably in terms of the level of concern for the impact of climate change. Agricultural dependency and environmental vulnerability are common across the cases. What factors then might explain the remarkable disparity in attitudes toward climate change? How can we understand why Zambians seem to be less worried about climate change and related environmental problems than Burkinabe?

To address these questions, we use national-level measures of vulnerability and adaptive capacity based on UN and World Bank data. Our measures are based on the conceptual framework proposed by Fussel, which includes six generic and sector-specific vulnerability factors as they apply to four key climate-sensitive sectors: coasts, water, food, and human health (see Figure 5.2) (Fussel, 2009: 22). The factors include greenhouse gas emissions, climate change, biophysical sensitivity, socioeconomic exposure, potential impacts, and lack of adaptive capacity.

	Coasts	Water	Food	Human Health
CHG Emissions	Cumulative CO2 emissions per cap. since 1990 from fossil sources Cumulative CO2 emissions per cap. since 1990 from all sources			
Climate Change	Climate Change Index (Baettig et al. 2007) National Climate Change Index (Diffenbaugh et al. 2007)			
Biophysical Sensitivity	Share of coastal area	Current temperature Water resources per capita	Changes in crop yields	
Socioeconomic Exposure	Coastal population	Water use ration	Agricultural GDP and labor force	Population in disaster hotspots.
Potential Impacts	Increase in population flooded	Change in runoff	Ricardian impacts	Mortality from climate change
Social Vulnerability (Lack of Adaptive Capacity	Human development index Physical capital stock per capita Government effectiveness			
	GDP per capita	Households with improved water supply	Prevalence of undernourishment	Vulnerability index for mortality from natural disasters

Figure 5.2 Fussel's Conceptual Framework of Vulnerability Factors. *Source*: Author Generated.

RESULTS AND DISCUSSION

We supplement this analysis and explore the climate change beliefs among Africans in Burkina Faso, Ethiopia, Mali, and Zambia using public opinion data from the fifth World Values Survey. The fifth wave of the World Values Survey was conducted between 2005 and 2009 and included respondents from several sub-Saharan African countries, including the four under examination in this project. Face-to-face interviews were conducted in a range of languages with a representative cross-section of between 1,500 and 3,000 residents of each country aged 16 and older. Table 5.1 presents methodological information for each of the four countries under examination in this project.

In the fifth wave of the World Values Survey, respondents were asked about their levels of concern about range of environmental problems in their community and in the world. Among the problems in their community, Africans were asked about water quality, air quality, and sewage and sanitation. At the global level, respondents were asked about climate change, the loss of biodiversity, and pollution of rivers, lakes, and oceans.

There is considerable variation in levels of concern about environmental problems across the four countries, as Figure 5.3 shows. Concern about all of these issues tends to be highest among Burkinabe and lowest among Zambians. At least seven out of ten Burkinabe are concerned about all of the issues, with poor water quality topping the list of concerns. Levels of concern among Malians are only slightly less than among Burkinabe, with pollution of the world's oceans, lakes, and rivers topping the list of concerns. Ethiopians are generally less concerned about environmental problems than Burkinabe and Malians, although solid majorities consider all six problems to be very serious, with concern about poor water quality topping the list. Zambians are considerably less concerned, with less than a majority believing that any of the problems are very serious. Just about four in ten Zambians say that poor water quality, poor sanitation and sewage, and the pollution of the world's rivers, lakes, and oceans are very serious problems.

Table 5.1 World Values Survey Methodological Overview

	Burkina Faso	*Ethiopia*	*Mali*	*Zambia*
Field Dates	*March 2007*	*March–April 2007*	*March 2007*	*March–April 2007*
N	1,534	1,500	1,534	1,500
Margin of Error (%)	±2.5	±2.6	±2.5	±2.5
Suggested Weight	Gender, Urban/Rural Distribution	Population characteristics unspecified	Gender, Urban/Rural Distribution	Gender

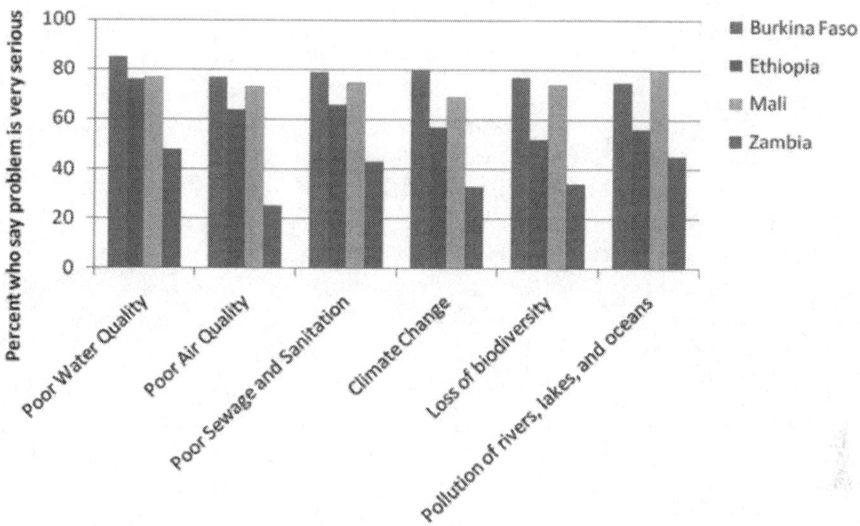

Figure 5.3 Concern about Environmental Problems among Burkinabe, Ethiopians, Malians, and Zambians. *Source*: World Values Survey, fifth wave.

Our quantitative and analysis of African attitudes regarding climate change allow us to explore the impact of risk and adaptive capacity on environmental attitudes. We find that concern about climate change and related environmental problems is highest among Africans in countries with high risk and low adaptive capacity. Specifically, we argue that environmental concern is greater the higher the magnitude of regional climate change, the greater the biophysical sensitivity and the socioeconomic exposure, and the lower the adaptive/coping capacity due to poor governance.

CONCLUSION

This study explores the link between vulnerability and environmental attitudes among Africans and concludes that concern about climate change and environmental problems is elevated in African nations with higher levels of climate change risk and lower levels of adaptive capacity. Understanding this connection is important because it sheds light on the complex relationship between the public's understanding of the risks of climate change and the structural capacity in place to adapt to or mitigate those risks.

The consequences of climate-related disasters may be more severe in regions with a history of political violence, as both conflict and weather events can spill over borders. Dealing with climate change effects in these regions therefore may be particularly problematic in terms of eliciting cross-border cooperation and the damage wrought to governance and development in areas plagued by perennial conflict. The neighborhood effects of political violence may be included in subsequent iterations, as well as indicators other than the political atrocities data to capture more large-scale violence such as civil wars.

Climate change disproportionately affects African countries which are more vulnerable to its impacts. Because of its capacity to disrupt national economies, mitigating the effects of climate change is critical to sustainable development. If the United Nations' Sustainable Development Goal 13 for climate action is to be met by the year 2030, policies must be developed and targeted to specific contexts. Many of the SDGs are focused on the core drivers of climate change. But also, crucial to developing effective policies is understanding public perceptions of climate change among those most affected by it. For climate action to work, it must be supported internationally and sustained locally. Understanding attitudes toward climate change, particularly among those most vulnerable to its impacts, will allow policymakers to better design policy options that will be viewed as acceptable by the public and may face better chances of implementation success as a result of regional and community-level buy-in.

NOTE

1. Surveys in African countries were conducted in 2006 and 2007.

REFERENCES

Alexander, David. (2009). Theoretical Notes on Vulnerability to Disaster Planning and Emergency Management. January 31. Available from http://emergency-planning.blogspot.com/2009/01/theoretical-notes-on-vulnerability-to.html.

Baettig, M. B., Wild, M., and Imboden, D. M. (2007). A Climate Change Index: Where Climate Change May Be Most Prominent In The 21st Century. *Geophysical Research Letters* 34. doi: 10.1029/2006GL028159. issn: 0094-8276.

Basher, Reid, and Briceño, Sálvano. (2005). Climate and Disaster Risk Reduction in Africa. In *Climate Change and Africa*, edited by P. Low. Cambridge, UK: Cambridge University Press, pp. 271–84.

Burg, Jericho. (2008). 'Measuring Populations' Vulnerabilities for Famine and Food Security Interventions: The Case of Ethiopia's Chronic Vulnerability Index. *Disasters* 32(4): 609–30.

Burke, M. B., Miguel, E., Satyanath, S., Dykema, J. A., and Lobell, D. B. (2009). Warming Increases the Risk of Civil War in Africa. *Proc National Academy Sciences USA* 106: 20670–74.

Cardona, Omar D. (2004). The Need for Rethinking the Concepts of Vulnerability and Risk from a Holistic Perspective: A Necessary Review and Criticism for Effective Risk Management. In *Mapping Vulnerability: Disasters, Development and People*, edited by G. Bankoff, G. Frerks, and D. Hilhorst. London, UK: Earthscan, pp. 37–51.

Collier, Paul, Conway, Gordon, and Venables, Tony. (2008). Climate Change and Africa. *Oxford Review of Economic Policy* 24(2): 337–53.

Diffenbaugh, N. S., Giorgi, F., Raymond, L., and Bi, X. (2007). Indicators of 21st Century Socioclimatic Exposure. *Proc Natl Acad Sci USA* 104: 20195–98.

Ermert, V., Fink, A. H., and Paeth, H. (2013). The Potential Effects of Climate Change on Malaria Transmission in Africa Using Bias-Corrected Regionalised Climate Projections and a Simple Malaria Seasonality Model. *Climate Change* 120(4): 741–54.

Fearon, James D. (2006). Ethnic Mobilization and Ethnic Violence. In *The Oxford Handbook of Political Economy*, edited by Weingast and Wittman. New York: Oxford University Press, pp. 852–68.

Flores, Alejandro Quiroz, and Smith, Alastair. (2010). *Surviving Disasters*. New York University, unpublished manuscript. Available from http://politics.as.nyu.edu/docs/IO/14714/Surviving_Disasters.pdf.

Fox, Louise, Haines, Cleary, Muñoz, Jorge Huerta, and Thomas, Alun. (2013). *Africa's Got Work to Do: Employment Prospects in the New Century*. IMF Working Paper, October.

Fussel, Hans-Martin. (2009). Review and Quantitative Analysis of Indices of Climate Change Exposure, Adaptive Capacity, Sensitivity, and Impacts. Background Note to the *2010 World Development Report*.

Gall, Melanie. (2007). Indices of Social Vulnerability to Natural Hazards: A Comparative Evaluation. PhD thesis, Department of Geography, University of South Carolina.

Gurr, Ted Robert. (1970). *Why Men Rebel*. Princeton, NJ: Princeton University Press.

Horowitz, Donald L. (1985). *Ethnic Groups in Conflict*. Berkeley, CA: University of California Press.

Hsiang, Solomon M., Burke, Marshall, and Edward Miguel. (2013). Quantifying the Influence of Climate on Human Conflict. *Science* 341(6151), 1212–28.

IPCC. *Climate Change 2014: Impacts, Adaptation, and Vulnerability*. Summary for Policymakers. Available at: http://www.ipcc.ch/pdf/assessment-report/ar5/wg2/ar5_wgII_spm_en.pdf.

Low, Pak Sum. (2005). *Climate Change and Africa*. New York, NY: Cambridge University Press.

Niang, I., Ruppel, O. C., Abdrabo, M. A., Essel, A., Lennard, C., Padgham, J., and Urquhart, P. (2014). *Africa in Climate Change 2014: Impacts, Adaptation, and Vulnerability. Part B: Regional Aspects. Contribution of Working Group II to the Fifth Assessment Report of the Intergovernmental Panel on Climate Change* [Barros, V. R., C. B. Field, D. J. Dokken, M. D. Mastrandrea, K. J. Mach, T. E. Bilir, M. Chatterjee, K. L. Ebi, Y. O. Estrada, R. C. Genova, B. Girma, E. S. Kissel, A. N. Levy, S. MacCracken, P. R. Mastrandrea, and L. L. White (eds.)]. New York: Cambridge University Press, 1199–265.

Parry, M. L., Canziani, O. F., Palutikof, J. P., van der Linden, P. J., and Hanson, C. E. (eds). (2007). *Contribution of Working Group II to the Fourth Assessment Report of the Intergovernmental Panel on Climate Change*. New York: Cambridge University Press.

Peixe, Joao. (2017). Can Mali Maintain Its Gold Mining Status? October 4. https://oilprice.com/Metals/Gold/Can-Mali-Maintain-Its-Gold-Mining-Status.html.

Posner, Daniel N. (2005). *Institutions and Ethnic Politics in Africa*. New York: Cambridge University Press.

Raleigh, Clionadh, and Jordan, Lisa. (2008). *Climate Change, Migration and Conflict*, August 28–31. Boston, MA: American Political Science Association.

UNDP. Sustainable Development Goals. Available at http://www.undp.org/content/undp/en/home/sustainable-development-goals/goal-13-climate-action.html.

Von Uexkull, Nina, Croicu, Mihai, Fjelde, Hanne, and Buhaug, Halvard. (2016). Civil Conflict Sensitivity to Growing Season Drought. *Proceedings of the National Academy of Sciences of the United States of America* 113(44): 12391–96.

Wisner, Ben. (2004). Assessment of Capability and Vulnerability. In *Mapping Vulnerability: Disasters, Development and People*, edited by G. Bankoff, G. Frerks, and D. Hilhorst. London, UK: Earthscan, pp. 183–93.

World Values Survey. (2005). Official Data File, v.20090901, 2009. World Values Survey Association (www.worldvaluessurvey.org).

Chapter 6

Financing Sustainable Development?

How International Tax Reform Is Failing Africa

Brian Dill and Heba Khalil

"Without resources, commitments will amount to paper promises," warned Ban Ki-moon, secretary general of the United Nations, at the opening of the Third International Conference on Financing for Development (FfD3) in Addis Ababa, July 13, 2015. Heads of State and other global leaders had assembled in the Ethiopian capital to reaffirm their commitment to address the challenges of both financing and creating an enabling environment for sustainable development. While they agreed that the resources required to fund the post-2015 development framework would have to come from diverse sources, such as foreign aid and the private sector, they placed particular emphasis on domestic resource mobilization (DRM). The prevailing consensus among global actors is that achievement of the Sustainable Development Goals (SDGs) will require that developing countries step up efforts to finance their own development.

The importance of DRM is not new to the post-2015 development agenda. The United Nations estimates, for example, that three-fourth of the Millennium Development Goals were funded domestically (UNRISD, 2016: 3). DRM now provides more funding for development than foreign aid or private flows. In 2010, countries in Sub-Saharan Africa (SSA) were collecting \$10 domestically for every \$1 they received from foreign aid (World Bank, 2013: 9). Overall, the first decade of the millennium was noteworthy with respect to the improved mobilization of domestic revenues across the global South; tax receipts grew 14 percent annually in emerging and developing economies (Ibid.). Nevertheless, DRM remains a challenge for many reasons in the world's poorest countries. In spite of the recent progress, the ratio of taxes to GDP in low-income countries (an average of 13 percent) is less than half that (35 percent) observed in high-income countries (Moore, 2013). Governments in the former are hobbled by a limited capacity to collect tax revenues from large informal economies and agricultural sectors, as well as from multinational corporations, particularly those engaged in the extraction of natural resources. This is particularly problematic given that developing countries derive a greater proportion of their total revenue from corporate tax than do advanced economies (International Monetary Fund, 2014).

The Addis Ababa Action Agenda (AAAA) that was produced at the conclusion of the FfD3, and endorsed by the General Assembly of the United Nations on July 27, 2015, acknowledges the need for reform in order to improve the mobilization and effective use of domestic resources deemed central to the pursuit of sustainable development.[1] It spells out numerous action areas that require attention including building the capacity of national tax administrations and broadening the tax base (item 22), combatting tax evasion and corruption, as well as opportunities for tax avoidance (item 23), countering illicit financial flows (item 24), and scaling up international tax cooperation (item 27).

While much of the focus of the AAAA and other proposals to increase DRM is limited to helping developing countries to help themselves, we argue in this chapter that the real place to begin is by reforming the international corporate tax system. The chapter reviews some of the obstacles to increasing DRM across SSA and suggests that international cooperation on tax is, in fact, the key to mobilizing the domestic public resources required to achieve the SDGs. We are not the first to draw attention to the importance of crafting a global agreement on corporate tax abuse. As evidenced by the release of the Panama Papers and the recent European commission decision concerning Apple's tax obligations in Ireland, corporate taxation has become a matter of global concern. Ongoing efforts to eliminate corporations' capacity to avoid taxation are being led by multinational actors such as the International Monetary Fund (IMF), the G20, and the Organization for Economic Co-operation and Development (OECD). Although framed as unprecedented international collaboration on tax reform, the program, unfortunately, does not presently align with the preferences and demands of African countries. Working across national boundaries, a diverse network of actors, has argued that the process is flawed and that the proposed reforms bear little resemblance to the interests, needs, and capacities of governments across SSA.[2] Rather than being merely consulted as stakeholders, for example, African actors would like the power to take decisions, to vote on OECD proposals. And rather than view tax reforms as simply a means to achieving the SDGs, they suggest that such reforms should be actual targets of the SDGs. In this chapter we draw upon African critiques not only to highlight the shortcomings of the current reform process but also to advance an alternative set of proposals.

OBSTACLES TO INCREASING DRM

Taxation has long been viewed as an essential condition of statehood. For those concerned with contemporary state-building in developing countries, effective and equitable taxation at the national level has been deemed critical for sustainable economic and political development. Tax revenues underwrite the capacity of rulers to incorporate more people into state institutions, to implement their political decisions, and thus to extend control throughout their territory (Levi, 1988; Mann, 1988). The stability and predictability of tax revenues enables governments to provide security, meet basic needs, and plan ahead with greater certainty, all of which are essential for the achievement of the SDGs. The political importance of taxation, however, arguably has more to do with the source of the revenue collected than its quantity. The dependence of governments on broad taxation rather than foreign aid or natural resource rents has, for example, been found to improve the quality of governance, which encompasses the capacity, responsiveness, transparency, and accountability of government (Bräutigam et al., 2008; Moore, 2007). Where there are robust and reliable tax structures, citizens are empowered politically and thus better positioned to hold their governments accountable for their decisions (Prichard, 2015).

Unfortunately, most states in the developing world exhibit tremendous difficulty at mobilizing domestic revenue. Burdened with tax authorities of limited capacity and large informal economies, some governments barely manage to collect sufficient taxes to cover more than a fraction of their annual budgets. The world's least developed countries remain highly dependent on foreign aid. The consequences of widespread revenue loss and subsequent fiscal powerlessness have been enormous. States lacking the capacity to extract consistent and sufficient revenues from their citizens and private sector actors have found themselves trapped in "punishing cycles of unserviceable national debt" (Slater, 2010: 35). As a result, they have often failed to provide basic essential services, such as potable water, sanitation, and basic protections against hunger and disease. More distressingly, "the inability of a state to generate significant revenue through taxation is often a precursor to state failure or even collapse" (Lieberman, 2003: 6). Managing debt, meeting basic needs, and securing the state, not to mention financing the SDGs, are all therefore compelling reasons for developing countries to improve their overall "tax take," namely the proportion of GDP that is collected as public revenue (Moore, 2013). Also, of considerable importance to these countries is the ability to mobilize domestic resources in the service of development agendas that they have decided upon themselves. That is, the significance of taking and implementing decisions that are not beholden to donors and lenders should not be underestimated.

Notwithstanding the considerable global attention now being given to DRM, we are not likely to witness a significant change in revenue collections in African countries for the foreseeable future. On the one hand, this is because there is a certain "stickiness" to tax revenues (Ibid.), meaning that they tend not to vary much from year to year. Tax administrations are, after all, one part of a complex bureaucratic structure; in the absence of coordinated reforms across the organizational network in which revenue agencies are embedded, we should expect the proportion of GDP raised as public revenue to remain consistent from year to year. On the other hand, like many developing countries, African nations confront a range of durable obstacles to increasing revenue collections in the short term. In this section of the chapter, we summarize and discuss three key constraints on improving DRM in the immediate future: (1) the structure of national economies, (2) colonial legacies, and (3) the scale and prevalence of transnational economic transactions and the related issue of illicit financial flows (IFFs).[3]

Writing about taxation more than four decades ago, French scholar Gabriel Ardant made some key observations that help to account for the low tax take in many developing countries today. In particular, he stressed the importance of complementarity between a state's tax regime and the structure of its economy (Ardant, 1975: 166).

An analysis of the system of taxation in contemporary times as well as in the past shows that tax collection and assessment are indissolubly linked to an exchange economy. The flow of goods and money are necessary for the understanding and especially for the evaluation of taxable materials. It is not enough to be aware of the volume of production because the economic structure sets a much lower limit. Agrarian societies of the past furnished the states with only minimal tax potential.

This suggests that tax structures evince a clear path dependency. A state's economy strongly limits what forms of taxation can be imposed (Tilly, 2009); economic transformation tends to be evolutionary rather than revolutionary; and dramatic changes to tax systems are rare (Fjeldstad and Moore, 2008). Although the international community has made a commitment to bolster Africa's DRM capacity with foreign aid, there are several enduring obstacles to realizing the desired transformation of tax administrations. In a recent assessment of constraints on DRM, for example, Mick Moore (2013) draws attention to two sets of structural variables that help to account for differences in the tax take across countries, both of which have to do with the ease of taxing. First, states are much better positioned to collect public revenues from citizens who have high average incomes, are primarily urban, and work outside of the agricultural sector. Second is a state's openness to international trade, as captured by the ratio of imports and exports to GDP. Trade, he notes, has long been central to state income, largely because "rulers have found it relatively easy, both politically and organizationally, to raise much of their revenue at their borders" (Ibid.: 16). Countries in SSA tend to fall short on both of these indicators. The region is consistently overrepresented at the bottom of GNI per capita tables, comprising, for example, 25 of the bottom 30 countries in 2015.[4] And although urbanization rates are currently faster in SSA than other regions, the majority of Africans still live in rural areas and make their living via (subsistence) agriculture. With respect to trade, African countries' integration into global and regional markets remains limited. Africa's share of world merchandise imports and exports has been less than 5 percent for the past four decades although the continent is home to 16 percent of the total world population.[5] Moreover, trade imbalances as a percent of GDP are very high for many countries in SSA.[6]

Although African countries are, taken as a whole, structurally disadvantaged with respect to taxation, there is, in fact, considerable variation across the region. For example, whereas tax revenue constituted almost 60 percent of GDP in small, rural Lesotho in 2008, it was less than 2 percent of GDP in oil rich Nigeria in 2112.[7] Broadly speaking, the differences in African countries' tax take appear to reflect differences in colonial heritage. While acknowledging that some of the variance can be attributed to the former colonial power—for example, there are differences between Anglophone and Francophone Africa—Mkandawire (2010) notes that this fails to explain the dissimilarity observed among countries produced by the same colonizer. Instead, he argues that understanding why some countries in SSA are better able to gather more tax revenues today than others requires analysis of the distinct ways in which they were integrated into the colonial economic order in the past. "Where a country ends up in terms of both tax level and tax structure depends in large part on where it begins. To put it another way, how fiscal systems develop depends significantly on how they started" (Zolt and Bird, 2005: 24). Contemporary economic performance in Africa, as other scholarship has suggested, appears to exhibit a strong path dependence (Acemoglu et al., 2000; Grier, 1999).

Following a seminal piece by Samir Amin (1972), Mkandawire works from the assumption that African economies were incorporated into the colonial order in three distinct, ideal-typic ways. First, cash crop economies left peasants in control of production but metropolitan mercantile houses enjoyed monopsonistic positions in the economy. Tax collection structures were limited to what was required to extract revenues from marketers and to collect poll taxes. Second, there were colonies such as the Congo (Kinshasa), in which private concession companies were given vast tracts of land to produce cash crops and extract minerals. The third category is the labor reserve economy, which, by contrast, was associated with larger white settler populations, racial segregation, and migrant labor. These tended to have more elaborate state structures, extensive regulation, a more effective coercive apparatus, and more complex tax collection systems. At independence, it was the labor reserve economies that had higher levels of direct taxation and thus greater levels of state capacity. The bottom line for Mkandawire (2010: 1648) is that "the end of colonialism left an institutional and infrastructural residue that still plays a major role in the determination of tax policies and the capacity to collect tax, and that may account in part for the differences in tax performance."

In addition to being saddled with colonial legacies, developing countries are losing billions of dollars every year in IFFs from money laundering, corruption, and tax evasion. Although many of the practices that erode governments' tax bases are unlawful, some of the mechanisms that corporations and individuals employ to extract wealth from developing countries and avoid paying tax are, in fact, perfectly legal. Base erosion and profit shifting (BEPS), for example, refers to tax avoidance strategies that, while legal, serve to exploit gaps and mismatches in international tax rules. The existence of low or no-tax locations "enable multinational companies to take advantage of tax rates that are lower than in the country where the activities take place and value is created by artificially shifting profits across borders" (OECD, 2014: 172). Observers agree that the actual magnitude of revenue losses attributable to IFFs is impossible to calculate with complete accuracy, yet recent estimates are cause for considerable concern. For example, a 2015 report published by Global Financial Integrity estimates that "as much as US$1 trillion flows out of developing countries every year" (GFI, 2015: 5). This is approximately seven times the total volume of foreign aid that flows annually to these same countries. Africa alone is losing more than $50 billion annually through illicit financial outflows (UNECA, 2015: 2). The OECD estimates that BEPS, which harms both developed and developing countries, causes annual revenue loss for governments of $100 billion to $240 billion.[8]

Both forms of outflows can be viewed as a consequence of globalization, insofar as technological innovations and increased global economic integration have opened up opportunities for multinational companies (MNCs) to minimize their tax obligations. Although the global community is very far from establishing World Tax Organization that was first envisioned at the end of the last millennium (Tanzi, 1999), we are in the midst of ongoing, multilateral efforts to address IFFs and to reform corporate taxation more broadly. The next section of the chapter provides a general overview of these efforts; the final section discusses the shortcomings of the process from the perspective of developing countries.

EFFORTS TO REFORM THE INTERNATIONAL CORPORATE TAX SYSTEM

Four years after leaders of G20 nations declared, in 2009, that "the era of banking secrecy is over" and committed themselves to ensuring the coherence of corporate income taxation at the international level (Barker et al., 2009), they endorsed a detailed plan "to restore confidence in the international tax system and to ensure that profits are taxed where economic activities take place and value is created" (OECD, 2016). Developed by the OECD, the resulting BEPS package includes 15 domestic and international measures intended to curb profit shifting and other forms of tax avoidance that are undertaken by MNCs. Although only a small portion of African countries (16 of 54) had joined the BEPS framework by the time of the first inaugural meeting in June 2016, proponents contend that the BEPS reforms have the potential to be particularly significant for the continent due to its heavy reliance on corporate income tax, particularly from MNCs. Operating concurrently with the BEPS process was the High-Level Panel (HLP) on IFFs from Africa, which was chaired by South Africa's former president Thabo Mbeki. Mandated by the 4th Joint African Union Commission/United Nations Economic Commission for Africa (AUC/ECA) Conference of African Ministers of Finance, Planning and Economic Development that was held in 2011, the HLP's focus was similar to but distinct from the OECD's. Both were concerned with a global problem—the ability of private sector actors to deprive states of tax revenues—requiring global action. But whereas the OECD focused on tax avoidance schemes that are, for the most part, legal, the HLP limited its recommendations to IFFs, which it defines as "money illegally earned, transferred or used" (UNECA, 2015: 15). Recognizing that not all activities that contribute to IFFs are strictly illegal in every circumstance, the HLP nonetheless chose the term "illicit" to reflect the fact that they run counter to established rules and norms.

Following the convention established by Global Financial Integrity, a non-profit research group that has looked closely at IFFs, the HLP takes the position that illicit flows of money have three distinct modes: commercial activities, criminal activities, and corruption. IFFs originating from commercial activities primarily involve the intentional manipulation of import and export transactions. MNCs are able to avoid tax by falsely declaring the value of goods that are imported or exported, as well as by manipulating the price of transactions that occur between related companies, in particular those that a part of the same MNC. Criminal activities are also central to the prevalence of IFFs, insofar as the relevant transactions are intentionally kept from the view of law enforcement agencies and the revenue authorities. The HLP observed that such activities included, but were not limited to "trafficking of people, drugs and arms to smuggling, as well as fraud in the financial sector, such as unauthorized or unsecured loans, money laundering, stock market manipulation and outright forgery" (UNECA, 2015: 31). Finally, corruption is somewhat more complicated in that it involves the abuse of public office, such as the proceeds of bribery and theft. While revenue authorities are unable to tax these illicit proceeds, the actual flow of such monies may be limited because the officials involved may not be exporting their ill-gotten wealth.

Among the package of 15 BEPS measures that are intended to improve the coherence of international tax rules, four are of particular concern to African countries: (1) country-by-country reporting, (2) transfer pricing, (3) automatic exchange of information, and (4) a multilateral instrument to modify bilateral tax treaties. As will be discussed in the following section of the chapter, African observers argue that these measures have been crafted with insufficient input from developing countries and, as a consequence, disproportionately reflect and advance the interests of OECD countries. Before outlining the critiques, however, we briefly introduce each of the four measures.

Country-by-country reporting requirements require MNCs to disclose their profits, revenues, taxes, borrowings, and employees for every jurisdiction in which they operate. They also necessitate that MNCs provide information about all of their subsidiaries and affiliates that do business in a particular jurisdiction and the types of activities that they are engaged in. This is particularly important in the current globalized era, in which a single MNC can be comprised of multiple subordinate entities operating in numerous contexts. Given the capacity of MNCs to shift their profits internally from one country to another in order to pay the lowest tax bill, country-by-country reporting is particularly important, insofar as it reveals the profits that MNCs record in each country in which they operate and the taxes that they pay on them. This helps to ensure that they can be held accountable for what they do and do not pay.

In addition to exploiting the gaps, by shifting profits, that exist between the tax rules of different jurisdictions, MNCs are also able to avoid taxation by manipulating the prices of internal transactions. Transfer pricing occurs when two companies that are part of the same MNC trade with each other. In theory, such internal transactions are regulated by the "arm's length principle," which is the international standard agreed upon by OECD member countries. This asserts that prices for goods and services charged between related entities should be similar to those charged for similar transactions carried out between independent entities at arm's length. In practice, however, MNCs have considerable latitude in terms of (mis)pricing internal transactions and thus ability to reduce significantly tax obligations. "While deliberate transfer mispricing in theory constitutes unlawful tax evasion, in practice current tax rules allow companies to set the prices of many company-specific goods and services more or less arbitrarily, making them nearly impossible for developing country tax authorities to challenge" (Oxfam, 2014: 5).

Although the country-by-country reports discussed above are to be filed by a MNC in the country of its primary tax residence, the potential of these reports to impact the international taxation system favorably is contingent upon the information being shared widely. To that end, in July 2014 the OECD developed and endorsed a new, single global standard for the automatic exchange of information (AEI). The standard mandates the automatic exchange (i.e., not requiring a request from tax or law enforcement officials) of tax information between countries in which individuals and corporations hold accounts. It was noted in late 2015, during the Paris meeting of the OECD's Task Force on Tax and Development that 96 countries had already committed to the new standard (OECD, 2015). It has been recognized, however, that the standard is not likely to benefit all countries equally for the foreseeable future; only those that "have the administrative capacity and legislative framework to share data with others and meet the requirements of the standard" will find it advantageous to engage in the systematic and periodic transmission of taxpayer information (Oxfam, 2014: 14). Indeed, the G20 has mandated that the OECD "help developing countries identify their need for technical assistance and capacity building in order to participate in and benefit from automatic exchange of information" (OECD, 2014: 173). Over several decades, states have forged agreements to ensure that companies and individuals do not incur a tax liability on the same income in more than one country. More than 3,000 such bilateral tax treaties currently exist to address the issue of double taxation. Recognizing the need to amend these treaties in a rapid and synchronized manner so that they are in compliance with the package of 15 BEPS measures, the OECD has proposed "a multilateral instrument that would have the same effects as a simultaneous renegotiation of thousands of bilateral tax treaties" (OECD, 2015: 9). Because the multilateral treaty is intended only to modify the BEPS-related provisions of existing bilateral treaties, it would not entirely replace but rather coexist with them. The OECD has suggested that such a multilateral instrument is desirable, insofar as it will reduce but not eliminate the need to negotiate and amend all of the extant treaties individually.

AFRICA'S CRITIQUE OF GLOBAL EFFORTS

One of the key criticisms of the BEPS process is that it lacks global representation. African actors have asked, for example, why they should be expected to accept and implement new global tax rules if they have not been on equal footing in setting the rules. Why have they been simply invited to consultations like any other passive stakeholder, rather than as active protagonists of this reform to the global tax regime? After all, the reforms are anticipated to impact Africa more than any other continent (UNECA, 2015). By excluding African countries, the main losers of the current economic system, the concern is that the initiative will be unable to arrive at a truly global solution to the problem of BEPS (ICRICT, 2015b).

When the G20 mandated the OECD, an organization representing 35 developed countries, to address the issue of BEPS by proposing reforms to the international corporate tax system, they were acting on behalf of their member states. Non-member countries and their stakeholders were, to be sure, invited to consult and discuss the process at different stages. None of them, however, had any voting rights. As a member of the G20 (but not the OECD), only South Africa has had any hope of intervening in the BEPS process on behalf of its continental neighbors; a channel that many critical voices in Africa have tried to utilize (TJN-A, 2011). For African countries, critiquing the process is not just about drawing attention to the lack of equal representation or a questioning a mere procedural technicality. Rather, they are concerned that the structure of the process means that the global tax issues will be defined from the perspective of the developed world, and, as a consequence, the solutions will fail to address the scope of the problems as they stand for developing countries. In addition, the inclusion of MNCs in the very process supposedly designed to regulate their illicit practices has raised additional questions, as the BEPS public consultation meetings continued to be dominated by the MNCs "who consistently outnumber civil society, academic, labor and country representatives combined, and are often doubly represented by their tax advisers and special industry groups" (ICRICT, 2015b: 3).

Although African stakeholders have welcomed the BEPS process and many of the revenue issues it has brought to light on the global level, such as country-by-country-reporting and transfer pricing practices, many groups have continued to engage with the process in a very critical manner. They have, for example, attempted to feed suggestions into it, while also proposing alternative, more democratic global frameworks for undertaking this huge task; that of reforming the global corporate tax rules. Some African groups have, for example, called for a greater role of the United Nations, or one of its bodies, such as the tax committee, in carrying out the negotiations and the ensuing reform of the international tax regime. After all, the UN is the most representative and democratic body of global governance nowadays, they argued. In addition, many critical voices from Africa have called for the establishment of a multilateral tax body at the UN level, which can give equal representation to all countries, and give voice to African countries (TJN-A, 2014).

Among the various African actors engaged in the BEPS process, the organization that has arguably been the most prominent is the African Tax Administration Forum (ATAF), a regional platform for African tax administrations based in South Africa. Empowered by South Africa's presence in the G20, ATAF was commissioned with organizing the African stakeholders' consultation on the BEPS process, a consultative process that regional networks and NGOs across Africa have critically engaged with. One critical network of civil society actors has been the Tax Justice Network-Africa (TJN-A). Established in 2007, TJN-A is a Pan-African initiative with 26-member organizations working across 16 countries. The network represents a regional initiative that integrates the various tax-related issues faced by different African economies and works toward the exchange of knowledge and expertise.

Concerns about the lack of inclusiveness of the BEPS process have not been limited to African voices. Many international groups have voiced the same concerns and have acted on them by providing a forum for a wider, more inclusive discussions on reforming the international tax regime. This resulted in the formation of the Independent Commission for the Reform of International Corporate Taxation (ICRICT) in 2015. The commission aims to "to promote the reform debate through a wider and more inclusive discussion of international tax rules than is possible through any other existing forum; to consider reforms from a perspective of global public interest rather than national advantage; and to seek fair, effective and sustainable tax solutions for development" (ICRICT, 2017).

Particularly because the OECD is tackling the tax issues voiced by the member states of the OECD and G20, nearly all of whom are high-income countries, the process is not necessarily a solution to the DRM problems faced by African countries. The critical perspectives presented by African stakeholders vis-à-vis the BEPS process are therefore key in understanding how the global initiative led by the OECD is likely to fail in fully addressing the challenges of DRM in Africa. The potential lack of success is particularly problematic given the importance of DRM for financing sustainable development in the continent most in need of development. The shortcomings and missed opportunities of the OECD are therefore worth mentioning, as articulated by African groups.

The very definition of IFFs, which lie at the heart of the reform of global corporate tax rules, is a particular point of contention. While the OECD and other organizations treat IFFs as money "illegally" earned, transferred, or utilized, African groups point to the fact that the very nature of base erosion lies in the legal practices of MNCs shifting their profits abroad to other low-tax jurisdictions. For example, Third World Network-Africa (TWN-A), a research and advocacy group based in Accra, Ghana, speaks about the "net transfer of investible resources from the African Continent," not just financial flows, adding that the "centrality of the notion of illegality" is a main drawback of the "mainstream paradigm" on IFFs, including that promoted by the OECD (Homeku, 2015: 6).

TWN-A's critique extends also to the aforementioned report of the HLP that was chaired by Thabo Mbeki. The alternative policy group contends that the report does not adequately address capital flight, so long as capital transfers are entirely legal or licit. This methodological critique is also shared by different activist groups from around the world, who are fighting for a wider definition of IFFs to adequately capture the immoral activities of the MNCs, which are "flows forbidden by rules of custom and morality even if they are legal" (Cobham, 2016).

One key achievement of the OECD which continues to fall short of the expectations of African groups is country-by-country reporting, a process that will be required by entities operating across nations, where corporations disclose their activities in each country, in order to ensure that tax is being paid in the country where the economic activity is taking place. African groups have voiced two main problems with the country-by-country reporting standards offered by the OECD. First, the reporting is only required for entities with revenues above $845 million, leaving behind many subsidiaries and separate entities (that potentially form the same MNC) that are not obligated to report (ICRICT, 2015b: 3). Second, as the standard is currently written, the reporting would not be made public. This, unfortunately, denies one key avenue of accountability, especially in a continent with a record of entrenched corruption such as Africa. Transfer Pricing has not only been one of the crucial items on the OECD agenda but also been one where the OECD decided to build stricter regulations to the existing system, usually characterized by "the arm's length principle," without considering the need to approach MNCs differently. The transfer price is the book value of a book or service transacted between related entities, meaning entities subsidiary to the same corporation. This perfectly legal practice can be easily manipulated to shift profits from high-tax to low-tax jurisdictions, thereby allowing MNCs to dodge taxes in a legal way (TJN-A, 2011). According to the Tax Justice Network (TJN), an international research, analysis, and advocacy group based in the United Kingdom, the size of these transactions is enormous, potentially constituting at least 60 percent of all international trade, which suggests the importance of treating these issues at their core. However, by adopting the arm's length principle, TJN points out that the OECD does little to change the status quo, insofar as the arm's-length principle solely requires corporations to use market-value for the trade and transactions they do with their subsidiaries. But for so many transactions, such as those concerning intellectual property rights, it is impossible to set a market price, thereby creating the opportunity for profits to get shifted (Ibid.).

TJN, alongside other expert groups, has therefore recommended an alternative system of unitary taxation: a system by which MNCs have to operate as single entities, as opposed to separate entities (i.e., a network of subsidiaries) scattered worldwide. This would allow countries to set standards for taxing revenue of the same MNC according to where employment, production, and revenue were achieved. The ICRICT calls on states to "reject the artifice that a corporation's subsidiaries and branches are separate entities entitled to separate treatment under tax law, and instead recognize that multinational corporations act as single firms conducting business activities across international borders" (ICRICT, 2015a: 2). In particular, ICRICT, alongside others, has proposed formulary apportionment as a technique of unitary taxation; that is, developing a formula of certain factors so that a unitary, single multinational operating across jurisdictions is taxed accordingly. The formulary apportionment will be "based upon objective factors, such as sales and employment, and with adequate consideration of the source principle" (Ibid: 2). In this way, "instead of attributing income from the control or ownership of intellectual property to a low-tax jurisdiction, the income should be apportioned to the jurisdictions where the intellectual property was developed or, if sold, apportioned," using an unambiguous formula, "according to objective economic factors such as sales and employment" (Ibid: 2). AEI is another BEPS-related issue that African groups continue to struggle with. Although the OECD has, in its package of 15 BEPS measures, set a new standard for AEI, they have neither obligated governments to commit to nor adequately given the space for the developing countries to be part of the process. Instead, the OECD and the Global Forum have acknowledged the lack of capacity and know-how, as well as absence of interest in engaging in the AEI in the developing world. This has prompted them to ask developing countries to take their time with respect to adopting this particular measure. For TJN-A, this raises a big question concerning the willingness to have African countries on board; countries that could benefit a lot from gaining tax information from secrecy jurisdictions, which are predominantly, and incidentally, the law-tax secrecy jurisdictions in OECD member countries (Knobel and Meinzer, 2014).

Finally, the OECD has developed a model tax treaty that African actors have found to be problematic. As noted above, the proposed multilateral treaty is intended to replace automatically, in one fell swoop, the often-abusive bilateral tax treaties. While this treaty has been welcomed by many commentators for its attempt to shift the tax revenue balance to the countries where economic activities take place, TJN-A and its partners have argued otherwise. In a consultation brief, they have concluded that the proposed multilateral tax treaty advances the interests of OECD countries, because it favors residency-based taxation as opposed to source-based taxation (TJN-A, 2015: 4). In short, because most investors are in fact residents of the developed world, the treaty de facto gives crucial advantages to their residence country in taxing their activities, thus benefitting the developed world, once more, at the expense of the developing world, including Africa. This, in turn, begs the question of the potential role of the United Nations, and in particular the Committee of Experts on International Cooperation in Tax Matters, the subsidiary of the UN Economic and Social Council dealing with Model Tax Treaties.[9] Whether the UN is a more legitimate and representative space to work from when seeking to reform the global corporate tax architecture is a question many African groups continue to ask (Alemeyahu, 2015).

CONCLUSION

The recently adopted SDGs have drawn global attention to the importance of tax revenues in meeting the financing needs of the post-2015 development agenda. The first target of SDG 17, for example, claims that it is imperative to "strengthen domestic resource mobilization, including through international support to developing countries, to improve domestic capacity for tax and other revenue collection" (United Nations). Multiple actors are currently involved with the revision of tax regimes in most, if not all, developing countries. Although these actors have converged around the view that taxation is a critical component of state-building and poverty alleviation, they take competing positions about what constitutes a "good" tax regime and which reforms ought to be prioritized.

We have argued in this chapter that reforming the international corporate tax system should take precedence over all other tax-related reform efforts. This position is somewhat at odds with the first target of SDG 17, which is singularly focused on bolstering the administrative capacity of revenue authorities in developing countries. This is not to suggest that such capacity building is unwarranted. The low, overall tax take observed in most African countries is, to be sure, partially the consequence of weak institutions, insufficient training and resources for revenue collectors, and endemic corruption. But it is also the result of the long-standing structure of national economies. African countries are, taken as a whole, structurally disadvantaged with respect to taxation, insofar as their citizens have low incomes, are primarily rural, work in the agricultural sector, and are marginal players in global trade. To strengthen domestic tax authorities prior to reconfiguring both the national economies and the global environment in which they are embedded is to put the cart before the horse. We believe that reform efforts must proceed in a stepwise fashion, progressing from the global to the national and then to the sub-national scale.

Our position is in line with that of a range of African actors, including tax administrations that are members of ATAF and civil society organizations that constitute TJN-A. International tax reforms, it is agreed, must come first. And fortunately, as evidenced by the ongoing BEPS process, such reforms are being assiduously developed and promoted. The reform process falls short, however, because it is insufficiently inclusive. Countries which stand to gain the most from international corporate tax reform (i.e., African countries) appear to have the least influence over the process and its proposals. As we have suggested above, consultation should not be confused with decision-making. In the absence of the right to vote in the OECD-led process, or the creation of a more inclusive, UN-led process, African interests are unlikely to be advanced. Should African countries continue to occupy a passive and symbolic position in the reform process, the outcome is likely to fall short in two interrelated ways: the package of reforms will do little to improve African countries' ability to mobilize domestic resources; limited resources will hobble attempts to achieve the SDGs. In order to finance sustainable development, more needs to be done to ensure that international tax reform is succeeding for Africa.

NOTES

1. For more information, see http://www.un.org/esa/ffd/wpcontent/uploads/2015/08/AAAA_Outcome.pdf.
2. This network includes, but is not limited to, the Tax Justice Network–Africa, the African Tax Administration Forum, and the Independent Commission for the Reform of International Corporate Taxation.
3. For a more detailed discussion of the obstacles of increasing tax revenues, see Moore 2013.
4. See http://databank.worldbank.org/data/download/GNIPC.pdf.
5. See the World Trade Organization's International Trade Statistics 2015, https://www.wto.org/english/res_e/statis_ e/its2015_e/its2015_e.pdf.
6. See UNCTAD's Key Statistics and Trends in International Trade 2015, http://unctad.org/en/PublicationsLibrary/ ditctab2015d1_en.pdf.
7. See http://data.worldbank.org/indicator/GC.TAX.TOTL.GD.ZS.
8. See https://www.oecd.org/tax/background-brief-inclusive-framework-for-beps-implementation.pdf.
9. For more on this, see ICRCIT PowerPoint presentation available at http://www.un.org/esa/ d/tax/16.

REFERENCES

Acemoglu, D., Johnson, S., and Robinson, J. A. (2000). The Colonial Origins of Comparative Development: An Empirical Investigation. Technical Report, No. W7771, National Bureau of Economic Research.

Alemayehu, Dereje. (2015). Chair, Coordination Committee of the Global Alliance for Tax Justice Senior Economic Policy Advisor. Corporate Tax Dodging and other forms of Illicit Financial flows from Africa. Presentation for ICRICT, Independent Commission for the, Reform of Corporate Taxation on 18/03/2015.

Amin, S. (1972). Underdevelopment and Dependence in Black Africa – Origins and Contemporary Forms. *Journal of Modern African Studies*, 10(4): 105–20.

Ardant, G. (1975). Financial Policy and Economic Infrastructure of Modern States and Nations. In Tilly, C., Editor, *The Formation of National States in Western Europe*, 164–242. Princeton, NJ: Princeton University Press.

Barker, A., Houlder, V., and Anderlini, J. (2009). On Tax Efforts and Colonial Heritage in Africa, April 2. *Financial Times*.

Bräutigam, D. A., Fjeldstad, O.-H., and Moore, M. (2008). *Taxation and State-Building in Developing Countries: Capacity and Consent*. Cambridge: Cambridge University Press.

Cobham, A. (2016). Breaking the Vicious Circles of Illicit Financial Flows, Conflict and Insecurity. *GREAT Insights Magazine*, 5(1). Available at http://ecdpm.org/great-insights/prosperity-for-peace/breaking-circles-illicit-financial-flows/. Accessed October 23, 2016.

Fjeldstad, O.-H., and Moore, M. (2008). Tax Reform and State-Building in a Globalized World. In Bräutigam, D. A., Fjeldstad, O.-H., and Moore, M., Editors, *Taxation and State-Building in Developing Countries: Capacity and Consent*, 235–60. Cambridge: Cambridge University Press.

GFI. (2015). Illicit Financial Flows: The Most Damaging Economic Condition Facing the Developing World. Technical Report, Global Financial Integrity.

Grier, R. M. (1999). Colonial Legacies and Economic Growth. *Public Choice*, 98(3): 317–35.

Homeku, T. (2015). Illicit Financial Flows and Africa: Beyond the Mbeki Report. *Africa Agenda*, 18(1): 5–7.

ICRICT. (2015a). Declaration of the Independent Commission for the Reform of International Corporate Taxation. Available at http://www.icrict.org/wp-content/uploads/2015/06/icrict_ com-rec-report_eng_V1.4.pdf. Accessed October 23, 2016. Technical Report, Independent Commission for the Reform of International Corporate Taxation.

ICRICT. (2015b). Evaluation of the Independent Commission for the Reform of International Corporate Taxation for the Base Erosion and Profit-Shifting Project of the G20 and OECD, October 2015, Available at http://www.icrict.org/wp-content/uploads/2015/10/ icrict_beps-briefing_en_web-version-1.pdf. Accessed October 23, 2016. Technical Report, In- Dependent Commission for the Reform of International Corporate Taxation.

ICRICT. (2017). What's ICRICT? Available at https://www.icrict.com/about-icrict/.

International Monetary Fund. (2014). Spillovers in International Corporate Taxation. Technical Report, IMF Policy Paper.

Knobel, A., and Meinzer, M. (2014). Automatic Exchange of Information: An Opportunity for Developing Countries to Tackle Tax Evasion and Corruption. Available at http://www.taxjustice.net/wp-content/uploads/2013/04/AIE-An-oppor

tunity-for-developing-countries.pdf. Accessed October 23, 2016. Technical Report, Tax Justice Network–Africa.

Levi, M. (1988). *Of Rule and Revenue*. Berkeley: University of California Press.

Lieberman, E. S. (2003). *Race and Regionalism in the Politics of Taxation in Brazil and South Africa*. Cambridge: Cambridge Press.

Mann, M. (1988). *States, War and Capitalism: Studies in Political Sociology*. Cambridge: Basil Blackwell.

Mkandawire, T. (2010). On Tax E Orts and Colonial Heritage in Africa. *The Journal of Development Studies*, 46(10): 1647–69.

Moore, M. (2007). How Does Taxation Affect the Quality of Governance? Technical Report, IDS Working Paper 280, Institute of Development Studies.

Moore, M. (2013). Obstacles to Increasing Tax Revenues in Low Income Countries. Technical Report, ICTD Working Paper 15, International Centre for Tax and Development.

OECD. (2014). *Development Co-Operation Report 2014: Mobilizing Resources for Sustainable Development*. Paris: OECD Publishing.

OECD. (2015). *Developing a Multilateral Instrument to Modify Bilateral Tax Treaties, Action 15–2015 Final Report, OECD/G20 Base Erosion and Profit Shifting Project*. Paris: OECD Publishing.

OECD. (2015). Draft Summary Record of the 5th Plenary Meeting of the Task Force on Tax and Development Supporting the Sustainable Development Goals, OECD's Task Force on Tax and Development, November 2015 Paris, France, https://www.oecd.org/ctp/tax-global/draft-summary-record-plenary-meeting-november-2015.pdf.

OECD. (2016). Background Brief: Inclusive Framework for BEPS Implementation. https://www.oecd.org/ctp/background-brief-inclusive-framework-for-beps-implementation.pdf.

Oxfam. (2014). Business Among Friends: Why Corporate Tax Dodgers Are Not Yet Losing Sleep Over Global Tax Reform. 185 Oxfam Briefing Paper. Technical Report, Oxfam.

Prichard, W. (2015). *Taxation, Responsiveness and Accountability in Sub-Saharan Africa: The Dynamics of Tax Bargaining*. Cambridge: Cambridge University Press.

Slater, D. (2010). *Ordering Power: Contentious Politics and Authoritarian Leviathans in South Asia*. Cambridge: Cambridge University Press.

Tanzi, V. (1999). Is There a Need for a World Tax Organization? In Razin, A., and Sadka, E., Editors, *The Economics of Globalization: Policy Perspectives from Public Economics*, 173–86. Cambridge: Cambridge University Press.

Tilly, C. (2009). Forward. In Martin, I. W., Mehrotra, A. K., and Prasad, M., Editors, *The New Fiscal Sociology: Taxation in Comparative and Historical Perspective*, xi–xiii. Cambridge: Cambridge University Press.

TJN. Transfer Pricing. http://www.taxjustice.net/topics/corporate-tax/transfer-pricing/. Tax Justice Network. Accessed October 23, 2016.

TJN-A. (2011). Walking the Talk on Illicit Financial Flows: The G20's Responsibility in Combating Illicit Capital Flight. Available at http://www.taxjusticeafrica.net/wp-content/uploads/2015/11/policy-brief-illicit-flows-tax-evasi on-sa-g20.pdf. Accessed October 23, 2016. Technical Report, Tax Justice Network–Africa.

TJN-A. (2014). The BEPS Process and Africa: Views And Recommendations From African Civil Society. Available at http://www.taxjusticeacademy.net/wp-content/uploads/2015/09/ beps-process-and-africa-views-and-recommendations-from-african-civil-society1.pdf. Accessed October 23, 2016. Technical Report, Tax Justice Network–Africa.

TJN-A. (2015). Tax and Domestic Revenue Mobilization: A Potential Game Changer to the Financing for Development Process. Available at http://www.taxjusticeafrica.net/wp-content/ uploads/2016/02/ffd3-cso-submission-policy-brief-20151.pdf. Accessed October 23, 2016. Technical Report, Tax Justice Network–Africa.

UNECA. (2015). Illicit Financial Flows: Report of the High-Level Panel on Illicit Financial Flows from Africa. Commissioned by the AU/ECA Conference of Ministers of Finance, Planning and Economic Development. Available at https://www.uneca.org/sites/default/files/PublicationFiles/iff_main_report_26feb_en.pdf. Accessed September 8, 2016.

United Nations. Transforming Our World: The 2030 Agenda for Sustainable Development. Available at https://sustainabledevelopment.un.org/post2015/transformingourworld. Accessed September 10, 2016.

UNRISD. (2016). Mobilizing Domestic Resources for Sustainable Development: Toward a Progressive Fiscal Contract. In UNRISD 2016 Flagship Report: Policy Innovations for Transformative Change, Page Chapter 6. United Nations Research Institute for Social Development, Geneva.

World Bank. (2013). *Financing for Development Post-2015*. Washington, DC: World Bank.

Zolt, E. M., and Bird, R. M. (2005). Redistribution via Taxation: The Limited Role of the Personal Income Tax in Developing Countries. *UCLA Law Review*, 52 (5–22). Available at SSRN: https://ssrn.com/abstract=804704. Accessed October 23, 2016.

Part III

SUSTAINABLE CITIES AND COMMUNITIES

Chapter 7

Bridging the Health Divide

The Case of Holy Innocents Children's Hospital, Mbarara, Uganda

Florence Kyomugisha

5.6 million children under the age of five died in 2016, and more than 50 percent of the deaths in children occurred in sub-Saharan Africa (SDG Report 2017, 4). Malaria, diarrhea, preterm-birth complications, pneumonia, and acute respiratory infections are preventable or treatable diseases that are the major causes of death among children under five years old. The high mortality in African children is exacerbated by the increasing prevalence of malnutrition and HIV/AIDS among children as well as other problems arising from civil strife and natural calamities that put children at a high risk of mortality.

While there has been substantial progress in improving children's health as evidenced by the declining child mortality rate from 91 deaths per 1,000 live births in 1990 to 43 deaths per 1,000 globally in 2015, higher rates still exist in many African countries (SDG Report 2017, 20). In 2015, the United Nations (UN) adopted the Sustainable Development Goals (SDGs) that aim at ensuring and promoting health and well-being for children. SDG 3.2 focuses on reducing under-five mortality to as low as 25 per 1,000 live births in every country by 2030 (WHO, Media Centre, 2017). According to the 2017 UN SDC Report, 5.9 million children under age 5 died in 2015. The report further states that "Sub-Saharan Africa continues to have the highest under-5 mortality rate, with 84 deaths per 1,000 live births in 2015—about twice the global average" (SDG Report, 2017, 20). The Sustainable Development Goals agenda emphasizes the commitment to making healthcare services accessible to all people in society.

This chapter discusses the Holy Innocents Children's Hospital (HICH) in Mbarara, Uganda, which is making healthcare accessible to many children, especially those from impoverished communities. This is a case study of a children's hospital that was founded by small group of Ugandans, Americans, and Europeans who formed a partnership to establish a results-focused sustainable pediatric hospital in Southwestern Uganda. The HICH project strives to provide holistic, integrated healthcare services to all children including the vulnerable and the less privileged, subsequently targeting SDG 3.2. This chapter not only highlights HICH's achievements in less than a decade since it opened in 2009 but also discusses the still existing inadequate and inequitable health care resources and infrastructure in Uganda at large and the need to revamp the effort to establish a sustainable healthcare delivery system that will save the lives of children.

HOLY INNOCENTS CHILDREN'S HOSPITAL

The Catholic Archdiocese of Mbarara, Uganda, led the founding of Holy Innocents Children's Hospital, Mbarara, in July 2009. Uganda is approximately 93,000 square miles and has a rapidly growing population estimated at 40 million in 2017. Fifty percent of the Uganda population is below 15 years old and the country's child mortality rate was estimated at 131 per 1,000 live births in 2012 (Mukanga, 2012, 9). There has been some improvement in children's health in the past decade, and according to UNICEF reports, the under-five mortality rate was 53 per 1,000 live births in Uganda in 2017 (UNCEF, 2018). HICH is the only specialist children's hospital in the Southern and Western regions of Uganda, and the community and all stakeholders have embraced the hospital. To date, over 196,000 children have received care at the hospital in the inpatient and outpatient facilities (HICH Report, 2017). The hospital is also involved in community health programs and immunization of children against six diseases and illnesses including malaria, measles, malnutrition, diarrhea, pneumonia, and respiratory infections. HICH's success is attributable to the efforts of individuals from Uganda, the United States, and Northern Ireland who formed a partnership based on a mutual interest in children's health, complementary knowledge, abilities and skills, and the desire to make a difference. The availability of financial and human resources is enabling HICH to establish a full-fledged public health outreach program (community-based primary health care interventions) to help parents and enhance their ability to raise healthy children. HICH's goal is to develop the type of public health interventions that are best and most effective in enhancing children's survival and reducing the risk of illnesses which will ultimately lead to a safer and healthier population. The stakeholders of HICH acknowledge that establishing and maintaining a hospital and its public health community outreach programs will require monetary resources in addition to public health professionals who are suitably trained and skilled to work in an integrated healthcare system.

BACKGROUND

According to UN Millennium Development Goal 4 (MDG, 4), the UN planned to reduce child mortality by two-thirds by the year 2015 (Mukanga, 2012, 4). This was an especially daunting task in Africa. In 2007, although sub-Saharan Africa constituted 11 percent of the world population, it accounted for 50 percent of the global child mortality burden (UN MDG, 2010). The most resent 2017 UN SDG Report documents 5.9 million children under age five who died in 2015 (SDG Report, 2017, 4). Sadly, seen from a different angle this is an improvement in children's health considering that between 2000 and 2015, the global under-five mortality rate fell by 44 percent. This is a troubling phenomenon considering that most of those 5.9 million deaths in children every year could be prevented by low-tech and cost-effective healthcare interventions. For instance, timely administration of inexpensive treatments with anti-malarial drugs, antibiotics, and interventions of immunizations and malnutrition would significantly reduce child diseases and illnesses and subsequently reduce their mortality rates (Mukanga, 2012; Talisuna et al., 2015). Despite African governments' efforts to promote anti-malaria campaigns, malaria continues to devastate communities culminating in high child mortality rates. Furthermore, severe malaria infection in pregnant mothers cause anemia which often lead to miscarriages, still birth and low birth weight babies, thus compounding malaria's devastating effects on African communities (Roman et al., 2015, 63). Measles has hitherto been one of the major causes of childhood mortality, but its prevalence has waned thanks to many African governments' mass immunization campaigns. Despite the relative success of government health programs in controlling some diseases, the inadequate and inequitable healthcare system continues to put constraints on the implementation of healthcare programs that deliver lifesaving interventions to combat diseases and illnesses among children, especially those in poor communities (Mukanga, 2012, 8).

The Sustainable Development Goals agenda emphasizes that access to good health and well-being is a human right. Protecting and ensuring this human right for all people will require a strong commitment of economic and human resources in the global community. Arguably, an equitable healthcare system is only possible if the leaders of nations and organizations can redefine their priorities during their policies' decision-making. African leaders must answer the call to join in the effort to achieve the SDG goal of reducing mortality rates at a target to reduce the number of under-five deaths by 10 million between 2017 and 2030 (WHO, Media Centre, 2017). Looking at the history of the healthcare system, many of the current challenges in the healthcare delivery system in some African countries, such as Uganda, are a legacy of the colonial urban infrastructure. For example, the colonial planning and design of hospitals in Uganda did not leave room for expansion in regard to building more hospital buildings on site, thus resulting in existing hospitals having limited space for patient accommodation (limited capacity of patient beds) as well as being hampered by outdated infrastructure and an old, barely effective communication system. As noted earlier, the state of the infrastructure has been a recipe for an inequitable and unreliable health system delivery, especially in the areas of ambulatory surgery and intervention and treatment delivery to children.

While inadequate access to healthcare may be an expected fact for rural communities, it continues to be a problem in some urban areas. Over the years, Uganda has experienced accelerated migration to urban centers that have limited infrastructure and very limited industrial and real estate growth, mainly during a period of strife from civil wars of the 1970s and 1980s. As more and more people moved into this urban environment with a dwindling economy—a consequence of the global embargo on Uganda—the country experienced high levels of unemployment and subsequently increasing poverty in urban centers, as evidenced by the overcrowded slums with poor sanitation, no clean water, and food insecurity. The most vulnerable in poor communities in urban centers and in slums are children, many of whom turn into "street children" who beg and steal to survive. Furthermore, impoverished families face great financial challenges when their children need the basic forms of treatment or surgery, especially when they have limited access to healthcare and hospitals. In most urban centers in Uganda, children compete with adults for treatment and care at adult hospitals. Uganda's total expenditure on health was a mere 7.2 percent of the GDP in 2014. The country needs to reevaluate its policy priorities to be able to get a shot at meeting the goals set in the SDG3 (WHO, Media Centre, 2017). Neighboring Kenya has made substantial progress in the healthcare delivery system for children as evidenced by the existence of several Kenyan pediatric hospitals. For example, St Gertrude Children Hospital, the largest hospital in East and Central Africa, opened in Kenya in 1946. Flavia Lanyero documented that in 2012 the under-five years mortality rate was 131 per 1,000 live births in Uganda compared to 107 in Kenya.

THE BEGINNING OF HICH

The concept of establishing a pediatric hospital was born not only from Archbishop Paul Bakyenga's passion for the well-being of vulnerable and disadvantaged children but also from the fact that children in Uganda were marginalized in terms of healthcare. On one of his visits to San Diego, California in 2006, the Archbishop shared his concern for the plight of children in his Archdiocese in Mbarara, Uganda, with four people. Consequently, the people who listened to the archbishop's appeal for assistance realized that they could help to counter some of the children's healthcare challenges that many families were experiencing in Mbarara: this became his call to action. A small group of American citizens from San Diego decided that they wanted to make a positive change in the lives of families in Mbarara. They talked to friends and neighbors about the children of Mbarara and many people who had the economic means to help believed that the failure to play a proactive role in saving lives of children positioned them as part of the problem rather than part of the solution. As one donor explained, most people understand the responsibility we all have for each other and how the survival and flourishing of any country in the world is not limited to that country's physical and geographical boundaries but is directly related to all of us in the global world. That realization informs the need to have a common goal of fighting to end the health disparities in the world. There is no doubt HICH's services in Mbarara have contributed in some ways to the under-five years lower mortality rate of 53 per 1,000 live births in Uganda in 2017.

MISSION AND GOALS

The many people who have participated in developing and establishing HICH understand that the much-needed pediatric hospital in Mbarara will give thousands of children the opportunity to survive and thrive so that those children can one day participate in the growth and development of their communities and country. The mission of HICH is "to guarantee holistic, integrated and sustainable health services to children, especially the less privileged and vulnerable ones, in fulfillment of the teaching and healing mission of Christ" (HICH Records, 2011). Healthcare delivery systems must be adapted to the specific needs of children who are more vulnerable to dehydration, malnutrition, and respiratory infections, and who need professionals who specialize in pediatric care. There is a continuing effort to seek and mobilize resources (expertise, skills, equipment, medical supplies, and money) because HICH is still in its infancy stages and needs this support to grow and develop to its full potential. The Ugandan government and community will have to provide a strong commitment and investment of both human and economic resources to ensure the sustainability of the hospital. HICH's board of directors is already pursuing an aggressive donor program so that the hospital can achieve its intended goals that include: (1) establishing a health system that ensures adequate access to essential medicine and other medical products and technologies; and (2) getting to a stage where the hospital's financing system will raise adequate funds to allow families in the local community to use the needed services while being protected from financial catastrophes associated with having to pay hospital fees for the treatment of their children.

BUILDING PARTNERSHIPS: A WAY OF PROVIDING SUSTAINABLE HEALTH CARE

An all-volunteer small group of people in the United States contributed resources, expertise and time to help the Archbishop of Mbarara realize his dream of a pediatric hospital in Uganda. In 2007, they formed a 501 (c) (3) nonprofit and named it "Holy Innocents Children's Hospital—Mbarara (HICH)." An HICH board of directors in San Diego, CA, and a planning and steering committee in Mbarara, Uganda, formed during the first year of the project. The two bodies brought together a broad range of knowledge, expertise, skill and perspective, and more importantly worked tirelessly to raise funds and other resources from institutions, organizations, and individuals to start the construction of the hospital. In addition, the planning and steering committee and the board were responsible for identifying strategic priorities, objectives, actions, and outcomes of the HICH project. Operating from several corners of the globe, the planning steering committee and the board coordinated the effort; they worked together to identify and pursue opportunities of donors and tirelessly networked to form new and strong alliances that helped in generating and promoting ideas of how to develop and sustain the hospital. The author has been on the HICH board of directors since 2007. In 2008, the Ugandan and US stakeholders formed a partnership with a small group of people from Northern Ireland (NI) who became an auxiliary board. The Archbishop of Mbarara led the effort on the project in 2007 by providing a piece of land near the Archdiocese headquarters to be the site for the new hospital. The University of San Diego (USD) was one of the first institutions to help in the construction of the hospital, and, in 2007, USD funded a medical mission to travel to Uganda to evaluate the feasibility of building and operating the children's hospital in Mbarara. After several weeks of doing a feasibility check of the area and the land, the USD team endorsed the building of the hospital. USD also provided resources from the Graduate School of Nursing, Graduate School of Business, and Graduate School of Marine Science (for water issues) to assist in the planning and implementation of the hospital project. Phase one of construction involved the 60 bed capacity wards, the outpatient facilities and laboratory, and the administration block and was completed in barely one year; thanks to a team of committed and highly competent Ugandan engineers. In 2017, phase two started and involved the expansion of ward space to at least 120 beds, construction and equipping a pediatric surgical center and expanding laboratory services.

Several donor organizations and individuals in the United States and NI played a significant role in providing the equipment, medicines, and other resources required to operate the hospital such as an oxygen generating system that has become a successful and very cost-effective way to ensure a regular supply of oxygen for the hospital. The donors in the United States and NI provided guidance in identifying the best qualified hospital staff and trained them to ensure the best delivery of care and quality control systems that are robust and well maintained. The first hospital administrator of HICH came from NI: a specialist nurse with immense management skills, she worked as a volunteer for an entire year and helped to put in place most of the operational systems and particularly streamline nursing care in the hospital. With the help of other supporting health care professionals from NI, she assisted the Uganda nursing staff to establish and stabilize fundamental clinical policies, procedures, protocols, and practices for infection prevention and control; safe systems of using technology; implementation and management of assessments and vital signs; and documentation. Two universities from the United States, the University of San Diego and the Dominican University, have provided several nursing faculty and students medical and teaching missions to the hospital and surrounding communities since the hospital opened in 2009. These medical teams have had a significant positive impact on establishing HICH's public health community outreach programs. Water quality studies at and around the hospital were conducted by a US-led team of chemists and appropriate action was taken or recommended to resolve contaminated water issues and improve the quality of water available to the hospital. Provision of access to safe water and sanitation services is paramount, considering that polluted water causes water-borne diseases that contribute significantly to high child mortality rates in Uganda. Additional organizations and individual that provided funding, medicine, equipment, supplies and expertise include The Catholic Medical Mission Board, AmeriCares, and Medical Assistance Program (MAP) International, which provided free or steeply discounted medicines worth hundred thousands of US dollars. MedShare International and Providence International also donated medical equipment and supplies. Sabin Children's Foundation in San Diego has provided funding, equipment, and supplies; and San Diego Foundation's Casa Maria Fund has provided funding for construction and mosquito nets. Against Malaria Foundation in the United Kingdom provided low-cost insecticide treated mosquito nets; Rotary supplied x-ray equipment and funds for a drainage project; Kiwanis (San Diego) and Knights of Columbus (San Diego) provided funding for several projects at the hospital. Children's Hospital Oakland provided equipment and sent in teams of doctors and nurses on medical missions to the hospital; graduate students from the United States and NI defer graduate medical studies to come and help at the hospital; and many other individuals and organizations have joined the effort of establishing HICH.

Ugandan organizations that have partnered or collaborated with HICH include St. Francis Community Outreach and Education Center, an organization that carries out developmental assessment and intervention programs; CARITAS and Gender and Development (GAD), which help to develop and implement sustainable hygiene, health, and nutrition projects; as well as Mwana Mujimu, a national nutritional rehabilitation center in Kampala, which treats children with severe malnutrition and teach mothers food preparation methods. HICH has also collaborated with Healthy Child Uganda, a nongovernmental organization that offers child health programs in communities in Southwestern Uganda. In addition, HICH collaborates with the Uganda Ministry of Health to maintain a malaria prevention program that has enabled a constant supply of mosquito bed nets in poor communities. HICH aspires for such vital partnerships and strives to ensure that it remains a trusted and effective resource for health development and illness prevention among Uganda's children.

HICH OPERATIONS

The HICH management team under the leadership of the Medical Director and the Hospital Administrator and in consultation with the preexisting hospitals in the Uganda Catholic Medical Board (UCMB) network has successfully developed a sustainable plan for the hospital's operational expenses; this plan was established after careful consideration of the hospital's main priorities vis-à-vis the limited resources. HICH adheres to a policy of ensuring access to basic but good quality pediatric care as a way to prevent parents from paying for expensive super-specialized pediatric services. Thus, health care at HICH is highly subsidized and therefore affordable to most rural and poor families thanks to financial support from multinational partners, government aid through annual conditional primary health care (PHC) grants and support from the UCMB through access to their high quality but low-priced medicines and sundries at their medical stores.

At the end of 2017, just eight years in operation, HICH had treated 196,200 inpatient and outpatient children. The hospital had established a neonatal intensive care unit for resuscitation and treatment of sick newborn babies; it carried out routine immunization of infants; it built a pediatric surgical center; and established partnerships with other hospitals and organizations in the areas of clinical care research and student training. Notable among those partners are Mbarara University Faculty of Medicine, University of British Columbia, Canada, Epicenter Research Collaboration, St Mary's Business School and the USD. HICH has also attracted volunteer doctors, nurses, and specialists from the United States and NI to work at the hospital. HICH also reached out to the local community with health education messages through the mass media (radio and newspapers) and collaborated with the Uganda Ministry of Health to implement health-related activities like community health outreaches and immunization. In addition to the above achievements, HICH managed to maintain a high degree of professionalism and ethical standards despite having to work with limited resources. HICH has endeared itself to the public as the neatest and cleanest hospital in the region. These efforts have improved the quality of children's healthcare and have generated community buy-in from the families that benefited from access to good health services. A parent commented,

> My son became very ill so I took him to the government hospital. He got sicker and sicker as each day passed. After six days, he was near death. . . . I had heard about Holy Innocents, so I picked my son up, left the hospital, and brought him here. The doctor knew what to do. After treatment, my son is ready to go home after three nights. I am so thankful for Holy Innocents Children's Hospital. I will never return to a government hospital. (HICH Newsletter, 2017)

When parents take their sick children to HICH and witness the easier access to a doctor or a nurse and the quality of care they receive, through word of mouth they tell other people in their communities or social networks about HICH. Furthermore, the innovative and extensive use of mobile phones and motorcycle taxis (*bodaboda*) in Uganda has made health care delivery more accessible. For instance, mobile phones have made it easier for rural and low-income families to get information about health conditions and health services that are available in their communities and how to access those services. There is enthusiasm from the local community that informs the importance of a robust public health outreach program that is meeting the people's needs.

PUBLIC HEALTH COMMUNITY OUTREACH: A PILLAR TO SUSTAINABLE HEALTH CARE

As a society, we need to have a renewed focus on public health services that respond quickly and effectively to children and families' needs and expectations. The fact is that society not only requires better access to health care in terms of treatment, but also requires outlets for providing accurate health information for disease prevention, especially in geographically isolated locations and rural communities. HICH's service delivery area and community health outreach is expanding mainly due to the new innovations in the use of mobile phones and the *bodaboda* public transportation (mentioned earlier), thus making healthcare more accessible to impoverished and rural populations. Through its illness treatment and prevention activities, HICH is oriented toward creating a broad-based healthcare delivery network and it works to engender trust, maintain high ethical standards, engage the community, and strengthen the public health goals. HICH strives to meet Uganda's child health needs through efforts to address "core" public health issues, including improved availability and access to health care for sick children and access to adequate food and nutrition for children and pregnant mothers. HICH conducts community-based primary health care interventions to help mothers learn how best to raise healthy children. The interventions include a comprehensive package of services such as early infant nutrition, immunization, home hygiene, safe water, and proper sanitation among other services. HICH realizes the need and opportunity to work with the local community in a partnership that has the potential to substantially benefit members of the community by focusing on empowering and helping people in the local community through providing the knowledge and skills to utilize local resources to live healthier, safer, and longer lives. As mentioned earlier, in particular, through the community health outreach, HICH recognizes that important benefits accrue to the communities served by HICH through investments in public health capacity development and creating partnerships with other health providers in government and nongovernmental organizations in the country. Coordinated and collaborative result-focused approaches by health providers enhance the hospital's ability to have improved health outcomes and a significant reduction in child illnesses. These partnerships and the integration of public health services are a smart approach and thus build on what is already in place and help to strengthen the public health system's capacity through providing quality services. Where you have robust communication structures and the sharing of data between health authorities, providers, and the public, there is more likely to be an enhanced understanding of the problems and solutions associated with health in the community. HICH's partnerships with local organizations in the community have also resulted in an environment of mutual empowerment as the community realizes the hospitals social and economic value to the region. In addition to saving the lives of children, building HICH has ultimately bolstered the Ugandan economy through providing the much-needed jobs ranging from construction jobs to laborers on the hospital grounds to health professionals who run the hospital. The ultimate goal is that the community will support HICH and it generates income from patients' fees and funds from the Uganda governments, and HICH will attain self-sufficiency and sustainability in all operational areas and infrastructure.

The ultimate goal of HICH's public health programs is to help members of the community acquire the skills to establish essential empowerment and healthy behavior that enhance community members' well-being that are sustainable, especially after the public health educators have left. For example, the education provided, and the skills taught could incorporate information on social health factors such as traditional healing, home remedies, medicine, diet, and language. This approach is more likely to ensure respect for the positive traditions of local communities and the inclusion of information that is relevant to the community, and subsequently provide a concrete opportunity to use and revitalize the local people's way of life.

Uganda is on the path to benefit substantially from comprehensive immunization programs, which are embraced and supported in urban and rural communities. For instance, enhanced and integrated malaria prevention and control programs have a positive impact on reducing the mortality rates in children as well as adults. The integration of health services offers the best chance to ensure that families have access to treatment and prevention of illness wherever the children are—be it urban or rural communities. Particularly, Uganda is making progressive strides to improve the lives of children and enhance their survival. In 2007 and 2009, the Uganda Government developed and implemented the "National Child Survival Strategy" that involved the Ministry of Health and the Ministry of Local Government collaborating to deliver children health interventions, including immunizations, the distribution of mosquito bed nets and anti-malaria drugs in communities across the country (Mukanga, 2012, 6).

CHALLENGES

The global economic downturn of 2007 to 2010 had a negative impact on HICH stakeholders' ability to maintain this nonprofit project. At certain periods during the global economic downturn, it was challenging to raise the necessary funds for operating the hospital. For instance, it was ineffective to keep returning to those who had already been extremely generous and ask for more help, and this phenomenon was more evident in Uganda, as one US board member observed, "What we are experiencing as an NGO financially in supporting the hospital is the norm in the global development arena. When a typical Ugandan must live on less than US$2.50 per day to care for all members of the family, it is no wonder there is no money in the Mbarara coffers" (HICH Board Report, 2011). The potential challenge is how HICH will continue to acquire the quantity and quality of medications, staff, and supplies to meet the needs of major referral tertiary center that expanded from a small community-based pediatric hospital if it does not receive the continued support from the Ugandan government and the community.

Irregular electricity supply at the hospital due to power shortages is a common occurrence that requires running an alternative generator. HICH stakeholders are in the process of establishing surgical services but are wary of the unreliable and irregular supply of electric power that can lead to the risk of precarious surgeries. The hospital also has slow and often unreliable Internet and telephone communication; this is a national rather than an HICH issue. Delayed communication and contact with the outside world sometimes leads to frustration especially on the side of partners from areas where prompt communication and response is the norm. Amidst these challenges, building trust and credibility in a partnership did not happen without hiccups considering that the partnership involved people from different cultures with varying perspectives, agendas, and schedules. Nevertheless, most stakeholders appreciated these challenges and devised means to tackle them. For instance, in order to avoid stalling in the construction of the hospital, several strategies employed included setting appropriate timelines for consultation; establishing realistic multi-phased deadlines for various reports on progress of the project; and using creative communication methods to reach the people involved in the project. HICH stakeholders are attuned to the fact that good outcomes may persuade more people to help; likewise, a clash of cultures or agendas could turn away many people. As individuals or teams of people from different countries closely collaborated on a variety of hospital projects and tasks, they gradually got to know each other better, thus acknowledging each other's standpoint and the lens from which they view the world. As a result, there has evolved a high degree of appreciation and respect among the people involved in HICH.

There is an inherent challenge in serving a population that may not be familiar with technology and facilities of a modern urban hospital. While there have been strides toward maintaining cleanliness in the hospital, proper hygiene from patients and their parents is still a challenge in the wards. For instance, some of the families served at HICH have never used flush toilets, piped water supply, electrical appliances, indoor litterbins, and so on. As a result, there are common cases of blocked toilets and drainage channels due to inappropriate disposal of solid materials such as diapers. A lot of time and human resource are spent on parents' education and guidance on basic functions within the hospital. The hygiene challenge is compounded by water shortages during the dry season that necessitate trucking of water into the hospital, which provides an extra strain on the hospital's meager budget. Despite all these challenges, HICH remains one of the top cleanest hospitals in the country.

THE WAY FORWARD

HICH is providing a model of a Ugandan pediatric hospital focused on Ugandan community needs and children's health concerns. As a result of the credibility HICH attained in Mbarara and its ability to partner or collaborate with other health organizations in the region, HICH plays an essential role in strengthening the Ugandan healthcare system in the area of communicable and non-communicable diseases, as well as the delivery of safe and quality medicines, and patient access to healthcare. There is a chance for HICH to establish a partnership with a pediatric hospital in Europe or the United States, and such partnerships improve opportunities for Ugandan health professionals to go abroad and train in all aspects of operating a children's hospital in the twenty-first century. Furthermore, one of HICH's goals is to establish a computerized integrated medical information tracking system that will support a network of health providers and will allow the tracking and treatment of diseases in urban, rural, and remote places. Though there is nothing new about a hospital saving lives, what is novel are the over 196,000 children who have been treated in the inpatient and outpatient facilities at this 60-bed hospital in eight years (HICH Report, 2017). HICH is substantially improving the lives of children and promoting the well-being of all children, thus contributing to the effort in achieving the SDG goal of reducing under-five mortality to 25 per 1,000 live births in every country by 2030.

Health disparities between nations are glaring, and it is time to emphasize and promote action through community-based partnerships, as well regional and international partnerships and collaborations to bridge the gap between these health disparities. There is an urgent need for African governments to adopt result-focused approaches to create sustainable communities with enduing healthcare delivery sustainable system that will achieve equal access to all members of society. Reaching the SDGs targets to "reduce newborn mortality to at least as low as 12 per 1,000 live births in every country (SDG, 3.2); and reduce under-five mortality to at least as low as 25 per 1,000 live births in every country (SDG, 3.2)" seems like a steep hill that is impossible to climb (WHO, Media Centre, 2017). Indeed, African countries have the most challenging task. However, these countries must acknowledge that while private investment is crucial to meet the short fall in the health sectors, there is an urgent need for governments to partner or collaborate with public and private organizations in a cohesive and result-focused approach to create sustainable and enduring healthcare delivery systems to all their citizens.

REFERENCES

HICH. (2011). Holy Innocents Children's Hospital Board Records. http://www.holyinnocentsuganda.com.

HICH. (2016). Holy Innocents Children's Hospital Report 2016. http://www.holyinnocentsuganda.com.

HICH. (2017). Holy Innocents Children's Hospital Newsletter, Holiday Edition 2017. http://www.holyinnocentsuganda.com/.

Lanyero, Flavia. (2012). Child Mortality Rate Remains High in Uganda – Report. *Daily Monitor,* December 2012.

Mukanga, David. (2012). *Community Case Management of Malaria and Pneumonia in Children: Exploring use of Diagnostics by Community Health Workers in Uganda.* Karolinska Institutet, Stockholm.

Mukanga, David, James K. Tibenderana, Juliet Kiguli, George W. Pariyo, Peter Waiswa, Francis Bajunirwe, Brian Mutamba, Helen Counihan, Godfrey Ojiambo, and Karin Kallander. (2010). Community Acceptability of Use of Rapid Diagnostic Tests for Malaria by Community Health Workers in Uganda. *Malaria Journal* (9), 203.

Roman, Elaine, Augustine Ngindu, Bright Orji, Jeremie Zoungrana, Sarah Robbins, and William Brieger. (2015). Evolution of Malaria in Pregnancy Control: Jhpiego's 10-year Contribution. *International Journal of Gynecology and Obstetrics* (Supplement 2): 62–67.

Talisuna, Ambrose, Jane Achan, Albert Peter Okui, Adoke Yeka, Fred Kato, John Bosco Agaba, Seraphine Adibaku, John Bosco Rwakimari, Sarah Staedke, Grant Dorsey, Moses R. Kamya, and Fred Wabwire-Mangen. (2015). The Changing Landscape of Malaria Case Management in Uganda: Decades of Struggle with Evolving Malaria Case Management Strategies and Drug Policies. *Malaria Control and Elimination* (3), 117.

The Southern Cross. (2015). Ugandan Children's Hospital to Add Surgical Center: San Diegans were Key to Hospital's Founding. www.thesoutherncross.org.

UN. (2010). Millennium Development Goals Report 2010. New York, June 2010.

UN. (2017). The Sustainable Development Goals Report 2017. http://www.un.org/sustainabledevelopment/sustainable-development-goals/.

UNICEF. (2018). Data: Monitoring the Situation of Children and Women. https://data.unicef.org/country/uga/.

UNICEF, WHO, World Bank, UN DESA. (2017). Population Division. Levels and Trends in Child Mortality, 2017. http://www.who.int/topics/mortality/en/.

Wetaya Richard. (2016). Malaria Leading Cause of Death in Uganda. *New Vision,* May 6.

WHO. (2017). Media Centre, Children: reducing mortality, Fact Sheet, October 2017. http://www.who.int/mediacentre/factsheets/fs178/en/.

Chapter 8

Sustainable Path to Sub-Saharan African Urban Development

The Case of the Transportation Sector

Mintesnot Woldeamanuel

Sustainable transportation is essential to healthy urban development and to ensure quality of life in the fast-growing cities of the twenty-first century. For growing African nations in particular, it is of the utmost importance to invest in sustainable transportation systems to avoid the consequences of an automobile dominated lifestyle which many cities in Western countries are now coping with. The current general trend in major cities of African countries is a positive relationship between an expanding economy and increasing automobile travel (Kutzbach 2009). This causes several urban problems such as congestion, pollution, and accidents. For example, the Numbeo's 2016 Traffic Index shows that South Africa is the fifth most traffic congested country in the world. Also, road traffic accidents constitute 25 percent of all injury-related deaths in Africa (Nabalamba 2013). Africa has less than 3 percent of the world's motor vehicles, but more than 11 percent of global road fatalities (SEI 2013). Africa has the lowest historical greenhouse gas (GHG) emissions of any continent, but its emissions are now growing rapidly, driven by a sharp increase in fossil-fuel use in the transportation sector.

With globalization and rapid urbanization, there exists a particular urgency for cities in Africa to adopt sustainable urban and transportation planning principles. Cities in Africa are experiencing unprecedented population growth and rural to urban land conversion, outpacing much of the developed world. This has brought opportunities to African cities in the form of economic growth, however, is also exacerbating health, equity, and environmental problems (Sebego and Gwbeu 2013). Thus, failing to pursue sustainable travel modes and transit-oriented developments (TOD) will likely magnify these detrimental outcomes of rapid urban development in Africa.

While a number of developing cities in Africa are actively building in the eye of Western modernism, many modern cities in Europe, the United States, and some parts of Asia are now trying to reverse the pattern and effects of automobile-centric development. For decades, wealthy nations enjoyed cheap energy which fueled private transport demand and the expansion of automobile infrastructure. The passing of peak oil production as well as environmental and social concerns have forced governments to explore sustainable transportation alternatives (Vanderschuren 2010). Many developing cities have nonetheless followed the development pattern of the Western auto-centric style. In Lagos, Nigeria, for example, automobiles are the dominant mode, accounting for 90 percent of land-based travel. This has resulted from high-speed roadway construction and increased car ownership from the affluent classes. Automobile-oriented development and car ownership in Lagos has directly contributed to racial and class polarization in mobility; preventing participation by certain groups in economic, political, and social activities through a constriction of accessibility. Automobile pollution and congestion are omnipresent as well (Ibitayo 2012).

There are several reasons for the growth of auto-centric developments and life style in Africa. When people have more money and are tired of not knowing when the bus will arrive and, if they are lucky, sitting on a hard seat, they will purchase a vehicle (likely an old, highly polluting one) to avoid the daily ordeal of public transit, and that in turn will add to the traffic congestion (Sperling and Salon 2002). Moreover, owning a car suggests high social status. In many major cities in Africa, there is a downward stigma attached to using public transportation, walking, or biking.

With the growth of automobiles, there is a prevalence of suburbanization and urban sprawl that leads to the developments of more transportation infrastructure. For a long time, sub-Saharan Africa has been perceived as not having enough road networks as well as lacking transportation policies. The lack of roads, especially rural roads, is viewed as a major physical constraint propagating poverty in the continent. However, there are recent unprecedented improvements in the transportation sector. Cities of some countries in sub-Saharan Africa are exhibiting a remarkable overall economic growth, and it is reflected in the transportation sector. For example, in Ethiopia's capital city Addis Ababa, performance in the transportation sector had been so remarkable that the total road length grew from 1360 km (845 miles) in 1998 to 3192 km (1983 miles) in 2010, that is, 135 percent growth in a period of 12 years. Also, according to Tsitsi Mutamambara (2008), in the southern part of Africa each country has been taking initiatives to rehabilitate, upgrade and maintain existing road networks as well as building new roads. In Lesotho, for instance, the road network is constantly being expanded and upgraded, especially with the Lesotho Highlands Water Project as the development of road networks seeks to access the more remote areas. In Madagascar, reforms and rehabilitation are taking place through the Transport Sector Program. In Mozambique, the Roads and Coastal Shipping Program led by the World Bank has made developing the internal transport system a priority (Mutamambara 2008).

With this promising growth and development in transportation infrastructure, the important question is how cities in Africa implement sustainable practices in their transportation planning in order to avoid the socio-environmental consequences of an auto-centric culture. While cities in developed nations are trying to reverse their auto-centric cultures, is it possible for the newly growing cities in Africa to start with a clean sustainable path? Having this question in mind, this chapter will discuss the brief history of African transportation development followed by sustainable transportation practices. The challenges of African cities in creating sustainable transportation will also be discussed in this chapter. I will conclude the chapter with a case study of Light Rail Transit (LRT) development in Addis Ababa city as a sustainable transportation effort.

A BRIEF HISTORY OF SUB-SAHARAN AFRICAN TRANSPORTATION

Africa's transportation evolved through colonial influence that focused on the development of transport infrastructure that facilitated links with Europe.[1] This system was intended to support the economic interests of the colonial power which meant to providing raw materials to the "homeland." As a result, colonial Africa was characterized by limited internal linkages with only major cities linked to international gateways (seaports) that served foreign markets. Colonial authorities paid little or no attention to road building. For instance, as documented by Jeffrey Herbst (2000), in the case of French West Africa, there were hardly any roads outside a few urban areas in the region in 1914. The colonial powers invested almost exclusively in transportation infrastructure such as railways which brought them economic benefits. Their need to minimize costs led them to build only those roads and streets that were absolutely necessary for colonial governance. At the same time, colonial powers recognized the importance of their physical presence throughout the colonies as a critical element of control. Accordingly, they proceeded to build a few roads linking some hinterland areas to the colonial government centers. Only very few airports were developed in Africa during the colonial era. These airports were designed to link the colonies to the colonial master nations. Thus, little if any efforts were made to link African cities to each other by air.

Even several decades after independence, the transportation infrastructure of African countries did not show signs of remarkable growth and there was no single transportation policy that guided the development of transportation infrastructure. There were a number of reasons for sluggish growth including poor economic and political performance, topographic conditions, and administrative incompetence. In recent years, however, with the help of the global financial institutions and the involvement of China, many African countries are exhibiting remarkable growth in the transportation industry.

If there is one program that defines sub-Saharan Africa's transportation policy, it is the sub-Saharan Africa Transport Policy Program (SSATP). According to John Thompson (2011) from the World Bank, the conception of the SSATP started with a small group of African and international engineers and policy makers who were deeply concerned with the poor condition of the region's road network. Despite some nations investing billions in road network funds, these countries were running out of treasury funds and, by the early 1980s, only 20 percent of the classified road networks were in excellent condition (Martinez 2001). Another conundrum had been the reality that poor nations in the region could not afford to refurbish their existing networks, let alone help fund the construction of an extensive road network for the entire region. Countries with deteriorating road networks witnessed economic decline (Gwilliam et al. 2008). With these challenges present, the founders of SSATP devised policies that focused on institutional arrangements and capacity building. The policies were intended to stop the unproductive cycle of road building, collapsing, and rebuilding for African countries. In 1986, the founding group members met at the United Nations Economic Commission for Africa (UNECA) to develop a program that would address the neglect of the regions road networks. The 1987 inaugural meeting in Oslo led to the creation of the International Advisory Committee (IAC), which was a joint committee of the World Bank and UNECA. Offices were located in Addis Ababa, Ethiopia. However, program operations stalled due to funding limitations until 1988 when the IAC relocated to the World Bank's offices in Washington DC and renamed itself the sub-Saharan Africa Transport Program.

In its early days the SSATP addressed a wide spectrum of issues such as road maintenance, railway managements, low volume roads, rural travel and transport, development of agriculture and transport, taxations in transport, and many other issues. The program attracted several agencies from African countries and some international organizations. These stakeholders, in short time, limited the range of the program to focus on policy issues. By 1992, the program was implemented through seven components: Road Maintenance

Initiative (RMI), Rural Travel and Transport Program (RTTP), Urban Mobility, Trade and Transport, Railway Restructuring, Human Resources and Institutional Development, and Transport Data.

In 2001, reviews were conducted of five African countries impacted by the program and recommendations were made for the need for more African involvement in program management. The recommendations led to the implementation of national and African regional coordinators based in Africa. Hence, SSATP became a stronger partnership with a sound governance structure. By 2003, thirty African countries were engaged in different components of the program and an increase in donor confidence was restored. The RMI and RTTP were popular of all the components. By 2006, the number of members increased to 35 (World Bank 2003).

Since the program's implementation, SSATP reports that countries have economically improved, especially over the last decade. Ten of the 48 sub-Saharan African countries have had economic growth in excess of 5 percent each year since 2005. There is no doubt that better transport has contributed significantly to Africa's growth. The social landscape has improved with many more people having access to health centers and more children able to go to schools. The SSATP has a distinguished history of supporting information-gathering, analysis, and dissemination. This has led to development of principles, themes, and areas of focus that had a substantial impact on individual country's transport policy formulation and implementation. Some of the impact is being seen with the recent program resurgence and widening influence on the policies and operations of countries, regional economic organizations, aide agencies, and international organizations such as the World Bank, UNECA, and the European Community. On an overall program level, the SSATP is focusing efforts on national transport policies and programs that support poverty reduction strategies-specifically in clarifying the key role of transport in achieving the goals of other sectors such as health, education, and agriculture.

The influence of principles and themes championed by SSATP components on transport sector development has been strong and consistent. For instance, the influence can be clearly seen in Ethiopia, where an agriculture-led development plan triggered a comprehensive road sector development program (RSDP), which enjoys the support of many donors. The RMI principles-ownership, stable financing, responsibility, and good management, all supporting the theme of commercialization have been central to the Ethiopian RSDP. Similar principles championed by the RTTP such as ownership, good management, and adequate funding have been applied not just to policy but to actual or pending improvements in many country programs that enjoy wide support.

SUSTAINABLE TRANSPORTATION IN SUB-SAHARAN AFRICA

Roger Graham of the World Bank stated that

> when the term "sustainability" or "sustainable transport" is interpreted [or discussed], it is not normally associated with Africa. Indeed, in many respects, common images of African transport are synonymous with unsustainability—high rates of traffic growth and congestion (even in cities with comparatively low motorization rates), high traffic injury and fatality rates from substandard road safety practices, highly polluting vehicles, minimal formal public transport services, poor enforcement of road worthiness and vehicle overloading (Graham 2014).

This has been the case for several decades; however, the recent major effort on directing Africa on the path of sustainable transportation was the Africa Sustainable Transport Forum (ASTF), the first ministerial and experts conference held in the year 2014 at the UN Headquarters in Nairobi, Kenya. The event was hosted by the Kenyan Government with support from the United Nations Environment Program (UNEP), the World Bank, the SSATP program based in the World Bank and UN-Habitat. The goal of the ASTF is to integrate sustainable transport into the region's development and planning processes and increase the amount of funding going to sustainable transport programs in Africa (UNEP 2014).

The forum focused on the challenge, in terms of day-to-day realities of sustainable transport in Africa and discussed solutions in the context of green growth and emissions reductions. Concrete actions were grouped in four priority areas: road safety, vehicles and emissions, accessibility and sustainable infrastructure, and enabling conditions. The agenda also allowed for discussion on the future of the ASTF. The forum brought together representatives of 43 African countries, with 21 Ministers of environment and transport in attendance. The concrete outcome of the ASTF inaugural conference is a 13-point ASTF Action Framework which outlines a harmonized roadmap for achieving sustainable transport in Africa. The Action Framework is a compilation of priority areas for action as identified by participating African experts and approved by the attending Ministers. The Action Framework also outlines a set of enabling conditions required to ensure the effectiveness of activities in line with the Action Framework (UNEP 2014).

The ASTF was followed by Sustainable Development Goals (SDGs) adapted by United Nations Sustainable Development Summit in 2015. The SDGs build on the Millennium Development Goals (MDGs), the eight anti-poverty targets that the world committed to achieving by 2015. The MDGs, adopted in 2000, aimed at an array of issues that included slashing poverty, hunger, disease, gender inequality, and access to water and sanitation. Enormous progress has been made on the MDGs, showing the value of a unifying agenda underpinned by goals and targets. The new SDGs, and the broader sustainability agenda, go much further than the MDGs, addressing the root causes of poverty and the universal need for development that works for all people. Of the 17 SDGs, "creating sustainable cities and communities" includes a provision of improving transportation.

> The goal of creating sustainable cities and communities involves investment in public transport, creating green public spaces, and improving urban planning and management in a way that is both participatory and inclusive. (UNDP 2016)

The translation of these goals to actual projects of sustainable transportation and financial commitments are yet to be seen, however it is an indication that Africa is committed to build its transportation infrastructure on the principles of sustainability.

Challenges of Sustainable transportation in the Sub-Saharan Africa

Reducing Transport-Related Air Pollution and Greenhouse Gas (GHG) Emissions

Many think that the number of cars in Africa is so small and the percentage of car users are so insignificant that we should not worry about air pollution and CO_2 emissions. The truth on the ground is that the car fleet in sub-Saharan Africa's streets is growing faster than anywhere in the world, except China, with a high proportion of imported used vehicles. When China is excluded, Africa is leading in global vehicle sales growth rates (Kamau 2009). For example, South Africa's car fleet increased 4.1 percent annually during the 1980s and 2.2 percent in the 1990s. Although the number shows a decrease, the annual rate of growth in the number of cars (2.1 percent) between 1995 and 2000 is somewhat similar to the 2.5 percent annual growth in the nation's human population during the same time period (Prozzi, Naudé, and Sperling 2002).

With Africa's middle-class growing, owning a car is becoming a norm and the environmental impacts of driving is apparent in several major African cities. The challenge lies in the fact that car inspection and maintenance to conform to environmental standards is often absent or insufficient. This means there are poorly maintained and inefficient vehicles on the roads, increasing not only the greenhouse gas emissions but also exhaust emissions which affect urban air quality. On top of that, countries have limited financial resources to address these issues. The current financing priorities in many sub-Saharan African countries are toward funding road construction and motorization which will lead to more car-dependent mobility patterns and higher emissions. Climate finance could help support more sustainable transport options, but investments in such projects to date have been limited (SEI 2013).

Some initiatives in developing a transportation system with limited environmental impact include Tanzania's Urban Development and Environment Management Program that raised understanding of local government authorities in planning and integrating environmental management in their development plans. Dar es Salaam Rapid Transit Agency implemented a Bus Rapid Transit (BRT) Project that improved public transport services and reduce associated air emissions. The country also phased out of leaded fuel in 2005 (Mbwambo 2010). Addis Ababa's light rail system is this first of its type in the sub-Saharan Africa paving the way of sustainable transportation for other African countries to follow suit.

Bringing Social and Economic Equity through Transportation

Transportation is one of the very important components of economic and social development. Without transportation, it is hard to imagine long-term improvements in local and national economic development and quality of life. Transportation promotes sustainability by providing interconnectivity, learning, and development, all of which are essential to the empowerment of socially marginalized and disadvantaged groups. To ensure sustainability, Africa's transportation system should bring equity through accessibility, safety, and environmental protection. Not everyone has equal access to transportation and the well-to-do have unprecedented access to the transportation infrastructure. *The poor* not only have longer commuting time and sometimes lateness or absence from work but also are victims of transportation externalities such as accidents, congestion, and environmental pollutions (Starkey and Hine 2014). For *the extremely poor*, affordability is a big issue. Even the relatively cheaper public mass transit is not affordable for the majority of urban dwellers. An important factor contributing to poverty in rural areas is low accessibility of key resources and services. The hours spent in collecting water, obtaining fuel, or getting to the school, the clinic, or the market are unproductive or "wasted" time (SEI 2013). The high-step doors on buses make it impossible, and often unthinkable for the *elderly* and the *physically disabled* to use public transportation. The household responsibility of *women* force them to make several short trips a day, but there is no frequent public transit system during off-peak hours, and the public transit is overcrowded during rush hours.

Road financing mechanisms and investment priorities are inequitably distributed among drivers (car owners) and non-drivers (people who walk, bike, and/or use public transportation), therefore, a new financing mechanism is needed to make transportation pricing fair, equitable, and economically efficient. By doing so, the transportation system should grant all people satisfactory living conditions and opportunities such as access to education and health services, irrespective of their socioeconomic status, religion, ethnicity, or physical condition.

Africa needs a new planning approach that supports the provision of affordable transportation for the poor, and special transportation services for economically and socially disadvantaged groups such as elderly, disabled, and women. The current planning, which is adapted from the Western car-oriented culture, values mobility over accessibility and prioritizes personal vehicles over public transit, walking, and cycling. With developed countries now focused on improving the planning tools for equity, safety, and environmental protection, Africa must adopt a similar approach in order to maximize the benefits of better transportation while minimizing the negative effects of pollution, congestion, and inequality in accessibility.

There are several initiatives in sub-Saharan Africa that show how a focus on increased accessibility and mobility can integrate equity and development. For example, Mozambique has implemented a program that provides microfinance for rural women to buy bicycles; a "Miracle Health Train" now brings critical services to rural South Africa; and motorbike "ambulances" are providing emergency maternity care in Zimbabwe. Though the evidence of these and other initiatives' impact is still just circumstantial and location-specific, the case studies show how transport measures can help address equity issues (SEI 2013).

Addis Ababa: A Showcase for Sustainable Transportation in Sub-Saharan Africa?

The State of Transportation in Addis Ababa

Evidence from Addis Ababa, Ethiopia, can help us better assess the possibility for sustainable transportation in a rapidly urbanizing Africa. Addis Ababa is the administrative, economic and social capital of Ethiopia. With the current population of 3.3 million people, Addis Ababa is projected to be an African megacity in the next 50 years with an estimated population of more than 10 million people (AACPPO 2012). The city serves as an important political hub for the African continent as it houses the headquarters of the African Union, the UN Economic Commission for Africa and regional offices of several international organizations. Like many other African cities, Addis

Ababa's economy is undergoing a rapid expansion; the Ethiopian government estimates national economic growth at 11 percent annually (USDS 2012). While GDP, foreign investment and incomes are rising, the city has substantial unmet demand for public services such as access to quality transportation. Additionally, the city has undergone substantial rural to urban migration and land conversion in the previous decades, which will be perpetuated by population and economic growth (figure 8.1).

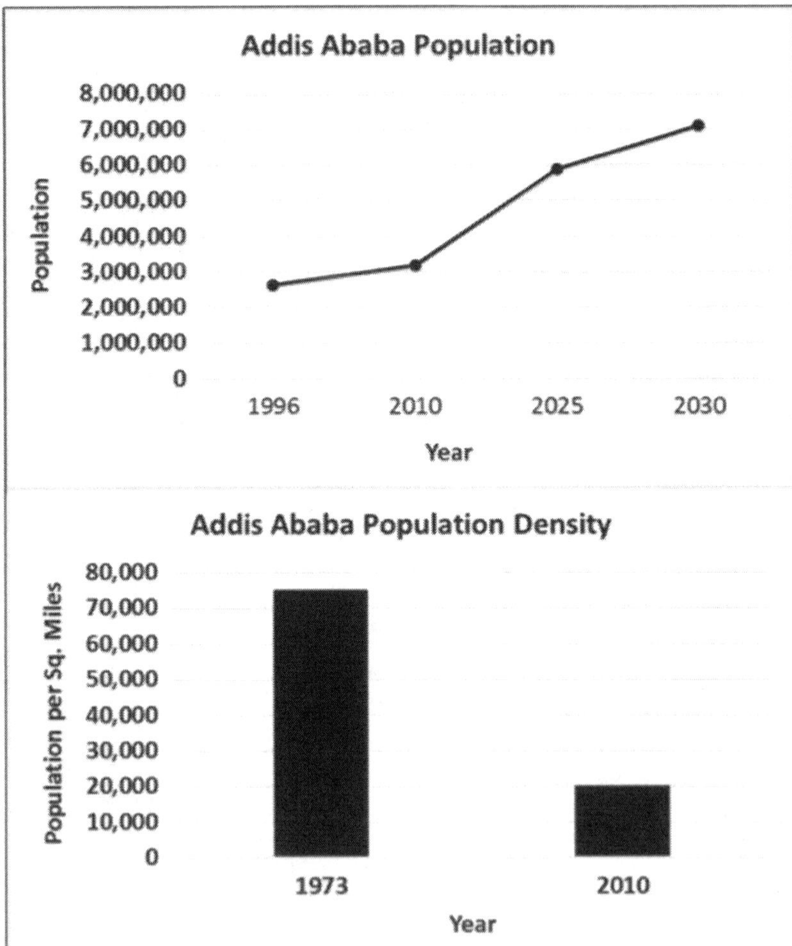

Figure 8.1 Addis Ababa's Population Growth. *Source*: Demographia available at http://www.demographia.com/ and population density (Population per Square Mile). Wendell Cox, New Geography 2012.

Between 2002 and 2012, Addis Ababa's municipal revenue grew by $1 billion, granting the city government one of the largest local budgets in Africa for its relative size (AACPPO 2012). There is, however, a deficit of public services to low income earners who make up a large portion of the city. Economic and population growth has created a shortage of affordable housing near the urban core, greatly reducing accessibility to employment and service centers for low income earners. In the midst of interminable real estate development, there exist large areas of informal housing which pose health, safety, and environmental concerns (Wubneh 2012). There is also a lack of adequate road infrastructure and poor street conditions which have resulted in traffic safety and circulation problems (Berhanu 2004). The local government has a daunting task of correcting these issues and providing adequate services in the wake of massive population growth.

One may think that with only small percentage of travel made by private cars in Addis Ababa it is not necessary to engage in the arduous task of reversing auto dependence. However, according to Mekonnen (2015), while the total number of vehicles used for personal use was no more than 100,000 in 2011, close to 48,000 such private cars have joined the roads of Addis Ababa every year between 2011 and 2014. The total number of all kinds of vehicles registered under the ownership of city dwellers has now surpassed the 400,000 mark.

> According to 2007 World Bank data, the ratio of motor vehicles to people in Ethiopia was one of the lowest, at three motor vehicles for every 1,000 individuals and one passenger car per 1,000 people. The number of vehicles per km of road was only five. This is considered low, even by sub-Saharan Africa standards. Sudan, for example, had 34 motor vehicles per 1,000 persons, while Tanzania and Uganda had seven in the same year. Kenya had 25 motor vehicles per 1,000 persons, according to data from 2011. [Well], this is a national data of Ethiopia, a country with less than 20 percent of its population lives in urban areas. Also, with the increasing number of cars entering the country, it's safe to assume that the ratio is high. But when it comes to the city of Addis Ababa (the primary city) car ownership certainly has a different picture. Based on calculating the data found at the Ethiopian Transport Authority, there are close to 100 motor vehicles for every 1,000 people living in the capital. This increase in vehicles on the roads has changed the lifestyles of people of Addis Ababa. A few years ago, for many people, cars were considered a luxury item, a symbol of high class status. These days, however with the expansion of the middle class, many consider cars a basic necessity. (Mekonnen 2015)

This auto-centric development and way of life decreased the density and increased sprawled developments. The city now faces the challenge of limited transportation infrastructures that have not grown with the rise in personal automobiles, congestion, accidents, and environmental pollutions. As per capita income increases, automobile ownership also continues to increase, creating a greater demand for travel. Although car ownership is still low in Addis Ababa, it is rapidly increasing mainly due to economic growth and the introduction of low-cost private vehicles into the local market. The key determinant of rising automobile use in developing countries is rising per capita income (Kutzbach 2009). Income inequality may also increase automobile use over time. As the wealth of Addis Ababa grows and low-cost automobiles are introduced, it is expected that the demand for private transport will substantially grow as well as infrastructure to support automobiles. Also, as indicated in the population and density chart, as urbanization rates increase, density is decreasing which can be translated to longer commuting time and more demand for cars.

Like many African cities, Addis Ababa still has the possibility of beginning sustainable transportation development with a clean slate. The city has the ability to leap frog such obsolete development patterns and ineffective policies that African cities try to adopt from cities in Western countries (Vanderschuren 2010). Addis Ababa, like other cities in the region, is culturally primed for sustainable development principles and mass transportation. Under the current transportation paradigm, walking, buses, and taxis dominate the modal split. Pedestrian activity and public transit accounts for 45 percent and 46 percent of transport, respectively. The Anbessa City Bus Service transports about 400,000 passengers daily (AACPPO 2012). Even with low automobile ownership, auto related congestion is already a problem in Addis Ababa's dense urban center and significantly impacts bus efficiency. The result is negative feedback which further stimulates demand for cars (Kutzbach 2009). Thus, when automobiles begin to dominate local roadways, they create a self-reinforcing effect by reducing the utility of public transit. The rising use of automobiles presents an apparent threat where they share the roadway with buses; which comprise a major transport share in Addis Ababa and in much of Africa. By 2020, Addis Ababa will have in the vicinity of 486,000 vehicles, 82 percent of which will be for private transport and only 12 percent projected to account for taxi cabs, buses, and trucks (Haregewoin 2010). This growth in automobile travel will greatly overextend the limited street infrastructure currently in place. Additionally, many of the streets are dilapidated and only about 35 percent of the current road network is pedestrian accessible (Demdime 2012). Currently, there is a rail system to transport passengers from the periphery to the urban center. This is important since a larger portion of the city's workforce live away from job centers and must cover a significant commute distance (Tafesse 1989).

Planning for Sustainable Transportation

Within the city's transportation planning objectives, the Addis Ababa municipal government has recognized the need for sustainable land use and transportation planning as essential to the success of the city. As a response to increasing automobile use, lack of infrastructure and a need for mass transportation, the city government of Addis Ababa has adopted a city-wide transportation master plan in order to modernize public transport, improve pedestrian environments, and tackle the congestion that is generated from the increasing use of private vehicles (Voukas 2012). Addis Ababa's transportation plan is rather ambitious; however, it is necessary to meet the immense population and development driven demand on the city. The plan calls for the organization of a strong mass transit backbone to serve a city of 12 million people. The transportation master plan includes the construction of seven BRT and two LRT corridors, as well as improvements in pedestrian facilities, non-motorized transport, and parking management (Voukas and Palmer 2012). The plan also calls for an integration of land-use planning and transportation planning, which is essential for maximizing returns on transit investment. Under the framework of sustainability principles, the city plans to develop new transit corridors and terminals into an integrated multimodal transportation system. The construction and upgrading of primary roads is planned with pedestrian infrastructure and designated transit lanes (AACPPO 2012). The separation of buses from vehicle traffic, through designated lanes, will help to maintain transit as a drive alternative as the city accrues wealth by maximizing consumer surplus for transit riders (Kutzbach 2009). These designated lanes will accommodate all transit modes, including the Anbessa buses, minibuses, and taxis. The master plan also embraces a highly connected polycentric model that the municipal government hopes will alleviate congestion in the Central Business District (CBD) with all major destination sub-centers aligned with planned mass transit corridors. The plan also calls for complete street design and TOD principles, such as mixed-use development, which should serve as effective planning methods for enhancing mobility while preserving the city's current transit and pedestrian orientation (Demdime 2012). Implementing such projects requires a strong political will and commitment to overcome numerous financial and logistic obstacles, which Addis Ababa has, as well as, growing public demand for mass transportation (Jemere 2012).

Addis Ababa LRT: The First of Its Kind in the Sub-Saharan Africa

Addis Ababa's LRT project is comprised of a North-South line (16.9 km) and an East-West line (17.35 km) which will juncture at the meticulously planned La Gare station in the CBD (AACPPO 2012; Jemere 2012). Addis Ababa's light rail is able to transport 60,000 passengers per hour with an eventual 90-second headway capability (Jemere 2012). The LRT project has 10 main hubs located at important service centers and intermodal nodes. The transportation master plan integrates the LRT at these major hubs with BRT routes, regular bus, and the taxi services. Additionally, pedestrian infrastructures are upgraded to supply the major walking mode with adequate access to the LRT terminals and surrounding land uses. The LRT stations and corridors under the master plan would be integrated into public spaces in terms of urban design, landscaping, and pedestrian needs. To the East and South, the LRT lines extend out of the urban core, providing peri-urban residences access to the economic and social center of Ethiopia. Addis Ababa is also engaging in regional planning efforts to coordinate future LRT extensions with the national rail network and the Oromia state government which would establish better connectivity to the rest of Ethiopia (AACPPO 2012). The LRT grants improved topographic accessibility by providing transport over the steep elevations which are common to the city. Precisely, the LRT is engineered to traverse 5 percent grades, necessitated by Addis Ababa's location at 1.5 miles (2400 meters) above sea level (Jemere 2012). The LRT system has several environmental benefits as it is fully powered by electricity. In addition to meeting the ever-expanding transportation demand of the city, it plays a significant role in providing access to different parts of the society. The LRT system is still in its infancy, and so more time is needed to evaluate its benefits, challenges, and problems (figure 8.2).

Figure 8.2 Addis Ababa Light Rail System Station. *Source*: Photo courtesy ©Mintesnot Woldeamanuel.

CONCLUSION

Africa's economy is becoming increasingly important in the global system. Rapidly growing economies across the continent have led to urbanization and a larger demand for transportation. With increasing demand, several social and environmental issues associated with the transportation sector must be considered. Thus, there is a substantial need to address urban transport-related socio-environmental issues in sub-Saharan Africa. This includes reducing air pollution, greenhouse gas emissions and associated health impacts, reducing traffic injuries and fatalities, relieving congestion, and promoting equity and quality of life. It is critical for rapidly urbanizing cities in Africa to begin their urban development with a sustainable philosophy.

Sub-Saharan Africa must pursue policies, strategies, and financial resources that provide a sustainable transportation system that is affordable and minimizes negative social and environmental impacts. The strategy to achieve these goals includes reducing travel by restructuring the existing land-use system. Mixed-use zoning, for example, encourages walking and biking (when topography allows) to fulfill daily activities. Transport needs should be met not necessarily by cars but by public transport, walking, and cycling. The infrastructure that would allow for this must be the focus of transportation policies. The major challenge sub-Saharan African countries must overcome is financing a sustainable transportation system that improves accessibility and quality of life. African countries therefore need to seek resources to improve the fuel-efficiency of cars on the street and shift from fossil fuels to the cleaner and fuel-efficient mode of transportation. Regulatory framework and enforcement mechanisms are needed to ensure the efficiency of vehicle fleets.

A knowledge sharing program with developed nations and among African nations is also important. There is tremendous local and global knowledge about proven strategies for sustainable transportation that reduces the social, economic, and environmental impacts of the transportation sector. Measures such as bus regulation and planning, promoting non-motorized transport, land-use planning, BRT, and light rail system can help sub-Saharan countries avoid the auto-centricity associated with development.

Numerous sub-Saharan African nations are attempting to imitate the car-dependent development patterns of many Western cities. It is time to subscribe to a model developed to counter the negative attributes of auto-centricity. The success of Addis Ababa implementing formal mass transit as a primary travel mode is a good example of building on sustainability principles. This transit system has the potential to serve as a positive model for growth, environmental health, and equity in the future development of African cities. In the wake of rapid economic and population growth, projects such as BRT, LRT, and TOD have a significant added value in creating sustainable cities. Residents of African nations have a long-standing culture of public transit use so with transportation projects that keep in mind the goals of affordable transport and enhanced access and mobility, sustainable urban transportation is not far from reach.

NOTE

1. This brief history of Sub-Saharan African Transportation is adapted from article written by the author for Encyclopedia of Transportation and the book *Concepts in Urban Transportation Planning: The Quest for Mobility, Sustainability and Quality of Life* © Mintesnot Woldeamanuel (2016).

BIBLIOGRAPHY

Addis Ababa City Planning Project Office [AACPPO] and Lyon Town Planning Agency. (2012). *Transportation Challenges in a Booming City; Coordination of the Mass Transit Network and Urban Development in Addis Ababa*. Addis Ababa City Government.

Berhanu, G. (2004). Models Relating Traffic Safety with Road Environment and Traffic Flows on Arterial Roads in Addis Ababa. *Accident Analysis & Prevention, 36*(5), 697–704.

Cox, Wendall. (2012). *World Urban Areas Population and Density: A 2012 Update*. New Geography.

Demdime, F. (2012). Integrating Public Transport Networks and Built Environment: The case of Addis Ababa and Experiences from Stockholm. *KTH-Royal Institute of Technology, School of Architecture and the Built Environment, Master Thesis in Environmental Engineering and Sustainable Infrastructure.*

Gwilliam, K., V. Foster, R. Archondo-Callao, C. Briceño-Garmendia, A. Nogales, and K. Sethi. (2008). *The Burden of Maintenance Roads in Sub Saharan Africa*. The International Bank for Reconstruction and Development/The World Bank.

Haregewoin, Y. (2010). Impact of Vehicle Traffic Connection in Addis Ababa. *Master's Thesis, Ethiopian Civil Service College.*

Herbst, Jeffrey. (2000). *States and Power in Africa*. Princeton University Press.

Ibitayo, O. (2012). Towards Effective Urban Transportation System in Lagos, Nigeria: Commuters' Opinions and Experiences. *Transport Policy, 24*, 141–47.

Jemere, Y. (2012). *Addis Ababa Light Rail Transit Project*. Presentation, Ethiopian Railways Corporation.

Kamau, H. (2009). *Trade in Second-Hand Vehicles: Sustainable Transport Africa*. Sustainable Transport Africa.

Khayesi, M., and A. Amekudzi. (2011). Kingdon's Multiple Streams Model and Automobile Dependence Reversal Path: The Case of Curitiba, Brazil. *Journal of Transport Geography, 19*(6), 1547–552.

Kutzbach, M. (2009). Motorization in Developing Countries: Causes, Consequences, and Effectiveness of Policy Options. *Journal of Urban Economics*, *65*, 154–66.

Martinez, A. (2011). Road Maintenance Policies in Sub-Saharan Africa: Unsolved Problems and Acting Strategies. *Transport Policy*, *4*(8), 257–65.

Mbwambo, K. (2010). *Impacts of Air Pollution and Progress Made By the Region to Reduce Air Pollution*. Tanzania Bureau of Standards (TBS).

Mekonnen, B. (2015). *Too Many Cars Spoil the Roads*. Ethiopian Business Review.

Mutambara, Tsitsi. (2008). *Regional Transport Challenges Within the Southern African Development Community and Their Implications for Economic Integration and Development*. Monitoring Regional Integration in Southern Africa Yearbook.

Nabalamba, Alice. (2013). *Mortality in Africa: The Share of Road Traffic Fatalities*. Market Brief Statistics Department, AfDB.

Prozzi, J. P., C. Naudé, and D. Sperling. (2002). *Transportation in Developing Countries: Greenhouse Gas Scenarios for South Africa*. PEW Center on Global Climate Change.

Sebego, R., and T. Gwbeu. (2013). Patterns, Determinants, Impacts and Policy Implications of the Spatial Expansion of an African Capital City: The Greater Gaborone example. *International Journal of Sustainable Built Environment*, *2*(2), 193–208.

Sperling, D., and D. Salon. (2002). *Transportation in Developing Countries, An Overview of Greenhouse Gas Reduction Strategies*. Pew Center on Global Climate Change.

Starkey, P., and J. Hine. (2014). *Poverty and Sustainable Transport: How Transport Affects Poor People with Policy Implications for Poverty Reduction: A Literature Review*. UN-Habitat.

Stockholm Environment Institute (SEI). (2013). *Transport and Environment in Sub-Saharan Africa*. A Policy Brief.

Tafesse, T. (1989). The Patterns and Problems of Work Trips in Addis Ababa. *Journal of Ethiopian Studies*, *22*, 75–96.

Thompson, John. (2011). *1987–2011 SSATP Africa's Transport: A Promising Future*. Sub-Saharan Africa Transport Policy Program.

UNEP. (2014). *Africa Sustainable Transport Forum*. Full Meeting Report, ASTF Inaugural Forum, held in Nairobi, Kenya, from 28 to 30 October.

USDS. (2012). *2012 Investment Climate Statement – Ethiopia*. U.S. Department of State, Bureau of Economic and Business Affairs.

Vanderschuren, M., T. Lane, and W. Korver. (2010). Managing Energy Demand Through Transport Policy: What Can South Africa Learn from Europe? *Energy Policy*, *38*(2), 826–31.

Voukas, Y., and D. Palmer. (2012). *Sustainable Transportation in East Africa: The Bus Rapid Transit evolution in Addis Ababa, Ethiopia*. Conference CODATU XV.

World Bank. (2003). *The SSATP Framework*. World Bank Publications.

Wubneh, M. (2012). Addis Ababa, Ethiopia: Africa's Diplomatic Capital. *Cities*, *35*, 255–69.

Chapter 9

Expectations of Public Space

Attachments, Environmental Responsibility, and Urban Sustainability in Dakar, Senegal

Suzanne Scheld

After Asia, Africa is the fastest urbanizing area in the world, with many cities growing on the average of 4 percent annually.[1] Due to this growth, African cities run the risk of developing in disorderly ways if they are not carefully planned. For this reason, when the United Nations announced its new Sustainable Development Goals in 2015, the UN-Habitat immediately released its new urban agenda in 2016. Among the UN-Habitat's principles for effecting urban sustainability is the need to plan for public space. From the UN-Habitat's point of view, public space is a resource that can aid the health, economy, environment, social cohesion, and the civic identity of cities. Public space is deemed as critical to the future sustainability of African cities. Can public space do so much good in developing cities, however? Is public space the new silver bullet for urban sustainability in Africa?

In this chapter, I explore the expectation that public space can aid urban sustainability by examining several popular public spaces in Dakar, Senegal, and the extent to which they are likely to engender environmentally responsible behavior. Environmental psychologists argue environmentally responsible behavior is engendered by strong place attachments (Vaske and Korbin 2001). A place attachment is an emotional, social, and cultural bond forged between people and their environment (Eisenhauer, et al. 2000; Proshansky et al. 1983; Tuan 1977). Anthropologist describe these bonds in terms of a sense of belonging to a particular social environment or milieu. Such bonds are created through repetitive visitation as well as interactions, exchanges, and events that occur in the space. Sensory experiences, memories, images, and discourse also foster these bonds. In theory, the more citizens forge connections to public space, the more likely they are to participate in social actions that aim to support, nourish, and protect public space and its environs. Highly functioning and self-sustaining public space is ultimately a benefit to sustaining a city overall. One can see how this theory applies in instances where citizens with long-term relationships to a public park, for example, are motivated by their connections to become engaged in protecting the environment or "green" space of the park. But, does this idea apply to citizen's relationships with other types of public space, such as markets and stately plazas, where "nature" is not a prominent feature of the space? Does it apply to public spaces that are managed with limited input from the public? Does it apply to public spaces in African societies where the history of public space differs from the history of public space in Western societies? Contemporary public space significantly contributes to urban sustainability when it is designed and used to host healthy and productive activities instead of destructive activities. The literature demonstrating the benefits of public space is vast.[2] Are there additional ways that public space contributes to the goal of fostering urban sustainability apart from standing as islands of productive human interactions in the broader city? In the pages below, I explore these questions through an analysis of several public spaces in Dakar, Senegal, where nature is, for the most part, not the dominant feature. These spaces include plazas, a shopping area, and an art space. Studies that probe how public space engenders environmental responsibility are often conducted in the context of green spaces where trash collection and recycling are examples of citizen stewardship. In the public spaces that I examine, the dominant features in the built environment are designs that engender group gatherings, limited movement, observations of one another and things, and conversation. Therefore, "environmental responsibility" may be interpreted as acts that welcome others into the space, acknowledge and engage others, and encourage others to have a sense of belonging. I find with one exception, old and new public spaces tacitly and explicitly exclude others, and in this sense, even when there are healthy place attachments, these examples of public space do not engender environment responsibility or citizen stewards that contribute to urban sustainability. It is possible for these forms of public space to engender place attachments that transform into stewardship, but this is dependent upon diverse members of the public having access to public space, citizens embracing a shared notion of public space, and public participation in meaningful "place-making" of public space.

In the sections that follow, I define public space, urban sustainability, and relationships between these two concepts. I briefly describe Dakar, and then I discuss several examples of old and new public space including of *Place de l'Indépendance*, a "traditional" plaza in the middle of the city, and Sea Plaza, Place du Souvenir, and a public art installation, three new forms of public space on the city's corniche. I conclude the chapter by reflecting on patterns observed in the aforementioned examples of public space, and the notion of public space as the UN Habitat's new tool for effecting change.

There are many forms of public space in Dakar (e.g., plazas, parks, markets, soccer fields, transportation hubs, sidewalks, beaches, etc.). I focus on plazas, market spaces, and public spaces along the corniche because they are examples that best highlight public, private, and community intersections and the changing meanings associated with public space as the city is undergoing rapid urbanization. Environmental psychologists typically study place attachments in public space using mixed methods, with a focus on quantitative data. In contrast, this chapter adopts an ethnographic approach to studying public space. This perspective conveys the experience of being in certain public spaces, which is knowledge that is highly relevant to understanding how some individuals and communities form deep attachments to public space while others are subtly and explicitly excluded from public space. The discussion in this chapter is based on participant-observation, open-ended interviewing, and archival research which was conducted in Dakar in July 2013 and June 2016. It is also informed by ongoing ethnographic research in Dakar since 1996.

PUBLIC SPACE AND URBAN SUSTAINABILITY INTERSECTIONS

Public space and urban sustainability are complex and contradictory concepts. Public space is traditionally conceived as open, outdoor space that is publicly owned and managed, such as plazas, parks, streets, sidewalks, beaches, and so on. New forms of public space that have developed within modern times challenge this definition. For example, do transportation hubs qualify as public spaces since many of them are indoors? Are indoor shopping centers or outdoor parks public spaces if they are accessible to the public but owned or managed by private companies? According to Stéphane Tonnelat (2010), the contemporary concept of public space tends to be based on the notion of private property and access, and in this sense, it is akin to the concept of early English commons whereby the rights to use pastures for animal grazing and subsistence were granted to farmers under the law of the manorial system. Ironically, Tonnelat points out such spaces no longer exist in the western world since nearly every inch of physical space is owned and regulated by a state or private entity.

"Urban sustainability" is an equally tricky concept. It is oxymoronic from one point of view. Urban centers are often associated with the notion of progress, movement, growth, and expansion. They were once conceived as closed systems, in opposition to "rural areas," the "countryside" and "hinterlands." They were also considered as part of a closed system when they were characterized as "the engine of the nation" (Jacobs 1961). However, the sustainability of a city depends on it having access to material and human resources in diverse parts of the world. Thus, cities are global in nature, and constantly changing. In Africa in particular, ongoing rural-urban migration results in ongoing urbanization and the need to frequently redraw city limits. Sustainability, in contrast, is associated with a closed system, self-sufficiency, and fixed resources. Expanding the boundaries in which limited resources will be consumed threats the vitality of resources. So, is it possible to create urban sustainability when "urban" and "sustainability" are based on contradictory forces?

In addition to the problem of contradictory meanings, sustainability is defined in diverse ways, which makes the meaning of "urban sustainability" even more of a moving target. Based on the United Nations' definition, sustainability refers to meeting "the needs of present generations without compromising the ability of future generations to meet their own needs" (Brundtland Commission 1987). This definition is prompted by concern for the rapid depletion of natural resources in the world. A similar concern certainly applies to culture since globalization is undermining indigenous languages, lifeways, and local knowledge that can contribute to the preservation of natural resources. David Throsby (1995) argues there is a need to add "cultural sustainability" to the general notion of sustainability. This form of sustainability entails the preservation of the arts, and society's attitudes, practices, and beliefs. Throsby furthers extended this idea to social sustainability, which entails the preservation of social relations, meanings, histories, and values of contemporary people (Arendt 1973 [1958]; Habermas 1991).

Despite the broad range and contradictory meanings associated with urban sustainability and public space, there is wide spread agreement that urban sustainability is critical to achieve, and public space can contribute to this goal. Presently, the UN-Habitat is at the fore in promoting the development of public space as a means to improve urban sustainability in the global south. The organization enlists the help of the Gehl Studio in Copenhagen, the Knight Foundation in Miami, and the Project for Public Spaces in New York for insights and tools for studying public space in developing cities all over the world. This turn to public space is noteworthy because these organizations and many others have been studying, designing, and advocating for public space as a tool for improving cities for several decades (Lewicka 2011). Why hasn't this literature been highlighted before?

Indeed, lay people intuitively have known the benefits of public space. Historians trace citizens' acknowledgment of the benefits of public space back to the Parks Movement in the nineteenth century in North America and Europe. Upper-class city dwellers were critical of industrialization and the deterioration of the environment, health problems, crime, and poor living conditions it produced for the working class and poor. They pressured their governments to create large landscape parks that they believed would uplift the poor and working classes, as well as protect their investments in the city. This movement resulted in the construction of Central Park in New York, Victoria Park in London, among other large parks (Low et al. 2005). Others chronicle citizen-led gardening movements in the United States and U.K. Studies of gardening movements in the nineteenth century reveal similar concerns for the negative effects of industrialization and urbanization on the health of the working classes and poor, and privileged citizens' belief that urban relief gardens would improve community health as well the overall look of the city (Lawson 2005; Burchardt 2002). The victory garden movement associated with both the world wars reflects concerns for the status and wealth of the nation, and often, the position of gardeners—typically women—within it. And, the Green Thumb and Green Guerilla movements in the United States reflect citizens' responses to urban decay and gentrification (Gowdy-Wygant 2013). Collectively, these studies highlight public space as a dynamic and contested social formation with "healing" as well as "controlling" powers. Diverse groups of citizens and urban authorities use public space as a tool to fulfill their needs and meet their goals. Diverse groups of citizens have also known the usefulness of public space all along. The UN-Habitat's promotion of public space represents the renewal of theories that have a long history. In this light, the UN-Habitat's promotion of public space for effecting urban sustainability can be interpreted from at least two perspectives. In practical terms, public space is a material resource that individuals and groups use for meeting others, recreating, exercising, procuring good health, and for developing a sense of community and belonging. As the host to these activities and interactions, public space shapes the day-to-day rhythms of a city, often in positive ways which contribute to its sustainability. In analytical terms, the renewed focus on public space coincides significant moment of urban transformation. In the past, public space received attention when elites needed to control the masses, or the working classes needed reclaim their space and legitimacy as cities underwent deindustrialization. What tension needs to be fixed today and masked by attention given to the politics of public space? Encountering the resilience of neoliberalism may be the source of this new tension. Neoliberal economic policies and programs have been thoroughly critiqued as inadequate to engendering economic development in the global south. Nevertheless, policies that encourage dependency on foreign investment, deregulation of the economy, and the retreat of the state remain in place. How will new opportunities for growth be created if political and economic relationships within African countries, and between African countries and the global economy remain the same? In short, the UN Habitat is in need of a new game plan to effect urban sustainability, and public space is available for use. The UN Habitat frames public space as dynamic tool for solving many ills, and in doing so masks the reality that the structural arrangements that undergird these problems is not changing. In this light, among the many cures a public space panacea can dispense is an anesthetizing effect when confronting resilient neoliberalism.

I now turn to introduce the reader to Dakar, a city that has been thoroughly shaped by resilient neoliberalism.

DAKAR

Dakar is located on the breezy, sandy Cap Vert peninsula of Senegal, Africa's westernmost point. It is a densely populated city with approximately three million inhabitants, which is almost a quarter of Senegal's population. The city is culturally diverse. Residents are of many ethnicities including Lebu (original inhabitants of the peninsula), Wolof, Fula, Serer, Jola, Manjaka, Soninke, Bassari, and Moors. Many are of mixed ethnic backgrounds. In the nineteenth century, Lebanese began migrating to Dakar and today, a large community of Lebanese-Senegalese lives in the city. There are migrants from Mauritania, Gambia, Guinea, Guinea-Bissau Mali, Ivory Coast, Liberia, and Sierra Leone. Others migrated to Dakar from as far away as India, Korea, and China. Dakar houses the headquarters of numerous international banks and development agencies which employ many Europeans, North Americans, Middle Easterners, and Japanese who add to the city's diversity. Dakar is also religiously diverse. Ninety-five percent of the population is Muslim who practice several varieties of Sunni Islam (e.g., Tijanism, Mouridism, Qadiriyya, Layenism). There is a small community of Shia Muslims, and about 4 percent of the population is Christian (mostly Roman Catholic, some Protestants). About one percent of the population follows traditional beliefs.

In addition to extensive cultural diversity in the city, Dakarois are economically diverse, although a great portion of the inhabitants are poor and struggling economically. 36 percent of Dakar's working-age population is under- or unemployed (ANSD 2015); 60 percent of the population earn less than $2/day. Many urbanites are illiterate and live in sub-standard housing. Because of limited job opportunities and poor living conditions, many younger people aspire to emigrate to other African countries such as the Gambia, Mauritania, or Ghana, and to countries in the global north (e.g., France, Italy, Germany, the United States, Canada). Many Dakarois try to make a living in the city's vast informal economy. A small number of urban residents are wealthy and live in luxurious homes in well-resourced neighborhoods such as Las Almadies and Fann.

Immediately after Independence in 1960, hopes were high for Dakar to develop into an industrialized, wealthy city. The new government

Africanized and further modernized the economy and state. By 1979, high hopes for industrial development evaporated as Senegal confronted a large deficit, collapsing growth, debilitating drought in the interior, and the global oil crisis which specifically impacted Dakar. In the 1980s, Senegal was deep in debt. The World Bank and International Monetary Fund offered to bail out Senegal with aid packages in exchange for several "structural adjustments" which, in theory, were to boost the economy. The adjustment included maintaining open borders, devaluing the currency, putting the government on austerity, and implementing cost-sharing approaches to public services. As a result of these policies, Senegal minimally benefited from hosting foreign companies within its borders, while its own companies were weakened by the new competition within Senegal and in the global market. Currency devaluations helped the economy in terms of prompting the Senegalese transnational migrants in Europe and North America to invest in Senegal; however, it drove the prices for sugar, bread, and rice through the roof thereby increasing food insecurity and poverty. In addition to this, as the government withdrew its support for education, health, and housing programs, causing the population to truly suffer. This accelerated transnational migration as well as prompted the deaths of many youth who with limited opportunities for visas for migration to Europe, opted for a clandestine route which entailed traversing the Atlantic Ocean on artisanal wooden canoes guided by inexperienced and broke, but ambitious captains. In short, structural adjustment programs did little to address poverty in Dakar or Senegal's dependency on other countries and low position in the global economy. If anything, it exacerbated poverty and normalized Senegal's marginal position in the world economy. Meanwhile, the well-to-do of Dakar continued to live comfortably. They drive the most expensive vehicles, live in large homes, and travel to Europe for shopping sprees.

Within this picture of uneven development in Dakar, public space is an ambiguous social formation. On the one hand, the public-private space dichotomy is a familiar concept in this city. On the other hand, definitions of public and private space vary in Dakar, thereby creating confusion over who has the rights to claim and use public space, and who has the obligation to protect and take care of it.

One reason the line between public and private space is unclear is found in the history of the peninsula. The Lebu, the first inhabitants of the peninsula, practiced customary land ownership prior to the arrival of French settlers. Arguably, their land *was* a form of public space until the French colonial administrators imposed Western distinctions between public (governmental) and private (nongovernmental) property. In 1858, this distinction was used to justify evicting the Lebu from their lands in order to build the first road in Dakar. Although the Lebu were afforded the right to use their lands in 1905 and the right to register for land ownership in 1932, by the end of the colonial period (1960) a good deal of Lebu land had been converted into French "public" land. Due to customary land laws, Lebu land was not easily registered in the French system. In 1964 when new Senegalese state passed a law to nationalize unregistered lands, the Lebu lost even more land. This compelled many Lebu to rapidly sell off collectively owned lands on the informal real estate market in order to derive some benefit before their lands were further appropriated. As a result, to this day land ownership in Dakar is sometimes unclear. Real estate buyers are commonly forewarned that a Lebu-initiated land dispute may crop up in the middle of a sale (Gaye 1992).

In short, the line between public and private space is a reworked historical invention that obscures the first inhabitants' attachment to the land. In the history of Dakar, "public" lands were "privatized" by two external, state entities, and in the process disenfranchised and marginalized its original inhabitants. Thus, unequal positions of power and varying historical perspectives of Cap Vert lands contribute to blurring the boundaries of public and private space in Dakar today.

Yet another reason the line between public and private space is blurred relates to the spread of informality in Dakar. Informality is often discussed with respect to the economy, the absence of formal employment, and individuals meeting their subsistence needs by performing work in an informal sector. There are other aspects to informality as well. They included the actions that individuals or communities take in response to the lack of state oversight of activities in many domains of society. Informality has always been an aspect of life in Dakar. In the colonial period, for example, even though French colonial administrators imposed a cash crop economy system in Senegal, African subsistence farming and bartering did not impact the French system and was therefore permitted to persist. As a result, it was common for a good deal of economic activity to take place outside of the French system.[3]

The scope of informality in Dakar was brought to a new level, however, in the 1980s during the years of structural adjustment. It has since remained high and a highly visible feature in the city. For example, informality is readily observed in the large number of itinerant traders roaming the streets at any time of the day, and the increased amount of public space that vendors appropriate for commerce. In the early 2000s, it was indeed difficult to walk down Avenue Pompidou (formerly Ponty) for the sidewalks were blocked by street vendors selling goods stacked on improvised wooden tables, tarps on the ground, and pinned to murals, trees, and umbrellas as well as bodies. Some vendors occupying street corners take advantage of cars that are forced to stop due to traffic. They extend these public vending spaces into the privacy of citizen's cars by thrusting an eclectic array of goods for sale through an open window when the cars stop at intersections. While sitting in the passenger's seat, one is often nose-to-nose with alarm clocks, packets of tissues, boxes of Kellogg's Rice Crispies, picture frames, mirrors, toothbrushes, kitchen cookware, sun glasses, and small plastic toys, among many other items coming in through the opening.

But informality is visible in other ways too. For example, it is common for private citizens to informally reroute traffic from a neighborhood in order to celebrate a family baptism or wedding. Plastic barricades rented chairs and awnings are among the objects employed to send taxis and buses down an unplanned, unofficial route. In downtown Dakar on Fridays, it is common for citizens to pray in the streets at mid-day. In this case, hundreds of bodies line themselves up in neat rows on the roads creating human barricades that prevent traffic from traversing the city.

Attention to informality is illuminated by citizens' appropriations of public resources when striving to meet social obligations and personal economic obligations. It is also illuminated by citizens' willingness to fulfill the government's role when the government does not take action. For example, Dakar's municipality collects garbage once a week. But youth have detected the desire for more sanitation services. So, many young men informally collect garbage by driving horse-drawn carts through neighborhood streets. They yell "*mbalit-mbalit*"[4] in a distinctive voice, and this prompts maids and other young women to dash out into the streets with bags of trash. The informal trash collectors then dump and burn the garbage in the open fields of Léopold Sédar Senghor airport. In this process, they expose themselves, others, animals and the soil to foul and toxic pollution. Yet, informality is normalized such that that youth willingly put themselves and the environment at risk as they clean the city.

The earlier descriptions are meant to introduce the reader to Dakar, and to convey that the concept of public space in Dakar cannot be taken for granted. Public space is a shifting concept shaped by the history of Cap Vert, by the spread of informality due to Senegal's position in the global economy and by many sets of unequal power relations. This results in public space being treated as available for private activities such as family celebrations and the intimate act of connecting with God, while activities typically relegated to public space, such as commerce, often invade citizens' privacy. The line between public and private space is vague and awaits clarification by city or state governments. However, citizens consider themselves among the governing bodies of Dakar and freely determine the boundaries of public space on their own. In the literature on cities of the global north, much ink has been spilled over characterizations of parks, places, sidewalks, and so on as contested public space.[5] In some instances, in Dakar, uses of public space are hotly contested. For example, there are periodic, violent sweeps of street vendors on Avenue Pompidou and other areas of the city, and market halls burned to the ground, a severe tactic for removing vendors from public space. The vast majority of public space appropriations in Dakar, however, have been without heated confrontations. After street sweeps and burned down buildings, vendors often return to "their" sites to reconstitute their work. In other words, the boundaries of public spaces in Dakar are highly fluid due to the movement of people, varying views of public space, the spread of informality, and the limited power of municipal authorities. Can fluid forms of public space engender forms of place attachment that are strong enough to mobilize citizen stewardship for urban sustainability? If attachments to public space are flexible, how do they result in producing enduring, proactive, and effective stewards? Let us now turn to public spaces in Dakar to examine if and how place attachments form, and if and how they are converted into citizen stewardship.

PLACE DE L'INDÉPENDANCE

The Place de l'Indépendance was part of the first master plan of Dakar which was designed by Émile Pinet-Laprade in 1862. The plaza was then named after the first governor of Dakar, August-Léopold Protêt, and was built on top of an abandoned French fort, and at the mid-point between the port and the governor's palace, Plateau (where French settlers predominantly lived) and the road to Medina, the African quarters on the outer limits of the town. In its early years, the plaza had a gazebo for musical performances and announcements, an enclosed garden and many shady trees that initially gave the plaza the look of a woody, romantic place where one could commune with nature. There were also benches to rest upon on out skirts of the park, and walkways around the entire plaza that were wide enough for strolling in pairs or small groups. Later, a monument in the form of a miniature Arc de Triomphe in Paris was added to mark the entrance for those coming from the Medina, and to commemorate soldiers who had died in World War I. Another monument was later added to commemorate the fallen solders of World War II. This monument was built into the sidewall of an elevated part of the plaza and remains in the plaza today, while the arch monument was removed and a large water fountain was added to the center to complete the symmetrical pattern of rectangular lawns and paths laid out on all sides of the fountain, effecting the look of the Tuiliers Gardents in Paris. At first, the Chamber of Commerce, courthouse, and a few cafés and shops surrounded the plaza. Before the end of the colonial period, modern high-rise hotels and an apartment building, each sitting on top of arcades, were built on both sides of the plaza, enclosing the area from the rest of the city, and providing photographers with opportunities to frame Dakar as a modern, French-influenced city.

The Place de l'Indépedance was specifically designed as a symbol of the French Empire. Aspects of the plaza's design were modified after 1960s to reflect the Senegalese state. The long and symmetrical grass panels and public space surrounded by administrative buildings symbolizes military power, rationality, and order. The natural environment is framed as subjugated by state power. Indeed, a small and enclosed section in the southern part of the plaza is designed to reflect a landscape of "untamed" nature whereby trees are not conservatively pruned, vines are permitted to grow on the fence, paths are narrow and asymmetrical, and due to branches drooping from the trees, views of the city are obstructed in unplanned ways.

Many citizens have formed attachments to this historic site of public space. On an ordinary day one finds local middle-aged men gathering under the shady trees in the middle of day. They use a spigot reserved for lawn maintenance to fill a plastic tea pot which they use to perform their ablutions for mid-day prayer. Youth in Catholic school uniform wait on benches in the shade for their friends. Elders stretch out and cat nap on the benches, while some also read books and newspapers. Other youth wander around offering for sale souvenirs, sun glasses, or their services as tour guides. Tourists meander through the center of the plaza, almost never entering the garden in the southern part of the park. They generally pause by the water fountain, which for the past two decades has not pumped any water, and spin around looking to the skyline for familiar landmarks by which to orient themselves.

From one perspective, the Place de l'Indépendance is a peaceful plaza where a wide range of locals and guests have equal access to the plaza. Groups in the plaza do not come into conflict with one another. There is ample space for visitors use, and locals continue to practice the cultural norm "teranga" (the Wolof term for hospitality for the visitor) as well. The plaza comes alive with action when it hosts significant cultural events such as New Year celebrations, international exhibitions, and an occasional political protest. The peacefulness, welcome, participation in cultural events, and lack of signs of destruction of the plaza suggests inhabitants value this public space.

From another perspective, the Place de l'Indépendance is a peaceful plaza because some citizens are *not* there. Individuals who grew up during the time of Senghor's presidency recall the plaza as an exciting place to visit, especially on the weekend when colored lights illuminated the spouting water fountain. When Abdou Diouf assumed the presidency in 1981 to distance himself from Senghor and Senghor's affinity for France, he limited funding for maintaining public spaces that referenced France. Therefore, the colored lights and water left the fountain. Then, as the economy weakened in the mid-1980s, the plaza filled with poor rural migrants seeking to eek out a living selling odd objects. The presence of "kaaw-kaaw" (a derogatory Wolof expression for rural youth coined by urban youth) in the plaza disrupted middle-class youths' enjoyment of the plaza, so they stopped visiting.

On the one hand, citizens appear to practice environmental responsibility at the individual and "green" level. Trash is generally properly disposed, locals are tolerant of the pause on water fountain use, and the trees in the plaza remain intact and valued for the shade and aesthetics they provide.[6] In terms of responsibility toward social environments, little sign that citizens feel the need to do more to protect the plaza or public spaces surrounding it.

Recent signs suggest the municipality feels the need to ignite citizens' place attachments. In 2013, the municipality permitted an exhibition in the plaza of approximately twenty postcards of Dakar, the plaza, and the surrounding buildings in the early colonial period. These nostalgic scenes were printed on large banners that were fastened to rebar driven into the dirt floor of a garden space in the plaza. Wind whipping through the plaza made the banners vigorously flap and twist around their rebar supports, making it challenging to fully view all of the images. But many of the images were already familiar to me since postcards of the African colonies are now a popular item for sale in e-commerce.

The sight of this exhibit in Place de l'Indépendance was both discomforting and curious. Why would Dakarois pine for the colonial past, a time of racism, exploitation, and the marginalized of Africans in the city? How could such an exhibit nourish viable place attachments among the citizens? On the one hand, I interpreted the postcard exhibit as a distasteful tribute to a time when aspects of urban growth may have been exciting despite the destruction of African culture that undergirded such growth. On the other hand, nostalgia for the colonial past may be viewed as displaced anxiety related to societal transformations occurring in the present.[7] For example, Place de l'Indépendance is currently being swallowed by urban growth. Due to the increase volume of traffic in the city and particularly circling the plaza, the plaza is marked by a layer of sand, dust, and particles from car emissions, and views of the sky are blocked by new tall buildings. At the same time, due to traffic in Dakar and the availability of amenities in the suburbs, it is increasingly unnecessary for inhabitants to visit Dakar's downtown and the Place de l'Indépendance. And since views of the plaza are available online, tourists do not need to wade through the traffic, crowds, and gritty air to view the Place de l'Indépendance either. In short, the plaza's position as the geographic and symbolic center of the city is currently shifting. The exhibition appears to be an attempt to "fix" the Place de l'Indépendance and downtown Dakar as the center of the city by taking control over representations of its history, however ironic the content of that history may be. This dynamic also suggests citizens' attachments to the plaza form and operate at one level, while the municipality works on another level to provide the context for these formations and their particular dimensions. Citizens are ultimately passive agents of place-making and in some cases they are against place-making efforts if they are too inclusive.

PUBLIC SPACE ON THE CORNICHE

In a recent wave of urbanization, developers moved from the center of downtown to the outer limits of the peninsula in search of new space to build on. New luxury hotels, apartment buildings, shopping centers, and recreation areas have been installed along the corniche. These developments are controversial because the beaches and ocean views are cultural significant landscapes to Senegalese, especially the Lebu fishing communities. Access and views have been blocked by the new structures, thereby disrupting access to cultural resources that are central to the cultural identity of so many inhabitants of Dakar. Indeed, from time to time there have been small groups protesting the construction of luxury hotels on the corniche.

One such new public space along the corniche is Sea Plaza, an underground shopping mall that is attached to the Radisson Blu hotel via tunnels. Sea Plaza was a 35-million-dollar project funded by Yerim Sow of Telyium Group, a wealthy Senegalese holding company that is constructing several other upscale housing projects on the corniche. Sea Plaza was designed by SAOTA, a South African based architectural firm that is known for their contemporary style and for building structures on cliffs. The mall hosts numerous brand name upscale retail shops, a spa, and several restaurants, a movie theater, and Dakar's only bowling alley.

While it appears to be a modern and inclusive public space, aspects of this space's signal it is meant to be used by a select population. This is first communicated by the presence of armed guards at the entranceway. Few other commercial centers in Dakar have this level of security. The security check may be for ensuring safety; however, it shapes the perception that there is something in the mall worthwhile to protect. Being searched at the security gate is a particular experience that is like passing through a threshold to a different and better world. Security guards trace visitors' bodies with beeping metal detectors. The detector is like a magical wand, and tracing the body is like a ritual through which one is transformed. Passing through a grand door that leads to mall's lobby, and then riding the escalator down to the first level of shops adds to the feeling of being transformed by one's entrance into a magical space. Indeed, on the lower level one is faced with many shops that are merely glass-enclosed spaces with fancy floor tiles and expensive goods. Glass walls signal that the mall is a highly modern and upscale place. They also permit a rapid socialization for new comers. Having unmediated views of numerous and diverse symbols of privilege, prepares visitors to quickly become familiar with these symbols and begin to incorporate them in their own self expressions. Glass windows also contribute to another ritual that orients visitors in the mall. As visitors stroll, they stop to take selfies next to window displays. The repetitive act of taking selfies inscribes familiarity, comfort, and desire for consuming and enjoying the upscale milieu. That said, a variety of physical features do much to filter this public space (Shephard and Smith-Simon 2011). A security check, stylish thresholds, reflective glass walls, expensive goods, and visitors taking selfies are aspects of shopping that are not found in many other markets in Dakar, least of all some of the most populated clothing markets such as Marché Sandaga. These features in the built environment may be inviting to some, but they signal to others that they do not belong. Therefore, some will not enter the mall. Sea Plaza is a form of public space that filters the public by threatening visitors' comfort zones in cerebral ways. It may provide opportunities for place attachments to develop among privileged city dwellers, but it limits opportunities for others. As such, it has a limited ability to contribute to the social sustainability of the city.

Place du Souvenir Africain is just south of Sea Plaza on the corniche. It is a multilevel and multipurpose public plaza and conference space which opened in 2009 during a time when the Senegalese government and Dakar's municipality made a concerted effort to improve the image of the city so as to maintain a foothold in the global tourist market. The mission of Place du Souvenir Africain is to commemorate national and Pan-African heroes through exhibits, conferences, and cultural events related to this theme. It is initially an inviting space because there are no check points or doorways to pass through in order to enter the space, and the promise of a view of the Atlantic is alluring.

The "Place du Souvenir," as it is commonly referred to, is a symmetrically organized space. The top level of the plaza is balanced by a line of flag poles on each side of the open space. A round water fountain with an asymmetrical arrangement of ceramic jugs is positioned in the center of the space. On the lower level, the space is balanced by two buildings with columns that reference Greek pantheons. In this space there are multiple water fountains and a large sculpture of the African continent in the center axis of the space and at the far end of the plaza. There is a restaurant on one side of the plaza with moveable chairs enclosed by a fence and set on a grass-like carpet, and an auditorium with modern glass walls on the opposite side of the lower plaza. The symmetrical organization of objects, nation state references, modern glass-paneled building, and the quaint but modern restaurant communicates that this plaza is part of a modern and orderly culture, while the asymmetrical sculpture in the center of the plaza suggests that this is also a space that honors spontaneity, creativity, nature, and African tradition.

While the Place du Souvenir appears to be open and accessible to all, there are a number of features that suggest the public is not welcomed unless they are tourists or conference participants. First, the plaza calls to mind a space that is needed for military columns to maneuver. This is not a space for ordinary citizens. There are no benches for sitting, only narrow ledges around the edges of the plaza. A view of the ocean is interrupted by the huge sculpture of the African continent that is placed in between the Greek-like meeting spaces. Unless one intentionally visits the plaza for an event, the spatial organization prompts a brief visit.

Some visitors, however, bond with the plaza. During one visit to the plaza, I noticed a thin, middle-aged man in dirty work clothes busily scraping tiles off of the floor of an unused water fountain. One of my friends said, "Hey he's stealing the tiles!" This prompted another friend in my group to say, "That's how it is. The patron in charge of the plaza is probably inside watching T.V. right now!" Indeed, while the visitor was scooping blue tiles into a brown plastic bag in plain sight, there were many people in the plaza setting up tents for an exhibition and discussing plans for an event. No one did anything to challenge the man as he appropriated material from this nationally significant public space. Was it problematic that someone was taking the tiles since the fountain is rarely used? Was this a new form of tax return? Who is hurt and who is helped by this act? Although the Place du Souvenir is designed to create memories that engender respect for Senegal's history and culture, some citizens form attachments that are based on the direct and immediate material benefit the state can give its people, with or without a governing mechanism to distribute its resources. Although inclusion is not an issue, it is doubtful this type of attachment is the basis for developing stewards of the city.

Cherif Mahktar Cissé's art installation on the beach underneath the Hotel Terrou-bi, just south of Place du Souvenir, is another example of compelling public space in the margins of the city. Cissé's art installation is also his home which he constructed in along a space in the cliff that coincides with an alcove on the beach. Thus, his house is not visible from the street. One has to walk down an informal path cut into a small slope to the beach to find it, or climb over many jagged and slippery boulders if approach the house from the sand.

Cissé's house is made out of light wood, card board, and tarps precariously nailed together. Inside his home he has stacked numerous pieces of art that he painted on wood and scraps of various sorts. He calls his home "Paradise by the sea." Upon meeting Cissé it is immediately apparent that he is an eccentric. He enthusiastically welcomes all who arrive and plays the role of a hospitable host who has been expecting the visit all along. He invites visitors into his home and offers them a place to sit (on the rocks). He exclaims many times how wonderful it is that the "world comes to him," and he finds indirect ways to indicate that world comes to him in the form of visits from curious international tourists and the trash that floats up on the shore which he uses for his art. The implied connection between international visitors and trash is delivered with humor and smiles, which is just one of the many ways that Cissé communicates his critical views of the world.

Cissé's art installation is comprised of approximately a dozen life-sized figures of famous Senegalese and Africans fashioned out of trash that he found on the beach. Water bottles, beer cans, plastic colanders, torn plastic bags, and ripped up soccer jerseys are used to affect the look of humans. If asked, Cissé informs his visitors of the name of the dignitary they confront—Senghor (Senegal's first president), Abdou Diouf (Senegal's second president), and Lat Dior (a nineteenth century resistance leader against the French) are among the dignitaries in Cisse's courtyard. This art installation is indeed an ironic parallel to the Place du Souvenir, which seeks to honor famous Africans but features none in the built environment.

Each time I travel to Dakar I try to visit with Cissé. My visit in 2016 was especially thought provoking. On the one hand, things were not going well for Cissé. He was in poor health and in need of money. On the other hand, he had taken his art to new level by creating costumes for his visitors to wear while taking selfies. He invited my companion to try on a "general's jacket" which was a green army-like vest to which he painted on strips and stars. He also gave me a "fez," created out of the bottom half of a large plastic soda bottle which he painted red. He also gave me a Senegalese flag to wave about. He had replaced the star in the center of Senegal's flag with large image of Abdou Diouf.

How does one classify Cissé's art installation? Is it an example of an artist's privatization of a public beach? Is it the reclaiming of public space for public art? The art installation is hard to define given the history of land and the ambiguous line between public and private space in Dakar.

Does Cissé's art installation exhibit signs of an existing place attachment or sense of belonging? If so, are their signs of environment responsibility possibilities citizen stewardship? Indeed, Cissé's work and approach to life is all about environmental responsible. In terms of responsibility toward the natural environment, Cissé's protects natural resources by reusing objects for his art before contributing to the demand for new goods. In terms of social responsibility, the goal of his art is to welcome everyone into his art space. Inviting visitors to engage in play with props made of recycled items prompts one to reimagine the notion of privilege and the effects privilege can have on one's natural and social environment. Ironically, Cissé's work takes place in the margins of the city where he is free but also inaccessible. With so few exposed to his work, his stewardship has a limited effect.

Public space along the corniche of Dakar is clearly developing in divergent ways. Public spaces are both more exclusionary and inclusive than ever before. This is exhibited by the welcome at Sea Plaza and Cissé's home. Yet in the margins, the state still aims to stamp public space with symbols that intend to orient citizens toward the nation. However, both the state and its citizens are ambivalent about their obligations toward one another. These themes are visible in the design, filtered access, and a citizen's anti-custodial reliance on the resources available in public space. As citizens are afforded the opportunity to develop attachments to these new places, connections to the beach and sea—part of the historic landscape for many long-term inhabitants of Dakar—will soon be lost. This message is communicated by Cissé who has installed himself on the beach to make art that expresses the need to care for the natural environment and a desire for an inclusive society. Ironically, this creative and fearless message is obscured, literally and figuratively, by shadows in the margins of the city.

CONCLUSION

This chapter began by asking if place attachments can engender environmental responsibility in public spaces that are not predominantly "green." Indeed, attachments are formed in nearly any type of public space, but this does not mean they can be transformed into significant acts of environmental responsibility. Local and Western notions of public space coexist and are evoked in different circumstances. Therefore, individuals' and communities' relationships to public shape are often shifting, giving the object of place attachments and citizen stewardship a certain ambiguity. It may be premature (and possibly not desirable) to target public space as a tool for engendering urban sustainability.

Environmentally responsible public spaces are meant to be inclusive, and in the examples above we have seen that in Dakar there are various issues related to accessing public space. Some public spaces are designed to purposely prevent access (e.g., Sea Plaza), or filter access (e.g., Place du Souvenir), or afford access to all, but some don't want to associate with others, and therefore limit their own access (e.g., the Place de l'Indépendance). Yet others are unaware of the access they are afforded (e.g., Cissé's art installation). Such diverse circumstances produce diverse opportunities for attachments to form. In some contexts, place attachments lead to citizen stewardship. For example, Cissé created an engaging way for the public to reflect on their own contributions to making art out of garbage on a beach. In other contexts, neutral place attachments form. Citizens care about public space, but don't see it as a place for social action, and in fact, are willing to leave it for other spaces in the city in order to avoid conflict. Yet others form connections that are detrimental to public space, as they remove pieces of it for their own use. In short, access is necessary in order for place attachments and stewardship to emerge. This would need to be addressed in order for these public spaces to become sites that engender inclusivity if not also an ethos of "green" environmental responsibility.

Based on the discussion above, it seems that the UN Habitat's hope for citizen involvement does not take into consideration the cultural or historical dimensions of the relationships between people and their environments. Nor does it propose consideration for the broader political, economic, and social dynamics that drive people to and out of public space, and shape people's perception of it and the environment as well. Without an understanding of these factors and their role in shaping public space, it will be difficult to move the needle toward urban sustainability.

The productive power of public space has been acknowledged by lay people since the nineteenth century and has been extensively documented by social scientists since the 1960s. So, how may we make sense of the UN Habitat and other international organizations' recent renewed interest in public space? Possibly, this renewed interest is similar to colonial nostalgia—a displaced desire to engage the past thereby masking anxieties about contemporary social tensions. In this case, the renewed interest in public space diverts attention away from the resilience of neoliberalism, a phenomenon that threatens the sustainability of Dakar by encouraging open border policies, deregulation, and the withdrawal of the state. One hopes that the renewed attention to public space in the name of urban sustainability will not result in a heightened enthusiasm for privatizing public space, for this will result in a built and social environment that does not take the history or culture into consideration and does not foster inclusivity. The municipality and citizenry should work together to determine the best to approach to creating and maintaining public spaces that "speak" to the people and history of the peninsula, and that engender social and natural environmental responsibility in culturally relevant ways.

NOTES

1. I would like to thank Isma Diaw and Khadim "Bu Mag" Diaw for their helpful contributions to this research.

2. On social cohesion and quality see Anderson 2011; Carr 1995 [1992]; Low, Taplin and Scheld 2005; Oldenburg 1989; Watson 2006; on improving physical development of children and adolescents, improving nutrition, and weight loss see Wolch et al. 2011, Black 2005; on improving mental health see Catlin et al. 2003; Kaplan et al. 1998; Popkin et al. 2005; Ulrich 1981; on civic identity see Projects for Public Space 2002.

3. For more on this idea in the context of Nigeria see Meagher (2017) Cannibalizing the Informal Economy: Frugal Innovation and Economic Inclusion in Africa. European Journal of Development Research.

4. In French, "balayer" means "to sweep." "Mbalit" is a Wolof derivation of this term.

5. For examples, see Low, S (1999) Theorizing the City: The New Urban Anthropology. New Brunswick, NJ: Rutgers University Press.

6. In Rethinking Urban Parks (2005), Low, Taplin, and Scheld document park visitors at Jones Beach, New York freely and extensively cutting down expensive trees and shrubbery in the park in order to have wood for their barbeques.

7. See William Cunningham Bissell's "Engaging Colonial Nostalgia" (2005) for an analysis of colonial nostalgia in Zanzibar.

REFERENCES

Agence Nationale de la Statistique et de la Démographie. (2015). http://www.ansd.sn/, accessed on February 15, 2018.

Anderson, E. (2011). *The Cosmopolitan Canopy: Race and Civility in Everyday Life*. New York, NY: W. W. Norton.

Arendt, H. (1973 [1958]). *The Human Condition*. Chicago, IL: University of Chicago Press.

Bissell, W. (2005). Engaging Colonial Nostalgia. *Cultural Anthropology* 20(2): 215–48.

Black, R. (2005). *Porta Palazzo, The Anthropology of an Italian Market*. Philadelphia, PA: University of Pennsylvania Press.

Brundtland Commission. (1987). *Our Common Future, From One Earth to One World*. Oxford: Oxford University Press.

Burchardt, Jeremy. (2002). *The Allotment Movement in England, 1793–1873*. Woodbridge, Suffolk, UK: The Boydell Press.

Carr, S., Francis, M. Rivlin, L. G., and Stone, A. M. (1995 [1992]). *Public Space*. Cambridge: Cambridge University Press.

Catlin, T. K., Simoes, E. J., and R. C. Brownson. (2003). Environmental and Policy Factors Associated with Overweight among Adults in Missouri. *American Journal of Health Promotion* 17: 249–58.

Eisenhauer, B. W., Krannich, R. S., and Blahna, D. J. (2000). Attachments to Special Places on Public Lands: An Analysis of Activities, Reason for Attachments, and Community Connections. *Social Natural Resources* 13: 421–41.

Gaye, M. (1992). The Self-Help for Housing and the Living Environment in Dakar, Senegal. *Environment and Urbanization* 4(2): 103.

Gowdy-Wygant, C. (2013). *Cultivating Victory: The Women's Land Army and Victory Garden Movement*. Pittsburgh, PA: University of Pittsburgh Press.

Jacobs, J. (1961). *The Death and Life of Great American Cities*. New York, NY: Viking Press.

Habermas, J. (1991). *The Structural Transformation of the Public Sphere: An Inquiry into a category of Bourgeois Society*. Cambridge, MA: MIT Press.

Kaplan, R., Kaplan, S., and Ryan, R. (1998). *Restorative Environments in With People in Mind*, 67–77. Washington, DC: Island Press.

Lawson, L. J. (2005). *City Bountiful a Century of Community Gardening in America*. Berkeley, CA: University of California Press.

Lewicka, M. (2011). Place Attachment: How Far Have We Come in the Last 40 Years? *Journal of Environmental Psychology* 31(3): 207–30.

Low, S. (2001). The Edge and the Center: Gated Communities and the Discourse of Urban Fear. *American Anthropologist* 103(1): 45–48.

Low, S., Taplin, D., and Scheld, S. (2005). *Rethinking Urban Parks: Public Space and Cultural Diversity*. Austin, TX: University of Texas Press.

Meagher, Kate 2017 Cannibalizing the Informal Economy: Frugal Innovation and Economic Inclusion in Africa. European Journal of Development Research 30 (4) DOI 10.1057/s41287-017-0113-4.

Oldenburg, R. (1989). *The Great Good Place: Cafés, Coffee Shops, Community Centers, Beauty Parlors, General Stores, Bars, Hangouts, and How They Get You Through the Day*. New York, NY: Paragon House.

Popkin, B. M., Duffey, K., and Gordon-Larsen, P. (2005). Environmental Influences on Food Choice, Physical Activity and Energy Balance. *Physiology and Behavior* 86: 603–13.

Projects for Public Space. (2002). *Public Markets for Social Integration and Upward Social Mobility*. Report. New York, NY. https://s3.amazonaws.com/aws-website-ppsimages-na05y/pdf/Ford_Report_2002-3.pdf, accessed on March 18, 2018.

Proshansky, H. M., Fabian, A. K., and Kaminof, R. (1983). Place Identity: Physical World and Socialization of the Self. *Journal of Environmental Psychology* 3: 57–83.

Shepard, B., and Smithsimon, G. (2011). *The Beach Beneath the Streets: Contesting New York City's Public Space*. Albany, NY: SUNY University Press.

Throsby, D. (1995). Culture, Economics, and Sustainability. *Journal of Cultural Economics* 19: 199–206.

Tonnelat, S. (2010). *The Sociology of Urban Public Spaces. Territorial Evolution and Planning Solution: Experiences from China and France, Paris*, H. Wang, M. Savy, and G. Zhai, eds. Paris, France: Atlantis Press.

Tuan, Y. (1977). *Space and Place: The Perspectives of Experience*. Minneapolis: University of Minnesota Press.

Ulrich, Roger S. (1981). Natural Versus Urban Scenes: Some Psychophysiological Effects. *Environment and Behavior* 13(5): 523–53.

Vaske, Jerry J and Katherine C. Korbin. (2010). Place Attachment and Environmentally Responsible Behavior. *The Journal of Environmental Education* 32: 16–21.

Watson, S., and Studdert, D. (2006). *Markets as Spaces for Social Interaction: Spaces of Diversity*. Report. The Policy Press for the Joseph Rowntree Foundation.

Wolch, J., Jerrett, M., Reynolds, K., McConnell, R., Chang, R., Dahmann, N., . . . Berhane, K. (2011). Childhood Obesity and Proximity to Urban Parks and Recreational Resources: a longitudinal cohort study. *Health and Place* 17(1), 207–14.

Conclusion

Theoretical Paradigms and Continuing Challenges

Jennifer L. De Maio, Suzanne Scheld, and Mintesnot Woldeamanuel

With its focus on eradicating poverty, protecting the planet, and ensuring that all people enjoy peace and prosperity, sustainable development dominates the global policy discourse. Ecological, social, and economic challenges threaten the majority of the world's population and are experienced most acutely on the continent of Africa. Sub-Saharan African countries are among the least developed nations and sustainable development has remained elusive for many. Some countries did make great strides in meeting the Millennium Development Goals (MDGs). The 2015 MDG report notes that "in many areas, especially related to health and education, the advance registered by sub-Saharan Africa was the fastest among all developing regions."[1] Despite progress, inequalities persist and development has been uneven. The child mortality rate in sub-Saharan Africa remains the highest among all regions, the majority of the population still suffers from lack of access to electricity, proper nutrition, clean and safe drinking water, and improved sanitation. Moreover, disparities between rural and urban areas remain significant. On the natural and built-environmental front, Africa also ranks high in terms of vulnerability and preparedness to mitigate and adapt to climate change.

The United Nations Sustainable Development Goals (SDGs) highlight the need to target least developed countries, small island developing states, and African countries with sustainable and resilient infrastructure development, official development assistance, and increased financial flows. The SDGs acknowledge the urgency of the challenges faced by African states and issue a call to action. Sustainable development as conceptualized by the SDGs emphasizes the links between energy, health, education, water, food, gender, transportation, climate change, peace and justice, and economic growth.

To ensure that these goals are implemented effectively, we must consider the fundamental theoretical, methodological, political, and cultural dimensions for sustainable development in sub-Saharan Africa. The three pillars of sustainable development—economic growth, environmental protection, and social inclusion—carry across all sectors of development, from urbanization to agriculture, infrastructure, energy development and use, water, and transportation. The question facing countries, cities, corporations, and development organizations today is not whether to embrace sustainable development but how. To that end, this book has focused on the foundations for an understanding of sustainable development in sub sub-Saharan Africa from an interdisciplinary perspective that combines approaches from political science, religious studies, anthropology, urban studies, and women and gender studies.

Several theoretical paradigms emerge from the analysis presented in this book. One of the most important themes that link the chapters is the idea that sustainable development must be broadly inclusive and environmentally sound to mitigate poverty and ensure prosperity for future generations. A key challenge in implementing strategies for sustainability has been the development of efforts that are broad, diverse, and culturally appropriate to effectively tackle the root causes of poverty. An important goal of this book has been to integrate principles of sustainable development with the application of politically, economically, and socially appropriate responses to ensure that the policies reflect the perspectives and prospects of the target populations. Community partnerships are therefore critical to promoting long-term sustainability. Local governments must take the lead in developing resilient community-based approaches to development, growth, and social justice. Local buy-in is fundamental and bottom-up strategies for sustainable development are essential to addressing economic, environmental, and social equity issues. Regional partnerships also play an important role as demonstrated by efforts initiated by the New Partnership for Africa's Development to emphasize the role of partnerships among African countries and the need for a shared and common vision to eradicate poverty through sustained economic growth and sustainable development. African governments have supported regional integration by bolstering existing regional economic communities and increasing the capacity of the African Union to respond in particular with regards to issues of justice and security. The international community has provided essential financial and technical support to regional efforts to advance the eradication of poverty through sustainable development in Africa. Partnerships between local governments, sub-regional and regional organizations, and international actors are critical to implementing sustainable development programs that are culturally and environmentally appropriate and will be supported by the communities affected.

An additional theoretical framework that emerges from this analysis is that some African countries are experiencing economic transformation with increasing fossil fuel based developments. This "growth by any means" attitude risks generating unsustainable practices that countries in the developed world are currently coping with. Therefore, for developing African countries, it is important to invest in socially, economically, and ecologically viable development projects.

Each of the chapters included in this volume advance our understanding of approaches to sustainability in sub-Saharan Africa. Divided by theme, they cover the history and regional context of sustainable development, the challenges presented by climate change and corresponding institutional responses, and the establishment of sustainable cities and communities. In the introduction, the editors highlight the importance of regional contexts and perspectives for sustainability discourses in sub-Saharan Africa. Chapter 1 includes authors Suzanne Scheld and Mintesnot Woldeamanuel's discussion of the "development" of sustainable development practices in general and in the context of African sustainability in particular. The chapter discusses how the discourse of sustainability develops from theory to practices, what Africa's place in the discourse is, and what the future holds. Chapter 2 highlights the ethical dilemmas of international relief and development work. Author Blaine Pope argues that explicit inclusion of business ethics issues in program planning, design, and implementation is critically important in the overall process of management and sustainability of development projects. He draws on his experiences in post-genocide Rwanda to conclude that sustainability in Africa must include African-developed mechanisms to address African issues.

In chapter 3, Mutombo Nkulu-N'Sengha explores the crisis of mining pollution in the Katanga province of the Congo and the shrinking of the rainforest, while reflecting on the political and social implications of promoting sustainable economic development. The study of the environmental situation in this part of the Great Lakes region is important not only for the sustainable development of Africa but also of the world. Indeed, the vast natural resources of this area play a crucial role in the global economy and have been at the center of major global and local conflicts. The author concludes that an African philosophy of sustainable development is a paradigm shift that calls for a profound and holistic shift of thinking and consciousness, a new way of defining human existence as it is constituted by relationships or community with others.

In chapter 4, author Chipo Dendere focuses on the intersection between governance and economic growth and examines the case study of Zimbabwe to assess the efficacy of sustainable development programs to address the political and economic drivers of poverty. Dendere concludes that critical to the successful implementation of the SDGs in Zimbabwe will be the increasing inclusion of women in governance and across all sectors of the economy as well sustained efforts to respect human rights and reduce corruption.

Part II of the book considers the impact of climate change on African states. In chapter 5, Jennifer L. De Maio and Kristy Michaud examine the attitudes of Africans toward climate change in comparative perspective. They conclude that to be effective, sustainable development policies must be developed and targeted to specific contexts. Many of the SDGs are focused on the core drivers of climate change. But also crucial to the discourse on sustainability is understanding public perceptions of climate change among those most affected by it. For climate action be implemented successfully, it must be supported internationally and sustained locally to ensure community-level buy-in. Authors Brian Dill and Heba Khalil argue in chapter 6 that the eradication of poverty and the promotion of sustained economic growth in Africa must begin with reforming the international corporate tax system. International cooperation on tax is, in fact, the key to mobilizing the domestic public resources required to achieve the SDGs. African countries are structurally disadvantaged with respect to taxation and are marginal players in global trade. Domestic tax authorities must be strengthened, but a critical first step is reconfiguring both the national economies and the global environment.

Part III of the text examines the development of sustainable cities and communities. Chapter 7 considers the partnership between communities and international partners to promote sustainable health initiatives. Florence Kyomugisha describes the Holy Innocents Children's Hospital Mbarara Project in Uganda and concludes that community outreach interventions can have a significant impact on improving the availability of adequate food and nutrition for children and pregnant mothers, child immunization, safe water, sanitation, and malaria prevention. In chapter 8, Mintesnot Woldeamanuel argues that in an increasingly important Africa's economy, there is uncontrolled urban growth which creates demand for urban services such as transportation. With increasing demand, several social and environmental issues associated with the transportation sector must be addressed, including urban transport-related socio-environmental concerns such as reducing air pollution, greenhouse gas emissions, and associated health impacts of auto-centric urban development. In chapter 9, Suzanne Scheld considers the contribution of public spaces in urban sustainability by examining several popular public spaces in Dakar, Senegal. The chapter examines the extent to which urban open spaces engender environmentally responsible behavior. Scheld contends that there is ambiguity in the idea that place attachments bring citizen stewardship. Environmentally responsible public spaces are meant to be inclusive and diverse circumstances produce diverse opportunities for attachments to form. In some contexts, place attachments do in fact lead to citizen stewardship. In others, place attachments may encourage connections that are detrimental to public space as citizens remove pieces of public space for their own use. Scheld concludes that access is necessary in order for place attachments and stewardship to emerge and for public spaces to become sites that engender inclusivity and an ethos of "green" environmental responsibility.

Economic growth over the past two decades has lifted millions of people out of poverty and has raised the income levels of millions more, but too often it has come at the expense of the environment and poor communities. To be effective, sustainable development programs must be accompanied by political systems that promote citizen participation in decision-making; economic models that support technological skills training, diversification, and sustainable self-reliance; social systems that prioritize equality and justice; production systems that preserve ecology; and regional and international partnerships that foster sustainable trade and finance.

NOTE

1. United Nations, Millennium Goals Report 2015. Available at: http://www.un.org/millenniumgoals/2015_MDG_Report/pdf/MDG%202015%20rev%20(July%201).pdf.

Index

About the Contributors

Jennifer L. De Maio is a professor of political science at California State University, Northridge. She has a PhD from the University of California, Los Angeles and is the author of *Confronting Ethnic Conflict: The Role of Third Parties in Managing Africa's Civil Wars*. Her research focuses on ethnic politics, civil wars and conflict management in Africa. She has also published and presented papers on elections and the use of social media, women and conflict, and sustainable development in Africa.

Chipo Dendere is a Zimbabwean political scientist. Dr. Dendere is currently Consortium for Faculty Diversity Fellow and Visiting Assistant Professor of Political Science classes at Amherst College. Dr. Dendere's research expertise is on democracy, elections, development and, migration, with a regional interest in African politics. She writes about the impact of voter exit, migration and remittances on the survival of authoritarian regimes. Her new research is on the role of technology and social media in new democracies.

Brian Dill is an associate professor of sociology at the University of Illinois at Urbana-Champaign. He has a PhD from the University of Minnesota and is the author of *Fixing the African State: Recognition, Politics, and Community-Based Development in Tanzania*. His current research focuses on the efforts of African states to tax the informal economy.

Heba Khalil is a PhD student at the Department of Sociology of the University of Illinois at Urbana-Champaign. Her research focuses in rural movements, class-based politics and the political economies of North Africa.

Florence Kyomugisha is a professor in the Department of Gender and Women's Studies at California State University Northridge, California. Kyomugisha has a PhD in Urban Studies and a Graduate Certificate in Women's Studies. Her research focuses on societal economic and cultural changes that are associated with health disparities in women, children, and other marginalized populations; and the functioning and variations in the family organization of people of African descent. She integrates her philanthropic and advocacy work against global health disparities in her teaching and scholarship. Kyomugisha has been on the board of Holy Innocents children's Hospital Mbarara in Uganda since 2009.

Kristy E.H. Michaud is a professor of political science at California State University, Northridge. She has a PhD from the University of California, Santa Barbara and is the author of *The Politics of Energy Crises*. Her research focuses on environmental politics and policy with an emphasis on climate change, energy, and sustainability policy.

Mutombo Nkulu-N'Sengha is a professor of in the department of religious studies at California State University, Northridge. He was trained in philosophy, history, religious studies, and African American studies in Africa, Europe, and the US where he received his PhD in 2002 at Temple University, with a dissertation on the philosophical and theological foundations of a theory of human rights in post-colonial central Africa. He speaks seven languages fluently including French and Italian, with a passive knowledge of Spanish and German. He has written extensively on the "Bumuntu Paradigm" of African philosophy. His recent publications include three entries in the *Encyclopedia Britannica on Bantu Philosophy and Cultures*.

Blaine Pope is lecturer in the Department of Management, at the Nazarian College of Business and Economics, at the California State University at Northridge (CSUN), where he teaches business strategy. Dr. Pope has overseen a wide range of emergency relief and economic development programs, mostly in Africa. More recently, Dr. Pope became involved in energy and the environmental policy issues, and related international political-economic issues. Dr. Pope has both a PhD and an MA in Human and Organizational Systems (Organization Development) from Fielding Graduate University.

Suzanne Scheld is a professor in the anthropology department at California State University, Northridge. She has a PhD from the Graduate Center of the City University of New York. She is co-author of the book Rethinking Urban Parks with Setha Low and Dana Taplin and has published and presented numerous papers on the politics of urban space in Dakar, Senegal including "Youth Cosmopolitanism: Clothing, the City, and Globalization in Dakar, Senegal" and "City in a Shoe: Rethinking Urban Africa through Sebago Footwear in Dakar, Senegal."

Mintesnot Woldeamanuel is a professor of the Urban Studies and Planning Department at California State University Northridge. He has a PhD from Hokkaido University in Urban and Environmental Planning and has conducted extensive research and written several journal articles on the relationship among travel behavior, the environment and urban form focusing on transportation mode choice and spatial analysis in Addis Ababa city. He is the author of *Concepts in Urban Transportation Planning: The Quest for Mobility, Sustainability and Quality of Life*.